• • •

ALL THE NEWS THAT FITS

• • •

HERMAN H. DINSMORE

. . .

ALL THE

NEWS

THAT FITS

. . .

A Critical Analysis of the
News and Editorial Contents of
𝕿𝖍𝖊 𝕹𝖊𝖜 𝖄𝖔𝖗𝖐 𝕿𝖎𝖒𝖊𝖘

ARLINGTON HOUSE   *New Rochelle, New York*

SBN 87000-051-9

Library of Congress Catalog Card Number 69-16945

MANUFACTURED IN THE UNITED STATES OF AMERICA

Contents

11790

Contents

Acknowledgements

The writer wishes to acknowledge his indebtedness to Long Island University for making him a Visiting Professor of Journalism so as to provide the opportunity for the gathering of data for the writing of "All the News That Fits." The chapter in this book on the assassination of President Kennedy was presented in 1966 in different form as a lecture to students of journalism at Long Island University.

The chapter on The Times' balance of power aims was presented originally as a speech before the Rotary Club of Greenport, Long Island, New York, in 1963. It then bore the title, "The Balance of Power Fallacy," and was not as completely formulated as it is now in Chapter 1. Meantime, it was published, in 1965, in the magazine U.S.A., again under the title, "The Balance of Power Fallacy."

For the many friends who have encouraged me to press on with this work, I have a deep and abiding affection, because their courage and their faith were most useful. Two of them, one a professor, the other an editor, were kind enough to read and endorse the manuscript.

Finally, I am indebted to the New York Society Library and to the New York Public Library for their never-failing courtesy and efficiency in providing books and papers for this work.

The truth is, to be sure, sometimes hard to grasp, but it is never so elusive as when it is not wanted.

H.H.D.

Preface

There is a joke in the composing room of The New York Times among the printers and make-up editors. It is often voiced when a compositor is locking up a page after he has helped to chip away stories in order to get the type into the steel chase. "All the news that fits," the printer will gaily remark after he has battened down the type with a wooden hammer and is closing up the page. Sometimes an editor will wince or look quizzical, knowing that there is more to the jest than meets the ear.

The New York Times motto is, "All the News That's Fit to Print." This implies that some news is not fit to print. Perhaps that was less true earlier than it is today. For the title of this book, I have used the printers' felicitous phrase, "All the News That Fits," as the more truthful of the two. But like some phrases and all generalizations, it does not tie everything neatly into a package.

There is more in The New York Times than is dreamt of in anyone's philosophy. My title will serve; it is not final.

H.H.D.

Introduction

The New York Times today is deliberately pitched to the so-called liberal point of view, both in its news and editorial columns. Although The Times still prints a large body of news, it is not as objective in its news as it was when it was making its name as the finest newspaper in the world. In its editorials The Times often takes a position above the battle, as for example, on November 21, 1965 when it commented:

"Even in Thailand and other countries under constant Communist threat, there may be second thoughts about whether conquest by Communists would be more painful than defense by Americans.

"In Vietnam itself more is involved than the deaths, the carnage and the alienation of peasant loyalty. The bombs that destroy South Vietnam's villages are smashing the social structure of the countryside.

"The final wreckage may be such that the Communists ultimately will be the chief beneficiaries in the South, however the conflict ends, while a badly battered North may fall entirely into China's grasp."

This is the ultimate and logically ultimate position of The Times in regard to America's defense of countries imperiled by the expansionism of the two great Communist nations, Red China and the Soviet Union. It is a clear bid to the non-Communist and anti-Communist nations of Asia to reject help from the United States and accept domination by the Communists. It is, moreover, a specific condemnation of the United States as a purveyor of death, in a way that could result in defeat both for South Vietnam and for the United States.

The New York Times has been a great newspaper, and no doubt will be one again. Its format today is largely the same as that of thirty and forty years ago, but the contents are different, and the editorials take a new and often depressing point of view. What happened to cause this change? And how is it that many seemingly perceptive persons still find The Times a most complete and useful intelligencer and guide?

There are cogent answers to these questions, and they should be stated. The Times is much too important an institution in the United States and in the world to be allowed to go undiscussed and unanalyzed. This is not, in fact, the first such analysis, but so far, most critical studies of The New York Times have been made by men who never worked inside The Times and could not know some of the points of view to be found there. Neither has there been any study of great depth.

Arthur Hays Sulzberger, the chairman of the board and former publisher, used to say that The Times had writers of many points of view and that it was this very condition that made The Times great and impregnable. That was true. It is less true today. There has been a subtle but massive change. It will be the purpose of this book to try to trace the transformation of The Times from an objective newspaper into one that slants and curves the news and takes tendentiously neutral editorial positions toward the Cold War.

There is an out of this world quality to Times editorials because they seem to assume that The Times should be neutral as between the United States Government and the Soviet Government (which The Times nearly always calls the Soviet Union, even when it is talking about the government) and, secondarily, Communist China, which it often calls merely China or mainland China in keeping with its editorial drive to get the Communist Peking regime accepted into the United Nations.

What will it profit a newspaper to maintain its space standards for news but to diminish the quality of the news columns? The New York Times has permitted various political currents to exist within its organization, but especially the Left-wing current, and there has been much distortion and omission of news. Some will question the use of the word "Left-wing." If it seems too severe, it should be recalled that the Times' copious use of "Right-wing" in its own headlines and news and editorials is even harsher. "Right-wing" has often been applied to the various Fascist parties of Europe and Asia and has meant something very different from either the John Birch Society or conservative Republicanism; indiscriminate use of the phrase in The Times may well be intended to frighten and alienate. My use of "Left-wing" will be justified by the facts.

This book will concern itself with what appears and has appeared in The Times. The aim will be to chart the course of a great newspaper from an indefinite point in the past down to the very definite present. Of especial concern will be the strange new directions followed by The Times during and after World War II. That was the period when the Soviet Government was taking over the countries of Eastern Europe, was stealing atomic secrets from the United States through its spies (this actually was going on during the war, apparently as early as 1942), was teaching and aiding the Chinese Communists to overrun all of China. It was the time when the Soviet Government was preparing, launching and sustaining the Korean War with the help of the Chinese Communists, and giving military support to the Communist forces of Indo-China under Ho Chi Minh, now the North Vietnamese leader. It was a period when the Russians were pursuing a policy of rule or ruin in the United Nations, and when they were seeking to gain control of newly-created governments in Africa, for instance, by giving military support to dissident forces in the Congo and sending very large shipments of military equipment to the United Arab Republic (Egypt) and Syria.

This book will undertake to show that The New York Times took no really effective steps to counter these Communist thrusts and all too frequently appeared to back them, as if to play the Soviet regime off against the United States and other democratic nations of the West. The New York Times in more recent years has stated that it wants a balance of power in the world—as if it were possible to maintain such a thing. Editorially, it has freely criticized the United States while but sparingly finding fault with Communist actions. For instance, The Times seems to accept without indignation the actions of the North Vietnamese Communists and their allies in South Vietnam; the Communist prison of Eastern Europe; and particularly, the Soviet Union. Does any one seriously believe that Herbert L. Matthews alone could have installed Fidel Castro and his Communist regime in Cuba without eager, massive and powerful support in The New York Times and the United States State Department?

Worst of all, as one turns the pages of The Times over the years since World War II, one is conscious of many opportunities missed because its appeasing, balance-of-power attitude precluded constructive thinking toward getting concessions from the Soviet enemy. The word "enemy" describes accurately how the Soviet Russian regime itself has wished to be regarded. Its hollow pretensions to superiority—moral to begin with and from there political and economic—should not have been lost on The Times. If they had not been tragic in their consequences, these pretensions would have been ludicrous, as for example, the Soviets' wild boast that their whole economic-political system was and is fundamentally freer and more productive than America's or that of any non-Communist country.

Yet the Russians for many years have sought in vain to learn American techniques of farming and industry—not because they have been excluded from studying the American procedures at first hand, nor because Americans have been forbidden to go to the Soviet Union to teach these methods (not all of them, to be sure, but some very important ones). Moreover, the Soviet Government has availed itself of great stacks of American patents, books of all kinds, all manner of agricultural and industrial documents, and the general openhandedness in the United States—not matched for American citizens in the Soviet Union or in the captive nations of Eastern Europe. The New York Times' policies precluded its seeking to bring about—peacefully, of course—the introduction into the USSR of the free enterprise system that has been so fruitful, both materially and spiritually, in America. It stands to reason that, if Russia maintained an open society, any need to seek a balance would diminish.

The attitude of The New York Times toward the Soviet Union has resulted in remarkable distortions in its news columns and in its editorial judgments. Among many examples, one that greatly depressed this writer (while he was editor of the International Edition of The Times) occurred on Christmas morning of 1952, when The New York Times presented Premier Joseph Stalin of the Soviet Government in 5-column headlines on the front page as a leader who wanted peace in the Korean War. These headlines read:

"STALIN FOR EISENHOWER MEETING
TELLS THE TIMES THAT HE FAVORS
NEW APPROACH TO END KOREA WAR"

Of course, there was not a grain of truth in anything Stalin said in reply to some questions put to him by James Reston. The story, however, gave Stalin the big Christmas Day play—and vanished. The quality of Stalin's sincerity and veracity is shown in one of his answers to Mr. Reston's questions:

Q.: Wherein lie the sources of present world contention, in your judgment?

A.: Everywhere and in everything wherever the aggressive actions of the policy of the "cold war" against the Soviet Union find their expression.

The no-victory war in Korea—fought under rules that defied every principle of common sense—was raging in December, 1952, even though truce negotiations were begun July 10, 1951, more than seventeen months earlier. That Stalin was a liar, a murderer, ever treacherous at home and abroad, and an intellectual crook who did not hesitate to borrow the mantle of Lenin publicly while denigrating him privately—that Stalin was all this, was well known long before a later Soviet Premier, Nikita Khrushchev, made the accusations officially before a gathering of Soviet Communist leaders, at their twentieth congress in February, 1956. To present this evil man in the role of a peacemaker on Christmas, of all days, seemed to be a cruel and painful hoax—a Soviet hoax, that is, made possible by the gullibility of The Times. A hoax, of course, is exactly what it turned out to be. Stalin died soon afterward, on March 5, 1953, and the armistice that ended the hostilities was signed on July 27 of the same year.

The story of the Korean War was never wholly told in The New York Times, or indeed even half told there. The role of the Russians was mostly suppressed, although the most elementary reasoning leads one to the view that the Soviet Government had to call the signals and stage the troops and planes for the Blitzkrieg drive that carried the "people's army" of North Korea so precipitately down the Korean Peninsula in the summer of 1950. That is one of the stories that this volume tries to fill out for the general reader. It is an alarming story.

Needless to say, there is no suggestion whatever here that Mr. Reston or any officials of The New York Times conspired with Stalin to perpetrate the hoax. Presenting this story in blazing 5-column headlines on the front page was a large error of editorial judgment. Given the orientation of The New York Times, however, it could be expected. It was nothing if not another heavy contribution to the theory of the expendability of the daily news.

Over the years The Times had earned a reputation for presenting facts daily that grew into an edifice of history. Even today The Times is read by members of the John Birch Society and by Communists, as well as by businessmen, housewives and persons in all walks of life, for news. A careful reader will be able to gain a great deal of information from The Times that he probably would not find in other newspapers, simply because few of them even make a pretense of giving "all the news that's fit to print."

On the same day that the objectionable story on Stalin appeared there was other news on that front page that was less complimentary to the Soviet Government. One headline read: "Tass Man Is Seized By Dutch As Spy." Tass is the Soviet press agency. Another story on that front page quoted the Washington Post as saying that V. K. Krishna Menon of India mouthed "almost the straight Communist line" in denouncing the United States for bombing in Korea when he said the Russians were on the verge of accepting his peace plan. (How familiar that cry sounds today! Except this time The Times itself took the lead in asserting that the Communists in Vietnam would talk peace if only the United States will stop bombing North Vietnam long enough.)

It is not possible that the Russians issued the Stalin story for publication on Christmas Day without believing that that would be the time for it to have the greatest impact upon the American people. Thich Tri Quang, the troublesome monk of South Vietnam, once said that he would "use the Americans to help us get rid of Americans" and that if this and other anti-American statements were quoted by the interviewer "nobody will believe you." * So, too, with the Russians.

That the Russians have taken advantage of American freedoms to gain the upper hand over the United States wherever the two nations meet is scarcely open to doubt. Is it not reasonable to expect the American press to defend itself against this kind of abuse? After all, the newspapers in a free country are themselves expendable if they lose the confidence of their readers. Even The New York Times could overstep the bounds of the permissible through design or negligence.

Yet nothing is so clear as The Times' determination to go to the brink of disaster in order to bring an end to a war (in Vietnam) that it does not understand, that it does not approve of, that it refuses to face up to, that it deplores editorially and misrepresents in its news columns. On July 22, 1965, The New York Times published an editorial containing the following lines in regard to the Vietnam War:

"There are such things as honorable defeats and dishonorable

* *Our Vietnam Nightmare,* by Marguerite Higgins, pp. 33 and 34.

victories. And in between are all kinds of compromises that are neither one thing nor another—but sensible and realistic."

If that is the "sensible and realistic" way to cope with the intransigent, warmaking Communists who have served notice upon the world that they intend to rule it, piecemeal at first and completely later—if that is sensible and realistic, then words have lost their meaning. But in truth the words do have meaning, and show the guidelines to which The Times adheres. The Times abhors the very mention of victory, specifically and vigorously excluding it as a desirable conclusion to the war in Vietnam. Victories can be— are, that is—"dishonorable" and defeat can be "honorable." This comes very close to introducing the upside-down language of the Communists into the editorial columns of The Times, and it accounts for the kind of news coverage that has been coming out of Vietnam from the beginning.

As The Times goes, so goes a large part of the nation's press. The Times strongly influences and often actually serves many newspapers and periodicals in the United States as well as some in Latin America, Europe, Asia and Australia. The editorial quoted above opposed "forcing Hanoi to sue for peace on American terms," (which terms, incidentally, are not as strong as those of the South Vietnamese) and it rejected the arguments of those "demanding a complete 'victory' over the Vietcong and North Vietnam." Thus The Times uses the word "victory" as if it were something undesirable or completely unattainable, though the British achieved it in Malaya, the United States gained it in Japan, and the Allies obtained it in Europe.

This no-win position is not a flash in the pan with The Times. It continues to the present. Moreover, it colors the views and news of The Times in many matters scarcely connected with international "balance." For instance, the assassination of President Kennedy by Lee Harvey Oswald, who called himself a Marxist and who had spent nearly three years in the Soviet Union, caught The Times flat-footed. Not that other newspapers were less irresponsible in taking at face value the reported Administration line that no "international plot," which would include Communism, was involved in the charges against Oswald. (This matter is taken up in greater detail in the chapter on the assassination.) The Times had been campaigning lopsidedly against the "Right Wing" in America, meaning members of the John Birch Society, anti-Communists generally, or roughly anyone to the right of Governors Rockefeller and Romney. Now that a Communist was named as the assassin of President Kennedy, it was doubly a shock. The Times called him a Leftist in its headlines in the first-day story, but it gave full coverage to his life as a would-be defector in Russia—that is to say, as full as its hamstrung policies of covering the news permitted.

The Times is nearly as allergic to the use of the word "Communist" in domestic affairs as it is to the word "victory" in foreign affairs. In connection with the assassination it printed a statement by the U.S. Communist Party, issued in New York City, without naming the sponsor of the release. No doubt this had some relationship to the Smith Act. Still, The New York Times' emphasis upon the great danger from the Right Wing, while soft-peddling any threat from American Communists, made it appear that The Times was anxious to create an alibi for the Left, in order to help it avoid the onus of connection with the assassination. Later, after the Warren Commission went to work, The New York Times made it clear in its news columns that it was going to support the view that Oswald acted alone, without confederates and without any conspiracy. Before the Warren Report was issued the news columns and headlines suggested that only Europeans, not Americans, felt that there had been a conspiracy. Thus it came as no surprise at all when The Times embraced the findings of the Warren Commission that Oswald and Jack Ruby each acted completely alone. According to a Harris poll taken in 1967, about two-thirds of all Americans do not believe that the Warren Report gave the whole story. Here again it appears The New York Times did not print and did not seek the full truth, but rather—reporting its editorial line instead of the facts—misrepresented the truth and misled its readers. Lately The Times has had some second thoughts about the Warren Report.

Obviously there are reasons in the atomic age why the newspapers should not wish to go out on their own and involve the nation in a further confrontation with the Communist world. But what *are* the ground rules for the press? How far can it afford to follow the Administration down the road to absolute news management? How can the press maintain its self-respect by telling its readers at one time that the Warren Report was entirely right, even impeccable, and then printing serially the book by Sylvan Fox, *The Unanswered Questions About President Kennedy's Assassination?* *

Throughout this book the reader will find light and shadow, for a newspaper with such extensive coverage of world events has much to commend it. Its errors become all the more egregious when they are set cheek by jowl with truthful and highly useful news. How upsetting, for instance, to read the story on the tenth anniversary of the noble Hungarian Revolt of 1956 that the Hungarians are now doing all right under the imposed Communist regime. It was a 4-column line on the front page, in October of 1966.

This volume will undertake to give news coverage and editorial views from other publications in order to make clear what is regarded herein as more complete news and more adequate, correct or useful opinion. In the area of commentary on the news a wide range of attitudes must be expected. The intelligent reader expects at least a body of thought that is based upon sound principles, openly stated; not a crypto-balance of power line that provides a shaky foundation for both editorialist and reader.

As a commercial vehicle The Times is unrivalled, no matter how befuddled its editorial line. It prints so much more news than any other paper in New York—and no doubt any other paper anywhere—and it is so diligent in seeking advertisements and print-

* This was done by the New York World-Telegram and Sun, later merged into the World Journal Tribune, both papers now defunct.

ing them attractively that businessmen look upon it as an indispensable medium. The Sunday paper is now so heavy with advertising that only the strong brave a trip to the newsstands for a copy. It often weighs 10 to 20 pounds.

The death of the New York World-Journal-Tribune in 1966, a hybrid created out of the New York Journal-American, The World-Telegram and Sun, and the New York Herald-Tribune a few months earlier, left The Times as the only full-size non-specialized newspaper in the city. Some New Yorkers feel that the World-Journal-Tribune did not really compete with The Times, being afflicted with a death wish and bound to fail (a strike provided the coup de grace). Nevertheless, it was a needless journalistic casualty, and, in a city of 8 million (wherein lurk more points of view than are offered in The Times), it was a painful deprivation for many newspaper readers. The World had stopped more than thirty years earlier and the people had had to get off—and read The Times or the Herald Tribune. Today the only other morning daily printed in Manhattan is the tabloid Daily News with a circulation of more than 2 million daily and more than 3 million on Sunday. Just before the Herald Tribune ceased publication its circulation was about 300,000 daily and 380,000 on Sunday. That would seem to be more than sufficient to sustain the life of a newspaper. It is a great deal more circulation than most American newspapers have, the vast majority of which make a profit. The New York Times circulation at the time of the Herald Tribune's demise was about 800,000 daily and about 1,500,000 on Sunday. The Times picked up some of the fragmented readership of the Trib, as it was generally called.

It may be that The Times mistakes its swollen circulation and revenues as signs that its readers solidly favor its commitment to a balance of power, to an end of the war in Vietnam with a victory for the enemy, and to a detente that would wash American hands even further of Soviet Russian cruelties in Eastern Europe. On the contrary, it is to be doubted whether even twenty per cent of Times readers follow it all the way. Many of them are captive readers who feel that they have no choice but to read The Times in the absence of other full-size morning papers. Many apparently do not read the paper cover to cover, for they are often shocked when told of some piece of news or a Times editorial position. For many years Times readers have bought the paper because of some feature or features that interested them; they ignore the rest. The Times does not control a bloc of any kind, but, unfortunately, it can willy-nilly put wrong ideas into people's heads and it can omit certain useful news. Hence this volume.

The reader is asked to remember that this book is half contemporary history and half critical analysis. History is usually thought of as the record of events in the somewhat distant past—at least a generation ago. Much of the sting and confusion of political or national differences or other colorations may have been removed from the writing of such history. The daily recording of the events of the world today, full of national animosities, nuclear fears, class and color divisions, political differences, and nationally-fostered ideological conflicts—this task is not as simple as it was in the days before World War II. At that time there was no atomic bomb, no missile that could carry such a bomb more than 4,000 miles in minutes, no need to get to the moon or to keep satellites orbiting the earth for self-protection—in brief, no necessity to watch every movement of our own and of our enemies in order to guard against doing too little or too much. Never before Korea in the 1950's did the United States fight a no-win war. (Right there we run into the problem of recording contemporary history. There are some journals and other publications that would not call the Korean War a no-win conflict. They would consider such a designation invidious. Yet it is a fair and factual characterization.)

However the reader may feel about that matter, he may be shocked to learn some of the information that was withheld from the American public by the press and the government acting in collaboration, allegedly in the interest of preventing the Korean War from becoming a general conflict. It is the intention of this book, through the weight of the evidence, to give neglected aspects of the Korean War more historical solidity. There is no need to wait for 99 years to do so. On the contrary, the sooner the better since many of the same misguided practices that were followed in the Korean War are now being pursued in the Vietnam War, by both the government and a large section of the press, including The Times.

It is contemporaneous events and developments that are recorded by the newspapers, news magazines, financial periodicals, picture publications, and other printed media. These accounts will differ enormously. Some of them are indeed highly superficial and unintentionally wrong or misleading. Repeated error in the treatment of some news matters, however, must be put down to the policy of the publication, not to the fault of a writer or writers. Because a publication would not allow such repetition if it were not deliberately sought by the management. The only check against being misled is to read several newspapers, news magazines and other periodicals. The reason for presenting the rather long "highlight" paragraphs at the beginning of each chapter of this book is to show various points of view in the handling and presentation of the news and to give certain insights into the subject dealt with. In many cases these paragraphs are in direct conflict with the news or editorial views presented by The Times.

Eastern Europe alone offers a subject for one book, and a large one, as regards journalism. This volume has touched upon that great region of more than 100 million population in only one chapter. The aim has been to show how these people have been disregarded in a great realignment of the more powerful nations of the world.

The New York Times achieves very considerable editorial effect by selecting and positioning the news. How far The Times has gone in this direction is described in this book.

If this volume helps to remove some of the mental and intellectual divisions in the nation, it will have performed all the service designed by the author. That lives can be saved by a greater understanding of international affairs is not to be doubted. Name-calling or personal attacks of any kind are not involved here. The great subsidiary aim has been to fill out large areas of contemporary history that are unknown or only vaguely understood by many, if not most, Americans.

CHAPTER I

The New York Times' Own World Balance of Power

• • •

"AS IN THE WHOLE EAST-WEST STRUGGLE, THE PEACE OF THE *Middle East, however precarious, depends on balance of power in the area."—From an editorial in The New York Times, entitled "Missiles to Israel," on September 28, 1962.*

"It (Indonesia) remains, politically and strategically, the key *country in the region even if its valuable oil, rubber and tin no longer are crucial factors in the world balance of power . . . Washington has seen India and Indonesia as the two most vital 'dominoes' it has feared would topple if Vietnam were to fall to Communism.*

"Yet the fact is that Indonesia's extraordinary gyrations in *recent years—first toward, then away from, Communism—have occurred in virtually total independence of the United States and the events in Vietnam,"—From an editorial in The New York Times, "The Indonesian Irony," on February 17, 1966.*

"Surely, without the U.S. defense of Vietnam, the military in *Jakarta never would have dared to challenge President Sukarno, revered as the father of Indonesian independence. Skeptics who ask what the U.S. has gained by its war in Asia should look at the sea of change in the Far East. The 180-degree turn in Indonesia, the bloody in-fighting among Chinese Communists and the reaffir-mation of Japanese-American friendship in last month's election are advantages which could not have been gained if the U.S. had abandoned its Vietnamese allies."—From Barron's, "The World at Work," February 6, 1967.*

Robert S. Elegant, writing in The New Leader of July 17, 1967, from Hong Kong: "Almost obsessive attention to the affairs of Communist China and the Far East during the past two years has convinced me that the American intervention in Vietnam has had profound, and largely beneficial, consequences elsewhere. Above all, fear of violent confrontation with the U.S. has stimulated the pragmatic revolt inside the Chinese Communist party against Chairman Mao's rigid and oppressive orthodoxy, with its absolute commitment to an aggressive and dangerous foreign policy.

"We cannot, in the end, prevent the extension of some form of primary Chinese influence over the Far East. We can, however, prevent the extension of direct Chinese influence until the Chinese have modified their ambitions; and we can assist that adaptation to the benefit of the Chinese people and the world. Already, because the United States has by military action demonstrated its determi-nation to prevent Sino-Communist expansion throughout Asia, two new factors have emerged: more determined resistance to native Communist movements; and an atmosphere more conducive to realistic social reform." (That could only refer to Indonesia among other countries, including Thailand and the Philippines.)

"The fifth and latest Chinese nuclear explosion does not fun-damentally change the balances of terror and power that provide such equilibrium as the world now enjoys."—From an editorial in The New York Times on December 31, 1966.

"There is another important similarity between Cuba and Turkey. The Soviet missile base in Cuba, like the U.S.-Nato base in Turkey, is of little military value. The Soviet military base in

Cuba is defenseless, and the base in Turkey is all but obsolete. The two bases could be dismantled without altering the world balance of power."—Walter Lippmann, from a column in the New York Herald Tribune on October 25, 1962.

"*There were already signs of trouble ahead in President Kennedy's years in office. The great majority of members of the Kennedy Administration held the world view for which (Vice President) Humphrey is now being denounced—a view, essentially, based on continuing concern for the world balance of power. But a minority, headed by the late Adlai Stevenson, did not hold that view. What is called 'world opinion' was their prime concern."— Joseph Alsop, in a New York World Journal Tribune column, entitled, "Is the New Left Spawning Another American Folly?" on October 31, 1966.*

"*De Gaulle seems to be trying to evolve for France a very complex version of the balance of power policy first practised by the Papal States and later taken over by England. As I see it, France would like, in a series of concentric rings, first to attain ascendancy in Western Europe and then to make Western Europe the leader in a Continental bloc between Britain and Russia."—C. L. Sulzberger, in a column in The New York Times Dec. 28, 1966.*

"*Back in the late 1940's when the cold war had begun, when Stalin was at his worst, I was invited to lunch in the Pentagon with a high official. The object of the lunch was to persuade me to write articles in favor of launching a preventive nuclear war against the Soviet Union. . . . I did not write the articles . . ." Walter Lippmann, in the New York Herald Tribune on June 24, 1965.*

"*In the words of Professor Hans Morgenthau, we should 'disengage' in Viet Nam so as to ensure our 'cooperation with the Soviet Union [against Communist China] in support of a Titoist [Ho Chi Minh] all-Vietnamese Government. Our interests in*

Southeast Asia are identical with those of the Soviet Union: to prevent the expansion of the military power of China.' He accepts China's political and cultural dominance over mainland Asia 'as a fact of life.' The only alternative: China has to be 'conquered.'

"These arguments against United States support for a treaty ally [South Vietnam] are designed to reward the aggressor or to offer a sacrifice on the altar of an illusory 'balance of power' thesis. Not one shred of evidence exists that the Soviet Union wants an alliance—even if it were desirable—against Communist China."—Prof. Frank N. Trager in his book (page 200) "Why Vietnam?" (Praeger, New York, 1966).

". . . today prime TV news and commentary spotlights are focused, in wartime, on a nonentity—'pacifist' Ronald B. Ramsey —who makes anti-American taped broadcasts for release in Hanoi.

"Why is this?

"The best explanation, I believe, lies in the intellectual influence which Marxists have been able to exert in our communications media. Recently, the present situation was clearly set forth by Professor Eugene Genovese of Rutgers University, who retained his post there after he had publicly welcomed the idea of a Vietcong victory. At a forum held last month [February, 1966] at the Riverside Plaza Hotel in New York City, under the auspices of the National Guardian, Genovese said that to achieve a Marxist revolution in the United States, the Left-wing intelligentsia must gain 'cultural hegemony.' He expressed optimism about their being well on the way, and said this is why there exists now in our country 'the necessity for open advocacy of socialism.'

"Hegemony is preponderant authority."—Alice Widener, from an article in the magazine U.S.A., entitled, "Needed: A Vietnam War Home Front," on March 18, 1966.

"By refusing to share the secret of the atomic bomb we are fostering Russian suspicions."—Herbert L. Matthews, member of

The New York Times editorial board, from an article in Collier's magazine in 1945.

A balance of power has been pressed upon the world since the end of the Second World War, and it is an organically functioning thing now. It is not believable that the balance as a whole was an accident. Not all of those who contributed to its emplacement are known. Not all are of like mind. The New York Times' conception of a balance of power is surely different from that of former Prime Minister Harold Macmillan of Great Britain.

On Nov. 1, 1961, The New York Times presented as its quotation of the day the following words by Mr. Macmillan:

"We have a duty to maintain the balance of power in the world and to insure that the deterrent still deters and that the security of free men is not overthrown because an aggressor suddenly becomes possessed of an overwhelming advantage."

Mr. Macmillan was speaking about the possibility that the West would resume atomic weapons tests in the atmosphere when he made those remarks. He wanted the balance tilted in favor of the free nations. Western agreements with the Soviet Government are tenuous things, without policing, easily evaded or broken, constantly under suspicion. They are part of the balance of power under which the world lives, amid brush wars, assassinations, Communist thrusts and perennial internal wrangling among the peoples of the non-Communist nations as to whether the Communists are really a threat at home or abroad.

A balance of power will hardly do now what it has never been able to do before—that is, maintain peace, as witness the 1967 war in the Middle East, where a balance had supposedly been set up. As it is set up today, the balance divides the world, including the United Nations. It divides the countries, including the United States. It has encouraged the Soviet Government to press in all directions to expand its empire, with the help of the balance-of-power forces in other countries. It encourages the Soviet Government not to make and certainly not to seek agreements with others. It accounts for the rise of Castro and the establishment of a Soviet base in Cuba. It was related to, if not the whole cause of, the fighting in the Congo. And it has a strong bearing on the war in Vietnam. It contradicts and obstructs the free world in its search for peace.

The balance-of-power movement tends toward the suppression of some truths and toward the shaping or re-shaping of others to suit the doctrine. Specific instances will be presented in this and other chapters of this book. Persons are upgraded or downgraded like cuts of meat in an abbatoir. The world becomes blurred as some of the shoddy malpractises of totalitarian life are transferred to the free countries.

What part The New York Times played in setting up or even helping to set up the world balance of power, no one can say. Nor, indeed, can one pinpoint the date on which The Times began advocating and pressing for a balance of power. All one can say with certainty is that it began in the news areas of The Times as World War II came to its inconclusive close, and as Russia under Stalin started the war with Greece, our ally, first of a great series of actions that made the Cold War a great deal hotter in fact than in name. The balance of power took firm shape during the period from 1945 to 1950. It proved its efficacy in 1950 upon the outbreak of the war in Korea, for by then it had been unalterably tilted in favor of the Russians and their Communist allies around the world. The United Nations' becoming corrupted, without exposure by the press, during the early period of the Korean War, was one of the fruits of this balance. Worst of all, the truth about this period has never been told to the American people by The New York Times or by most other newspapers. The truth became a double sacrifice to the balance, designed to keep a non-existent peace or to "prove" to the Russians and their Communist allies that the non-Communist countries wanted peace. As if the Russians did not know that—and use it for their purposes.

A printer at The New York Times who was making up a page

of the International Edition was asked, "Why do we appease the Russians as we do?" A small, wiry man, with bright red hair, a man of good habits and sure instincts, he replied at once: "Because we have dirt in our blood. That's why." That could be called the brute-force reaction to the balance-of-power policy. That policy, however, is based on something far more clearly thought out than naked fear. It has been followed, to some extent at least, by Democratic as well as Republican Administrations since 1945. The Truman Doctrine of containment in 1947 established some physical contours but did not attack the doctrine of the balance, which penetrated the Truman Doctrine as water flows through a sieve. The balance idea has been hard at work in recent years to prevent the Vietnam War from gaining vigorous support to extend the muted general acceptance that it has had in the United States. Let it be remembered that the same Americans who sang most vociferously, "The Yanks are not coming," in 1939-41, changed to "The Yanks are not coming too late," after the Germans attacked the Russians in June, 1941. A New York Times assistant editor on the Foreign Desk said at that time that he considered it entirely reasonable to argue that World War II was "a British imperialist war" until the Germans launched their drive into Russia, when it became "a people's war." If Moscow today gave the signal for general support of the South Vietnamese-American-Allied side in the Vietnam War, there would be some remarkable changes on the American scene.

For if the balance idea has set up an Iron Curtain in Europe and a wall in Berlin, it has built a curtain and a wall around the Communist party and its followers in the United States. And the two phenomena are related. Let us try to sketch how this thing called a world balance of power came into being around the time of the Second World War. We must first establish what it is, to come closer to defining its sources of support.

Before, during and immediately after the war the Soviet Government annexed parts of Germany, Finland, Norway, and Rumania, all of Estonia, Latvia, and Lithuania, Tannu-Tuva, the

Japanese half of Sakhalin Island, and the Kurile Islands of Japan. After the war it gained political and physical domination of such countries as Outer Mongolia, Poland, East Germany, Hungary, Czechoslovakia, Rumania, Bulgaria, Albania, and North Korea. By then the Russians were beginning to feel so strong that some expressed regret that Czarist Russia had ever sold Alaska to the United States. They demanded that Turkey cede two provinces, Kars and Ardahan, make other concessions, and sign a treaty of friendship. The Russian aim appeared to be to outflank Turkey and render her defenseless. The Turks rejected all the Russian demands. Then the Soviet Government sought to gain the same end by supporting the Greek Communist party, which formed a Liberation Front (EAM) and a Liberation Army (ELAS) precisely as was done later in Vietnam. United States and British efforts in 1947 curbed and eventually succeeded in halting this Soviet move, which involved control of the entire Eastern Mediterranean region.

"This [Soviet] support [for the Greek Communist 'war of liberation']," writes Professor Basyl Dmytryshyn in his *USSR: A Concise History*, "was contrary to the wartime Soviet-British understanding which made the British responsible for the liberation of Greece and for the restoration of order. A Communist regime in Greece, however, offered the Soviets a prospect of realizing complete control of the Balkans, seizing the Straits (Dardanelles), and establishing Soviet influence in the Eastern Mediterranean."

The Russians now have transferred their efforts to achieve the same aim to the Arab countries. Their defeat by Israel has in no way weakened the determination of the Soviets to extend their influence in the whole Eastern Mediterranean and Middle Eastern region. Their thinking involves getting the United States Sixth Fleet out of the Middle Sea.

With the collapse of the Soviet effort to get control of Greece in 1948, Stalin the Insatiable turned to the Orient. Largely with Russian help the Chinese Communists defeated the Chiang Kai-shek regime (which moved to Taiwan) and set up the Communist

Government in Peking in 1949. In the following year Stalin launched the war in Korea after he had held long talks in Moscow with the Chinese Communist leader Mao Tse-tung. They drew up a Chinese-Soviet treaty and undoubtedly discussed preparations for the ghastly war on the Korean peninsula. Gen. Curtis E. LeMay, former Chief of Staff, United States Air Force, afterwards wrote (in U.S. News & World Report Oct. 10, 1966):

"In Korea, where we also pulled our Sunday punch [he was then writing about the Vietnam War], there were 3.5 million military casualties on both sides during three years of drawn-out war. Over a million civilians were killed and other millions left homeless in this protracted land struggle. I can't believe that this is the most humane way to fight a war."

Many of those casualties can be laid to the balance of power philosophy, which divided the forces of the United Nations military effort in Korea and made a veritable shambles of the high command, which Gen. Douglas MacArthur valiantly tried to command while the ground was being cut from under him in the United Nations, the United States, the United Kingdom, and the Union of Soviet Socialist Republics, which country for a time actually participated in the Korean War from both sides of the battle lines. (This is explained at some length in the Chapter III dealing with Korea and the consummate treachery of the Communists of a number of nationalities.)

As will be seen, the balance-of-power establishment enlists the support of the Left Wing—Communists, fellow-travelers, allies, assistants—and rarely if ever since the end of World War II has it given wholehearted support to the free world as against the Communist expansionists and totalitarians.

A nearly incredible situation arose in the fall of 1956 when the United States and the Soviet Government found themselves on the same side in the Security Council of the United Nations, in the matter of the attack upon Egypt by the United Kingdom, France and Israel. The balance lost its balance momentarily in this improbable situation. The United States, a devoted and honorable member of the United Nations, sought to save the world organization as America followed its traditional moral course in foreign affairs and condemned the war on Egypt as a violation of the United Nations Charter. The Russians had no moral problems to be bothered with, since their ally was being attacked and they had shown complete indifference to the fate of the United Nations through vetoes, obstructionism, treachery, and espionage. They sided with Egypt because Egypt was their ally. Once the United States had succeeded in bringing the British, French and Israeli actions to a halt, President Eisenhower made it clear to the Russians that we would not tolerate any moves on Moscow's part to extend the war for purposes of retaliation. The Soviet leaders dropped their threats to send "volunteers" to Egypt. The United Nations was saved from a massive discrediting, but it faced added battering in the years ahead from the Communists, even though the balance of power had weighted virtually everything in the organization in their favor. John Foster Dulles, the American Secretary of State during the Suez affair of 1956, was still being reviled years later in various partisan quarters for the part he played in "humiliating" America's partners—Britain, France and Israel. It was entirely forgotten that he had upheld such integrity as was still left in the United Nations.

Coinciding with that Middle Eastern outbreak was the violent outburst of insurrection in Hungary, which the Russians put down with Draconian brutality and a quite un-Socialist lack of international brotherliness. They were making it clear for all Eastern Europeans to see that Russian nationalism was primarily ahead of Socialism, or Communism, or any other consideration. And all the world looked on, and did nothing. The United Nations made an investigation. Some 200,000 Hungarians were mercifully (but with conscious ulterior purpose) permitted by the Russians masters of the country to emigrate, minus their possessions. Many thousands of young Hungarians were shipped to Siberia. None ever returned, according to Hungarian persons who ought to know. No serious consideration was ever given by any of the free countries to intervening on behalf of the Hungarians whose daring and courage had electrified the world; and who had been encouraged to believe that they would receive help from the free countries if they did revolt.

The end of the Korean War—that is, the signing of the armistice—in 1953 was the signal for a general stirring of unrest in Eastern Europe. Poland's industry is said to have been almost wholly hitched to the war, and the country suffered. The death of Stalin in March no doubt brought a feeling first of relief and then of rebelliousness. The first outbreak occurred in East Germany, starting in East Berlin in June, 1953—after the death of Stalin but before the Korean truce. The East German Communist leaders were unable or unwilling to suppress the demonstrations of construction workers, who asked for "butter, not a people's army." [1] They received not butter but an extra people's army—the Russian people's army, as the East German Communists called for help. In characteristic disregard of common humanity, the Soviet leaders proceeded to show the East Germans who was boss.

Having learned in this hard way who were the rulers of East Germany, many of the ablest workers fled to West Berlin and thence to West Germany. In 1953 a total of 305,737 left East Germany, and by the end of the decade the figures of the emigrants by ruse and subterfuge added up to 4 million. [2] That did it for the Russians and their East German satraps. They decided to plug up the hole through which the brain and skilled brawn of East Germany were being drained to the West. The Great Wall of Berlin was erected in 1961—a monument to Communist cruelty and intransigence. The question whether this action "in defiance of international agreements," as former President Eisenhower put it, [3] would be accepted was not long in coming. The New York Times, which suggested no move to contest erection of the Wall, published on August 18, 1961, a semi-editorial type of news story from Berlin, saying that "the western Big Three—the United States,

1. *USSR: A Concise History,* by Basil Dmytryshyn, page 288.
2. Ibid., page 289.
3. *Waging Peace,* page 269.

Britain and France—are unable to do anything about ending Germany's division even if they wanted to."

"Troublemaking," wrote General Eisenhower in *Waging Peace,* page 628, "should not be confused with true initiative. Always hopeful of bringing significant parts of the Western or neutralist areas within their orbit, the Communists resort to advance—then retreat, then threat and cajolery. Measured against the background of the world struggle, these forays and blustering threats do not mean that the Soviets have and retain the initiative. However, should the Free World begin to accept and give way before these ventures, then indeed we should fear loss of initiative. This was the real tragedy of the Berlin wall, which, built in late 1961 and in defiance of international agreements, yet evoked no quick or effective response by the United Nations, the United States, or by any of our allies."

Then, as if to explain the balance of power and how to handle it, General Eisenhower continued (page 629):

"The major portion of world power—moral, intellectual, economic, and military—still lies outside the Communist bloc. This the Soviets well know. They cannot gain the initative unless they succeed in dividing us against ourselves. I confess I experience uneasy moments when I see major Free World nations disagreeing publicly and sharply among themselves in solving problems critical to their common future. The difficulties facing the Free World in Cuba, Vietnam, Berlin, and elsewhere *can* be handled with confidence and success if those who love freedom will work together in the knowledge that individual selfish interest must never prevail over the welfare of the total free community. The greatest single task facing the leaders of the major free nations is to weld their peoples into dependable, cooperative organizations, characterized by mutual respect and a willingness to share the responsibility of defeating each new Communist adventure, and in promoting the positive actions essential to building a world of peace, justice, and rising levels of living."

Secretary of State Dean Rusk recognized the balance-of-power school of thought when on August 12, 1963, he asserted that the nuclear test ban treaty with the Soviet Government was not designed to set up a balance of power—that the United States intended to keep superiority over Russia in atomic weapons. This statement seemed to be pointed to those sections of American opinion that emphasized a balance of power as all-important, even to the point of seeing that the self-declared enemy was as strong as the United States.

"It is a melancholy prospect to recall that when the moment in history came round to challenge the very heart of our conviction (and our persistent rhetoric) about the fight for liberty, we found ourselves too sophisticated or too fearful or too concerned with the worldly balance of power to act." That statement was written by Timothy Foote in an article, "The Road Back to Budapest," printed in The New York Times Sunday Magazine Nov. 20, 1966. Here a trained foreign correspondent recognized the heavy-handed power balance's ability to stay the hand of the whole free world while totalitarian hordes pounced upon an uprising in behalf of freedom and crushed it.

Although it seems likely that the balance of power school of thought saved the day for the Russians in Hungary, General Eisenhower, who was President at the time, makes out a strong case for United States inaction. He writes in *Waging Peace* (page 88):

"The Hungarian uprising, from its beginning to its bloody suppression, was an occurrence that inspired in our nation feelings of sympathy and admiration for the rebels, anger and disgust for their Soviet oppressors. No one shared these feelings more keenly than I; indeed, I still wonder what would have been my recommendation to the Congress and the American people had Hungary been accessible by sea or through the territory of allies who might have agreed to act positively to the tragic fate of the Hungarian people. As it was, however, Britain and France could not possibly have moved with us into Hungary [since they were involved in the Suez operation]. An expedition combining West German or Italian forces with our own, and moving across neutral Austria, Titoist

Yugoslavia, or Communist Czechoslovakia, was out of the question. The fact was that Hungary could not be reached by any United Nations or United States units without traversing such territory. Unless the major nations of Europe would, without delay, ally themselves spontaneously with us (an unimaginable prospect), we could do nothing. . . .

"So, as a single nation the United States did the only thing it could: We readied ourselves in every way possible to help the refugees fleeing from the criminal action of the Soviets, and did everything possible to condemn the aggression."

But General Eisenhower writes on a later page (pp. 98-99):

"Did the British and French actions [in Egypt] provide an excuse for the Russians to move with massive force into Hungary? If the Russians had moved into Hungary with no Suez problem preoccupying all Western Europe, would the reaction of the West have been more intense? To both of these questions my own answer has always been negative.

"Some critics have said that the United States should have sided with the British and French in the Middle East, that it was fatuous to lean so heavily on the United Nations. If we had taken this advice, where would it have led us? Would we now be, with them, an occupying power in a seething Arab world? If so, I am sure we would regret it.

"During the [American Presidential election] campaign, some political figures kept talking of our failure to 'back Israel.' If the administration had been incapable of withstanding this kind of advice in an election year (1956), could the United Nations thereafter have retained any influence whatsoever? This, I definitely doubt."

The United Nations was saved—to fight against the United States and the free world another day, while valiant Hungary was pushed back into totalitarian slavery through "the criminal action of the Soviets." The use of "totalitarian slavery" to describe the conditions in which Hungarians live today can easily result in the charge of intemperateness or anger. Let those who are tempted to feel that such language is intemperate consider for one moment how they would describe such conditions if Americans had to live under them in their own country. The best capsule description of the shaping of events and the carnage wrought by the Russians in Hungary in 1956 is given by General Eisenhower in *Waging Peace,* page 97:

"The Middle East crisis was now starting downhill. Gomulka and his government in Poland were hanging in midair with their revolution. And the Soviet Union had murderously throttled the Hungarian drive for freedom. On the morning of November 8, two hundred thousand Russian troops were still inside Hungary; Hungarian refugees were fleeing to Austria at the rate of three thousand to four thousand a day: the fighting there would leave forty thousand Hungarian families homeless and twenty-five thousand Hungarian patriots dead. It was not going to be easy to pick up the pieces of those twenty days."

Indeed, it was not easy. But it would be harder for readers to discover the miseries under which Hungarians lived, under their Soviet mentors and tormentors, in the pages of the New York Times. Still devoted to the balance of power as the way to tranquility in Eastern Europe, if not exactly peace, The Times addressed itself in the coming years to freeing the colonial areas of Africa, to the communization of Cuba, and other worthy works in behalf of the balance. The more than 100 million people of Eastern Europe were written off as human sacrifices to the great Moloch of Soviet power.

The pursuit of happiness is the greatest casualty on both sides in the Cold War, but can any one doubt which side is the larger sufferer? It is not accidental that such words and expressions as freedom, due process of law, pursuit of happiness, trial by a jury of one's peers, the two-party system, an opposition, separation of executive, judicial and legislative powers—these expressions are not part of the mental furniture of the people of totalitarian lands because words like those are anathema to dictatorship. If the political leaders, the press, the pulpit, the school teachers and university professors, labor union leaders, streetcorner orators and other practitioners of freedom keep telling the people that in them resides all the power of the state, the people come to believe it and to know what they can do to prevent tyranny or to free themselves from it if it overtakes them.

Stalin deliberately flouted laws in order to prove that there was none superior to his will. But it must always be remembered that the man who condemned Stalin unmercifully in 1956 in the Soviet Communist congress was the same man who in the same year directed the Russian tanks and troops in brutally crushing the Hungarians. His name was Khrushchev, and he proved that Stalinism was simply Russianism as far as the coordination of Eastern Europe into the Soviet system was concerned. True, Yugoslavia broke away—and later Albania. Those countries were a little beyond the reach of the Russians, who would have had to cross one or more Eastern European countries to get to Yugoslavia, and they would have had to cross Yugoslavia or Bulgaria and Greece to get into Albania. Hungary is contiguous with Russia and thus was entered direct from the Soviet border. The loss of Hungary by the Soviet Government could have introduced another Berlin into the Eastern European scene, and a far larger one. The successful working of the free enterprise system in Hungary after years of blight under Communism could well have made the other economies hitched to the Soviet milking machines unmanageable. This subject is dealt with in a later chapter.

For a graphic and unforgettable account of life under the Communists in Budapest, from 1945 to 1956, *A City in the Darkness,* by Dr. Andras Pogany, is heartily recommended. Dr. Pogany endured the conquest of Budapest by the Russians twice, in 1945 and 1956. No paraphrase here would begin to match the eloquent rage of Dr. Pogany. Only one who has suffered the barbarous outrages perpetrated by these crusaders for Communism can speak with unrestrained candor. Dr. Pogany, like so many other Eastern Europeans, looks beneath the veneer of Communism and discovers old-fashioned Russian nationalism masquerading as a bringer of the best on earth. Conquering Russian soldiers pillage and rape. Conquering Russian generals must provide their quota of prisoners. If the total of military captives does not equal the prescribed number, it is made up from the civilian population. The bumbling incompetence and geometrical brutality that are Communism make nonsense of inane newspaper dispatches telling of improved conditions ten years after the revolt.

On January 13, 1962, The New York Times published as its leading editorial, "The Varieties of Marxism." In this it told of the many types of Leftists, from Nehru Socialists to Nasser Socialists, from Guinea's Sekou Toure Marxists to the Chedi Jagan Marxists of British Guiana (now Guyana, an independent country); then on to Tito, Castro and Khrushchev Marxist-Leninists. It said they were all different and it concluded:

"This is but a simplified catalogue, and could readily be amplified and complicated. But the point should be clear. The 'Leftist' or 'Marxist' or even 'Marxist-Leninist' segment of the world today covers such a wide spectrum of opinion, often conflicting with others in this area, that these terms by themselves do little to enlighten us about the nature of a given regime and about its intentions or attitudes toward us. Rather than permitting ourselves to be panicked by its labels, we must study each country and its actual policies, and then on the basis of factual evidence make up our minds as to the appropriate American attitude toward it. This will be unpleasant to the peddlers of semantic confusion, but will add greatly to the clarity of our individual and national thinking."

The strange thing about that editorial is that, while most intelligent persons have been doing what it advocates all along, The New York Times has been the chief victim of the semantic confusion that it deplores in others. For instance, while The Times makes a large distinction between Castro's Communism and Russian

Communism, the fact is that Russian Communism shipped missiles to Castro's Communist Cuba and emplaced them there in a direct threat to the United States. That made the distinction between Castro Communism and Russian Communism worthless and dangerously misleading. The failure on the part of the United States Government, first of all, and The New York Times secondarily, to see this, caused the first nuclear showdown in the history of the world. But it was The New York Times that originally played a large part in presenting Castro to the United States as a non-Communist and even anti-Communist and a kind of Abraham Lincoln of Cuba. And after Castro revealed that he had hidden his Communist affiliation because he did not want the Cuban people to know it until he had become their dictator, The New York Times both in its news and editorial columns continued to introduce semantic and other confusion in order to conceal the facts.

A Times headline on December 8, 1961, read: "Castro's Embrace of Marxism Appears to Disturb Red World. Speech on Communist Ties Censored in Havana—Soviet Seen Wary." If the Red world was disturbed, it was over the timing, not the embrace, which had been going on for many years. That story quoted only a truncated version of Castro's statement. It said Castro had "declared himself a Marxist-Leninist 'until the last day of my life'" and asserted that the statement had caused consternation in the Communist world.

It recalled that Premier Khrushchev had said in November of 1961, a month earlier, "that he did not think Dr. Castro was a Communist." As it turned out, Mr. Khrushchev was not the most trustworthy authority to tell the world whether or not Dr. Castro was a Communist.

A trustworthy source of information on this matter was Secretary of State Dean Rusk. Speaking before the ministers of the Organization of American States at Punta del Este, Uruguay, on January 25, 1962, he said this:

"When Dr. Castro himself said on Dec. 2, 'I am a Marxist-

Leninist and I shall be a Marxist-Leninist until the last day of my life,' he could have surprised only those who have paid no attention to the evolution of the Castro regime. This public oath of fealty to Marxism-Leninism underlines Dr. Castro's commitment to the Leninist use of deception and violence, to the Leninist contempt for free institutions, and to the Leninist injunction that obedience to the international Communist movement is the highest duty.

"Driven by this Marxist-Leninist faith, the Castro regime dedicated itself, not to the struggle for democracy within the hemisphere or even within Cuba, but to the perversion and corruption of this struggle in the interest of world communism. . .

"The Castro regime has extended the global battle to Latin America. It has supplied communism with a bridgehead in the Americas, and it has thereby brought the entire hemisphere into the front line of the struggle between communism and democracy. It has turned itself into an arsenal for arms and ammunition from the communist world. With communist help, Dr. Castro has built up the largest military establishment in Latin America."

Despite everything that has happened since that speech was made, The New York Times hews to the line that the Castro regime has made a necessary revolution in Cuba and that the United States should help it along. The Times printed Mr. Rusk's address, even though it does not share his opinions. In recent years it has rarely resisted a temptation editorially to find fault with Mr. Rusk as a hardliner, especially on Vietnam. A separate chapter in this book deals with the part played by The New York Times in introducing Castro to American newspaper readers and the public generally. That The New York Times exerted an enormous and disproportionate influence—and an improper influence—in saddling Castro and his Communist regime upon the American hemisphere is not open to doubt. Moreover, there is no doubt that The New York Times is the single most influential newspaper in the United States and perhaps in the world—and influence is the measure of a newspaper's importance, for good or ill. It would hardly be worth writing—or reading—a book on a newspaper that had little influence or currency.

While the Soviet Government was building up its domains in Eastern Europe and in Asia, constructing military ties in the Middle East, dabbling in the affairs of the emerging African nations, and infiltrating Cuba for the eventual bedevilment of the Americas, there was a claque around the world to applaud the Soviet actions. The same claque that so often backed the Russians stayed the hand or softened the restraining moves of other countries, chiefly the United States. When the Soviet Union did not have the atomic bomb immediately after World War II, there were actually persons in the United States and Britain who advocated giving the secrets to the Soviet Government—to even up the balance. Among such persons was Herbert L. Matthews, a member of the editorial board of The New York Times, who was later to be such an important force, together with The Times, in presenting Fidel Castro to the American people as an anti-Communist. Mr. Matthews wrote in Collier's magazine in 1945:

"All they [the Russians] want is security. By refusing to share the secret of the atomic bomb we are fostering Russian suspicions . . . One can understand how they feel about our recognition of Franco, our seizure of Pacific bases, our exclusive policy in Japan, our Red-baiting press and our America-firsters. We have set up a vicious circle of mutual distrust and fear." * (Acting suspicious is a basic Soviet method of disarming others.)

At that time (1945) it was not known to the public that the Russians had already gained access to the secrets of the United States atomic bomb knowledge from as early as 1942. The brazen effort to induce the late Dr. J. Robert Oppenheimer, head of the atomic bomb construction project at Los Alamos, New Mexico, to join in a "coordination" of American scientific efforts with those of the Russians during the war is told in a pathetic book by Haakon

* *RUMBLES Left and Right*, by William F. Buckley Jr., page 68. G. P. Putnam's Sons, New York, 1963.

Chevalier—*Oppenheimer: The Story of a Friendship* (George Brazilier, New York, 1965). Chevalier wrote the book because he was angry with Oppenheimer, who reported to the FBI Chevalier's proposal—somewhat belatedly, to be sure, which is one of the reasons Oppenheimer incurred the hostility of many Americans with a knowledge of Soviet treachery.

At last the Russians succeeded in building and exploding an atomic bomb in 1949. All confirmation for the Russian atomic explosions comes from the United States Government. The Russians have announced some of the blasts, but there have never been any pictures of Soviet nuclear or thermonuclear explosions in American newspapers or periodicals.** On the other hand, every American atomic detonation has been followed by a veritable fall-out of pictures. The United States atomic bomb effort was assisted by a great international host, including Dr. Albert Einstein, a German who became an American citizen; Professor Niels Bohr, a Dane; Dr. Enrico Fermi, an Italian; Dr. Lisa Meitner and Dr. O. R. Frisch, Germans who fled to Sweden from Nazi Germany. There were British and Canadian scientists, still other Germans, and a number of other contributors of other nationalities. Last but indeed not least, there were the Americans, including Dr. Oppenheimer, Arthur H. Compton, E. O. Lawrence, Harold C. Urey and many others.

The Americans offered not only much highly advanced scientific effort but the tremendous industrial enterprise that has made the United States the leading entrepreneur in the world. The Russians would have been happy to strike an under-the-table bargain with any of the scientists to supply information on the work to the Soviet Government in the traditional Soviet, or perhaps Russian, manner—that is, without repayment in kind, if any were available. Where they failed in such an effort, the Russians were able to introduce scientific spies of various nationalities into the American

** United Press International told the writer on June 28, 1967, and *Life* magazine on June 29, that they had never seen any pictures of a Soviet bomb explosion.

project. It is believed that the secrets thus obtained enabled them to explode their first bomb some years before they would have been able to bring about such a blast through their own efforts. While it would no doubt be a mistake to attribute this Soviet achievement to the balance of power, it would not be wrong to note that a decidedly soft attitude was generally taken toward the Soviet Government in its spying. This can be ascribed to the balance.

The deep-seated fear that The Times printer found to be the cause of our yielding attitude toward the Soviets is not enough to account for this phenomenon. Everyone knows that we live under the cloud of atomic uncertainty. However, it is possible for the best of us to become a little mixed up in this matter. One of our better publicized historians, Professor Arthur M. Schlesinger Jr., wrote in a New York Times Sunday Magazine article Sept. 18, 1966: "If a Communist regime barely established in Peking could take a decision to intervene [in Korea] against the only atomic power in the world in 1950, why does anyone suppose that a much stronger regime should flinch from that decision in 1966?" The United States was not "the only atomic power in the world in 1950," since the Russians exploded an atomic bomb in 1949. Professor Schlesinger was buttressing up his case for the possibility that the Chinese Communists might join the war in Vietnam to aid an ally or to divert and discipline the Chinese people. He also held out the menacing possibility that the Russians would aid the Communist Chinese if they entered the war. Each school of thought can find reasons for opposite views of the future. Obviously, historians —even the best of them—are on their surest ground when they treat of the past. The only thing we can be certain of in regard to the atomic terror is that it has not prevented a great deal of conventional killing in a number of wars started by the Communists. The only atomic showdown was brought about when the Russians emplaced atomic missiles pointed at the United States in Cuba in 1962.

One of the most conspicuously able and independent members of the staff of The New York Times is Seymour Topping, now the Foreign Editor. For many years he served with distinction in posts around the world as a correspondent for The Times. A dispatch he sent from Moscow and printed on January 4, 1962, said this:

"Looking to the West, Moscow obviously is disturbed by the emergence of the European Common Market, which is rendering invalid certain of its (Moscow's) ideological premises. The depth of this feeling is shown by the severity of (Soviet) press attacks on the plans of the market for economic and political integration and by warnings (in the Soviet press) to such neutrals as Austria against joining it.

"Realization of the Common Market would militate against a trend foreseen by Moscow in which such countries as France and Italy would decline economically, leaving the way open for the assumption of power by their large Communist parties.

"The Common Market program also has disappointed some of Moscow's economic hopes. The Soviet Union looked forward to a time when its economy would be vigorous enough so that it could enter into more ambitious bilateral trade arrangements with individual West European nations and play one off against another competitively."

That is how the other side of the balance works. It is rare that such a candid and courageous dispatch comes out of Moscow. It describes an expansionist regime with a vengeance. It is, in a word, breathtaking. Here is the American nation, with Lend-Lease, the Marshall Plan and just plain Aid, seeking to rescue and uplift nearly all the world, and in doing so to save the whole world. And here is the Union of Soviet Socialist Republics counting upon an increase of misery in order to extend its totalitarian sway over Europe.

By condign chance, Soviet Russia suffered a disastrous grain crop failure the following year, 1963. "By late 1963 and early 1964, the Soviet people were subject to what amounted to informal bread rationing, but even that relatively mild deprivation was possible only because the Soviet Union had been able to buy

12,000,000 tons of grain from abroad, mostly from Canada and the United States," according to Harry Schwartz, a member of the editorial board of The New York Times. * Mr. Schwartz's book, *The Soviet Economy Since Stalin* (J. B. Lippincott Co. 1965), is an objective and most useful study of the vagaries of Russian Socialist economics. It is hardly matched by The Times newspaper coverage of the Soviet Union over the years, and it completely outclasses The Times' Eastern European news, which over the years has been a shambles of noninformation. Perhaps that had something to do with the decision of Seymour Freidin, who was foreign editor of the New York Herald Tribune, to write a book called *The Forgotten People,* those of Eastern Europe.

Writing about the raising of Soviet meat and butter prices in 1962, Mr. Schwartz stated:

"More dangerous [than mere discontent] was the spirit of open rebellion the price increases generated. The facts are best known about the pitched battles which took place in the city of Novocherkassk, near Rostov, where hundreds were apparently killed before rioting was put down."

It is pertinent here to present a quotation made by Mr. Schwartz because it would hardly be found except by a diligent scholar. It is from an article, "When the Kettle Boils Over. . . ," by Albert Boiter, in *Problems of Communism,* Jan.-Feb. 1964, as follows:

"The price increases had, in fact, been greeted everywhere with demonstrative anger. Sit-down strikes, mass protest demonstrations on factory premises, street demonstrations, and here and there riots involving bloodshed occurred throughout the Soviet Union. Some of the places from which evidence at hand speaks about such occurrences include Grozny, Krasnodar, Donetsk, Yaroslavl, Zhdanov, Gorky and even Moscow itself (reportedly a

* "State and collective farms have performed so badly that the Soviets had to buy around $2 billion worth of wheat, flour and other bread grains from Western capitalist democracies in 1963-64-65 to avoid distress or starvation in Russia."—U.S. News & World Report, p. 71, Nov. 6, 1967.

mass protest meeting took place in the 'Moskvich' Automobile Plant). And, despite guarded official denials, reports about street demonstrations and widespread looting of food stores in the Kemrovo area are solidly based. An outside observer cannot judge the intensity nor the extent of the various local disorders; neither can he affirm with certainty that Novocherkassk was the worst and bloodiest."

There was little coverage of these stirring events in the pages of The New York Times. And after weighing every one of the many factors that occur as explanations of the large omission, one comes back to the balance of power as the most logical and the most cogent. It is a little ludicrous to see the largest country territorially in all the world, the Soviet Union, now presenting itself as the strongest of all, and then posing as an undeveloped country that has hardly had a chance to show what Socialism can do. At any rate, it flies on these two wings. Mr. Khrushchev at that time, 1962, was rattling his nuclear sword and threatening to level even the Acropolis in Athens if necessary. No doubt he was telling the world that it had better not crow over the Soviet internal troubles. On balance, his warnings were superfluous.

That the Russians continue to follow a destroyer course in foreign affairs is shown by their actions in Vietnam. It is generally believed by realistic observers that the Soviet aim in that area of the world is not primarily to preserve or strengthen the Communist party or to save North Vietnam from the humiliation of its own folly, but to bleed the United States of men and money and tie down large American forces. The American casualties in 1967 were running at a rate of more than 60,000 yearly, the Russians none. (Some Russians may have been killed or wounded while manning or overseeing the operations of Soviet antiaircraft missiles and guns in North Vietnam, but none has been announced.) Russia's monetary cost for her unneighborly behavior is put by some at about $1 billion a year, against the American expenditure of more than $22 billion a year.

The Russians have demonstrated over the years that the Soviet Union differs little from Czarist Russia in following a nationalistic course in foreign affairs. Moscow's contemporary path bears little relation to Communist politics except as they contribute to Russian aggrandizement. The help given to the Russians in this sphere can hardly be exaggerated. This has resulted in clashes between The New York Times and other newspapers or periodicals—a new development in contemporary American journalism. It appears that a number of newspapers over the country follows the same general course as The New York Times, but it is remarkable that The Chattanooga Times, under the same ownership as The New York Times, differs radically from the New York paper in editorial positions. Time magazine and U.S. News & World Report make it a point to check The Times on a number of stories regularly. More remarkable still, this divergence in American journalism is a world phenomenon, more closely related to global events than to local affairs.

It is patently contradictory to advocate a strong United Nations and a balance of power. One cancels out the other. A balance that has to be maintained by diluting democracy with totalitarian Communism is repugnant. A balance that has to be set up with gifts of tribute from decency and freedom to tyranny and vulgar reaction can only be a makeshift, not a permanent arrangement. We cannot agree forever to one rule for the Soviet Government and another for everybody else.

In the United Nations one finds the same kind of balance of power in action that one sees in Europe, building in Africa and Latin America, and contested in Southeast Asia. When the world organization was created at San Francisco in 1945, it was never intended that the Russians should show distinguished leadership chiefly in vetoing, walking out, refusing to take part in the specialized agencies except those in which they can engage in politics useful to themselves and, finally, directing the United Nations Secretariat in ways to suit the Russians. (U Thant, the present Secretary General, has shown himself a consistent exponent of the position opposite that of the United States in the matter of settling the

Vietnam War and other vital issues.) We want and we need a world organization, but we can only wonder how long this house divided against itself will stand. There are built-in divisions in the United Nations machinery and one monkey wrench, the veto in the Security Council, available only to the United States, the Soviet Union, the United Kingdom, France and Nationalist China. The Russians have used the veto 104 times; the United States has not used it at all. That probably fairly expresses the respect or lack of it in which the two nations hold the world organization—the readiness or unreadiness of the two countries to act in concert with others to seek or to keep peace. There could be no question, however, in view of Russia's attitude, about the retention of the veto in the Charter.

Among the disparities of the United Nations, built-in or otherwise, are the following:

1. The Soviet Government has three votes of its own (the USSR, Byelorussia and Ukraine), while other nations have only one. With the votes of the satellite states, which Russia controls in defiance and contempt of the Charter, Russia has eight votes.

2. The Soviet Government pays as it pleases. While it has a tremendous voice and presence in the United Nations, it contributes only about a tenth of the budget, and it pleaded poverty early in this decade when a small increase in its dues was proposed. Russia paid none of the assessments for the United Nations guard in the Gaza Strip (which U Thant unilaterally and unaccountably removed in May, 1967, without consulting U.N. members or the Security Council). The Soviet Union also refused to pay assessments for the Congo operations, which the Soviet Union supported in the Security Council. (Other nations, like France and the Arab States, refused to pay assessments for the Gaza Strip or for the Congo operations or both, but no other country in this category plays such a large role of leadership or misleadership in the United Nations.)

3. The Soviet Government has a seat in the United Nations Trusteeship Council and has given expansive views on the territo-

rial affairs of other nations. Every country with territories or overseas possessions is supposed under the Charter to make annual reports to the Trusteeship Council on those lands. The USSR, with the greatest number of colonies of any nation, makes no reports on any of them, because, it says, they are annexed parts of the Soviet Union or they are independent nations, like the so-called democratic republics of Eastern Europe.

4. The Soviet Government has access to the United States and other countries through its officials and agents assigned to the United Nations, and this access is so massive as to constitute a free movement. Nothing of the sort is available to American or other officials in Russia. Here is an illustration of how this one-way traffic works: Soon after Moscow had cancelled an invitation to President Eisenhower to visit Russia in 1960, Premier Nikita Khrushchev entered the United States without a by-your-leave through his credentials to the United Nations. And here in the State of New York he denounced the United States and other nations to his heart's delight. That brought the United Nations dangerously close to being a Trojan Horse. (It was on that visit that Mr. Khrushchev took off his shoe and banged it on the desk before him to emphasize his views. This made a poor impression upon the Russian people as well as others. It was said to be one of the matters that contributed to Mr. Khrushchev's retirement from public life, since many members of the Russian public felt that he had not acted in a becoming manner. One report that leaked out of the Soviet Union asserted that Mr. Khrushchev never was accepted socially by the people of Leningrad, which is probably the most cultured city in the country. No one could argue that the balance does not tilt sometimes in favor of the free world.

5. No meetings of the United Nations are ever held on Soviet soil. The West has from time to time put out feelers for a meeting of the General Assembly in Moscow but they have come to nothing.

It was never intended that the United Nations should be used and abused in this fashion. Advantages and special privileges have been given to the Soviet Government in the United Nations as elsewhere in order to appease the Russians. This is what constitutes the balance. You give things to the fire-breathing Russians to mollify them, and this is designed to set up an easy relationship of quiet tension. But concessions have never worked to soften Moscow's attitude. It is in the United Nations as everywhere else—a steady rat-tat-tat of Soviet aggression, opposition, arrogance, intrigue and intransigence, not unrelated to killings around the world. The Russians and their compliant satellite aides continued their arrogant and insulting behavior at the United Nations General Assembly meeting on the Middle East in June, 1967.

The Soviet Government played a strange part in the wars of the Congo. Here again, as in Korea, the Russians were on both sides of the battle lines. In time of war the United Nations, therefore, not only has built-in divisions but a built-in Trojan Horse. It cannot be ignored or pooh-poohed. It exists, and there it is. It has already cost the lives of Americans and other citizens of U.N. member countries in Korea. Some American Communists joined this Trojan Horse but were forced out through the courage and perseverance of loyal Americans, members of a Federal Grand Jury, who received all too little help from the United States State Department.

Now figuring in the balance of power is the possibility of a split and even war between Communist China and Communist Russia. There can be no doubt that if these two nations should break apart completely and become deadly enemies, instead of strange allies (as they still were in Vietnam at this writing), the balance of power as we know it would be upset. There would indeed have to be some "agonizing reappraisals" all around. The largest of all would take place in the city of Moscow. At this point the Russians have not removed troops from East Germany. They have not lessened their help to North Vietnam. The internal turmoil in Communist China does not suggest that the Communists, if they should pull themselves together and then the country, would be capable in the early future of making war upon the Soviet Union. Except for the quiet cementing of ties between Russia and Great Britain and especially France early in 1967 through visits of Premier Alexei Kosygin to London and Paris, the Russians have given no sign of flexibility because of the chaotic situation inside Red China. (Instigating a war in the Middle East in 1967, besides increasing military help to North Vietnam, is hardly a sign of flexibility.)

The Communist party of the United States is the fair-haired boy of the balance of power in this country. The New York Times has frequently voiced its jealous concern over measures designed to hamper or discredit the party. The following section of a Times editorial is quoted, not because it is a good statement of The Times' position, but because it is a Times statement of The Times' position:

"The real Communist challenge is from abroad; and the sooner Americans get over the idea that we can solve the problem by persecuting the tattered remnants of American Communism at home, the better able we will all be to face the really hard decisions and hard problems posed by the genuine menace of Communism pushing outward from China and the Soviet Union."

That was printed on June 7, 1961. Since then The New York Times has vigorously opposed United States efforts to halt the expansion of Communism in Vietnam and in the Dominican Republic. It has also continued to express its support for the Castro revolution in Cuba,* even though it is now generally acknowledged to be Communist, with a considerable number (thousands) of Russian troops there. The truth seems to be that The Times opposes interfering with the Communists abroad or at home, as the record shows. The Communists at home have gained—and they maintain—an ironclad anonymity, with the concurrence of the press.

The balance of power requires a laissez-faire for the Communist party, even though this gives the Soviets a hand in the internal affairs of the United States. The Communist party is basic in any

* Herbert Matthews retired from The Times August 31, 1967.

understanding of the balance. The attacks that are made upon extremists are most frequently against the John Birch Society and other ultra-conservative groups, not against the arm of the Russian Government in our society. Even a whisper against Communists will bring cries of "McCarthyist!" All-out attacks on conservatives of all shades somehow are not regarded as McCarthyism in reverse. There is no gainsaying that Soviet ability to close off the USSR to others while the Russians operate openly and widely in every other country is no small achievement.

William S. White, a highly respected former member of the Washington staff of The New York Times and now a columnist, wrote in the New York World Journal Tribune on Feb. 22, 1967:

"WASHINGTON—This nation faces a creeping crisis infinitely graver than a dozen Viet Nams.

"It is nothing less than this: Can constitutional and responsible government and the undoubted will of a vast, inarticulate and tolerant majority in fact be long maintained under the unexampled challenges of a tiny, bitter minority which, in some cases unwittingly and in some cases with conscious purpose, seeks simply to drive this country from the field in the cold war?

"Even to put such a query in this rich and privileged land seems at first glance to be extreme beyond belief. But the unbelievable must sometimes be believed; for we live now in an Alice in Wonderland world.

"It is a world in which ugly mobism is only democratic protest; in which elected public officials are sometimes barely saved from physical violence; in which every agency of government entrusted with this country's physical security is persistently attacked and smeared . . .

"Campus 'demonstrations,' whose leaders openly wear the symbols of the Communist Viet Cong, are coddled and immensely publicized, and few of our great thinkers worry here about the 'integrity of American education.' Bearded peaceniks use their 'educational' exemption from the draft to ridicule other young men who are putting their lives on the line in Viet Nam to preserve the privileges of a nasty little lot who openly subvert the institutions of this country.

"It is a terrible tale—a tale of demonstrable Communist infiltration. . . ."

Indeed it is a terrible tale. It is one in which our greatest newspaper has played a part, sometimes positive and sometimes negative. The Times has given vast amounts of space to the activities of the beatniks, the peaceniks, the draft-dodgers, the hellraising monks who have encouraged self-immolation under burning gasoline, the news that the C.I.A. has helped American students as the Russians help theirs. The Times has done nothing to make the war in Vietnam popular or even tolerable. It has never once published an editorial encouraging entertainers to visit the fighting men. It has given precious little space to proclaiming the gallent deeds of Americans and their Allies in South Vietnam. On the contrary, it has done much to denigrate the South Vietnamese. Occasionally there is a niggardly piece about the South Koreans, the Australian and New Zealanders. In brief, The New York Times has rebuffed the war in Vietnam—sought to make it unpopular and advocated on many occasions that the United States Government follow a course that has in the past led to the erection of Communist governments and the loss of countries to the free world.

The arc of reasoning that is responsible for the balance of power stems chiefly from the Left side of the political spectrum. Of course, it draws full support from the Communist party, which in turn acquires strength from the power and resources of the Soviet Government, financial and otherwise. Unless we can say these things and discuss them without hysteria or blinders we shall be multiplying our dangers. Every form of appeasement is akin to dishonor and can only lead to defeat.

CHAPTER II

The Forsaken Peoples: Eastern Europeans

• • •

"TO THEIR BETTER EDUCATED AND MORE PRAGMATIC SONS AND *successors, the old [Communist] party leaders [of Eastern Europe] can offer a mixture of apology and uncertainty.*

"A decade or more of terror, dogmatism and isolation has had to be condemned as a terrible 'mistake.' The 'planned' but actually indiscriminate development of industry has had to be recognized as a terrible waste of resources. And agriculture has been everywhere and all too obviously a failure. . . .

"The resentment long felt for the Iron Curtain against contact with the West is shifting toward the even greater barrier created by the economic backwardness of the East."—Max Frankel, in a survey of Eastern Europe, "Wealth and Stability Still Elude East Bloc Nations," for The New York Times of January 14, 1965.

"The facts were all too plain. Eight years of Communist control [of Hungary] had reduced a country to penury and total desperation. When its people broke out, they were put down by the Red Army with what could only be described as Czarist ferocity.

"Almost overnight, the conception of the Soviet Union as the great leader on the road to a Socialist revolution in the condition of man was either permanently marred or destroyed outright. . .

"It is hard for us to grasp the genuine shock and deep grief for a lost ideal with which thousands of Parisians read the 1956 headline: 'A Budapest les Russes ont tiré sur le peuple.' The Communist world has never recovered from that shock—and it never will unless the Soviet Union proves, as it now shows some slight signs of doing, that it can change its ways and its power structure."
—Timothy Foote, in an article, "The Road Back to Budapest," in The New York Times Sunday Magazine of November 20, 1966.

"BUDAPEST, Oct. 22—It was just 10 years ago that the straw flame of the Hungarian revolt flared up in a dark and divided world and then rapidly burned out. It left almost everyone, including Hungarians, puzzled about what had happened."—Special dispatch, "Hungarians Find Life Better 10 Years After Revolt," to The New York Times of October 23, 1966.

"BACK TO BUDAPEST," yesterday's NBC documentary on life in Hungary 10 years after the bitter, hopeless uprising of 1956, turned a generally benign—albeit occasionally piercing—light upon the accommodation a rebellious people have made to an oppressive regime . . .

"What don't they have? Well, they have virtually none of the rights the freedom fighters died for in the streets 10 years ago. The primary demand—removal of Soviet troops—has not been granted. . .

"The second demand of 1956—free elections and freedom for the political parties—has not been granted, either. The most that has happened has been the sanctioning of a secret ballot within the Communist-dominated elections. Freedom of the press, the right to strike, the right to establish workers' councils, all are still absent from Hungarian life. In time, a new generation will not

know what it is missing."—Harriet Van Horne in the New York World Journal Tribune of November 14, 1966.

"The blood-drenched Communist juggernaut, which has crushed millions under its wheels in many lands, rolled again through Prague yesterday and took to the gallows eleven of the Communist conspirators who betrayed Czechoslovakia into Stalin's hands and now were hanged on the charge of betraying Stalin. These are the latest victims of the Communist party purges which Stalin introduced into Soviet Russia long ago and which have since spread to every country falling under Communist domination."— From an editorial in The New York Times, "Purge in Prague," on December 4, 1952.

"The Soviet Union observes this year the fiftieth anniversary of Russia's two 1917 revolutions. To those identified with the old order then, the abdication of the last Romanov Czar in March and the victory of Lenin's Bolsheviks in November seemed to promise only catastrophe ahead for the country they loved.

"Today, however, the Soviet Union is one of the world's two most powerful and influential nations; its people enjoy the highest standard of living in all Russian history; and the world is richer for Soviet contributions to science, technology, music and literature.

"These achievements have been purchased, of course, at enormous human and material cost."—From leading editorial in The New York Times of January 9, 1967.

"At the height of the Stalin-Trotsky struggle in the Soviet Union during the 1920's there were disturbances and demonstrations that briefly gave wishful thinkers abroad the impression that Lenin's heirs might be about to destroy their patrimony [the Communist society] through internecine conflict. The Trotsky adherents were quickly and easily put down; and since then none of their innumerable power struggles among ruling hierarchs of a Commu-

nist country has ever come close to exploding into actual domestic warfare."—From leading editorial in The New York Times on January 11, 1967.

"MOSCOW, July 14—Estonia, Latvia and Lithuania began week-long celebrations today to mark the establishment of Soviet rule 25 years ago in the former Baltic independent states. . .

"The Lithuanian Communist party leader, Antanas J. Snieckus, wrote in Pravda, the leading party newspaper:

" 'Our happy holiday has produced malicious reaction in the camp of bourgeois nationalists and their imperialist sponsors. This was to be expected. . . .'

"In honor of the occasion, the year's first shipments of apricots from the southern Soviet republics of Moldavia and Armenia are to reach the northern Baltic area. Carloads of Bulgarian tomatoes are also said to be on their way."—From a special dispatch headed, "3 Baltic Lands Mark '40 Incorporation into Soviet, Begin Week-long Celebration With Speech and Song," to The New York Times on July 15, 1965.

"I went over there with a great feeling and sympathy and respect for the Russian people for what they'd done in the war and what they'd been through in the war.

"I had never been particularly interested in the study of Communism.

"As a result, maybe I didn't really understand what a nightmarish system it is—the most oppressive place in the world.

"These marvellous people—the Russians—are very much, it seems to me, the way Americans were back in the 30's in the depression:

"Everybody's a little bit shabby, but cheerful. Although they're aware they don't have a lot of things that we have, at the same time they're not hostile and tense the way Americans are.

"But on top of these marvellous people is this political system that is just a vast lunatic asylum—just absurd. So I wound up not

liking it."—From excerpts from radio broadcasts by CBS Moscow correspondent Hughes Rudd during a visit home from Russia, printed in U.S. News & World Report on July 11, 1966.

"*It is ten years ago today since Nikita Khrushchev delivered his famous secret speech of Feb. 25, 1956, exposing to the Communist hierarchy the vicious criminality of Stalin; and the repercussions of that fateful address have not yet ended. Khrushchev knew he was playing with explosive material when he delivered his speech, but he could hardly have foreseen that he was setting in motion a train of events that would lead to the semi-liberation of Eastern Europe and to the bitter, world-shaking rift of Moscow and Peking. By demolishing the myth of Stalin's infallibility, Khrushchev swept away the moral and political basis for Soviet hegemony over world Communism with the result that this hegemony has disappeared.*

"*Within the Soviet Union itself, however, the evolution set off by Khrushchev's depiction of Stalin for what he truly was, a murderous paranoid and a monumental blunderer, has been more halting."—From an editorial in The New York Times on February 25, 1966.*

Samuel J. Fucello, B.A. and M.A., Seton Hall University; M.A. in history, New York University. "*Once cleared by customs, I entered East Berlin proper. Deserted! Where are all the people? It was Sunday and the shops, with their meagre wares displayed without chic in the windows, were closed. Ah! There are some people! A young man and woman with a child in a perambulator approached. I nodded as I passed. The baby smiled. The young man and woman looked away, unsmiling. They show both fear and pleading, I thought. Down two more blocks I went. One or two cars passed by. Where are all the people?*

"*The street led into the main boulevard, Unter den Linden, and there I saw the people of Communist Berlin. Literally thousands of them: old people, young people, teenagers, children—all promenading, as if it were a religious ritual, slowly, deliberately, up one side of the boulevard to the Brandenburg Gate, where they would pause and look into West Berlin, the old people waving, with tears in their eyes, the young with the resignation of caged animals.*

"After this ritualistic pause at the gate, the promenade continued down the other side of the street. No one was laughing. No one looked at the American stranger—except with sidelong glances. The tone of conversation was slow, lifeless and the few smiles were sad and wise. Zombies—living dead! I turned from Unter den Linden, retracing my steps to Checkpoint Charlie. I quickened my pace. It started to drizzle. It seemed the heavens were weeping.

"At the Communist point of departure I was informed that my East German marks would have to be spent. I relinquished the marks to the People's Democratic Party.

"The two blocks of no-man's land between sectors seemed interminable. I wanted to run away from this open grave. I wanted to be free."—From the Bulletin of the Student Institute on Communist Affairs, Seton Hall University, May, 1967.

"No one has to convince us that the contest between freedom and Communist imperialism is for keeps."—Secretary of State Dean Rusk, speaking in New York on August 2, 1964, as reported by The New York Times on August 3, 1964.

A senior student in an American university told the following story with some annoyance. He said he had been teaching some younger students in the year 1966 about Eastern Europe and had spoken of "the captive peoples," when he was interrupted by one of the pupils, who asked: "Who are the captive peoples?" That marks the road we have travelled since 1939. It is the full course. It shows how new generations look upon maps without knowing history. It demonstrates how nations can be seized by others, incorporated into new frontiers, and become dissolved. The massive suffering and travail of the change, unless experienced or read about in daily newspapers, periodicals or books, are forgotten by the outside world.

Finland, Estonia, Latvia, Lithuania, Poland, Czechoslovakia, Hungary, Rumania, Bulgaria, Yugoslavia, Albania—these have all known what it was to be captive countries since at least the end of World War II. Finland, Yugoslavia and Albania are not today captives of the Soviet regime, but Finland has been outflanked and rendered defenseless as a nation, while Yugoslavia and Albania are Communist regimes with little more regard for freedom and the dignity of man than is to be found in the Soviet Union. No doubt conditions are somewhat better in Russia than they were under Stalin, but Hungary and East Germany, another captive area, received a rude jolt from the Russians three years after the death of Stalin when Hungarians and East Germans thought the time was ripe for them to run their own affairs. Poland is part of the region characterized by The New York Times as "semi-liberated," and the impression is given by the same source that Rumania pretty much goes its own way. Yet it is obvious to the most casual observer with a professional journalistic or diplomatic training that neither Poland nor Rumania nor any other country under the domination of Moscow is free or even semi-liberated in the most meaningful sense of those words. It is bad enough to sell the Eastern Europeans down the river to the Russians. It is wrong and reprehensible to assert that they have freedom when they have little of the sort. The crushing of Czechoslovakia in 1968 may finally have impressed this on some of the optimists.

The nations of Eastern Europe drifted behind the Iron Curtain as a fleet of ships sails into and beyond the horizon. "Nations have no friends, only interests." "All generalizations are untrue, including this one."

The eclipse of the Baltic States—Estonia, Latvia and Lithuania—was sudden and final. Since 1939 there has not been any serious newspaper coverage of those countries by American correspondents. When the three countries "celebrated" their incorporation inside the Soviet Union "with speech and song," the report of this happy event by The New York Times was written in Moscow. There are no regular dispatches out of those Socialist Republics; indeed, there are almost never any dispatches at all from Vilna, Riga or Tallinn. But from time to time there is a piece of startling news that throws a flash of light like a bolt in the darkness, revealing things nearly every one had forgotten were there. For instance, on page 15 of The New York Times on the morning of September 6, 1947, there appeared a story from Philadelphia, under this headline:

STOP THIS 'TERROR,' LITHUANIAN URGES

Plea to World Women's Group Says Soviet Has Deported 150,000, Ended Liberty

A story placed that far on the inside of the paper—page 15—would hardly be calculated to stop the terror (with or without quotes) in Lithuania. The dispatch was written by Lucy Greenbaum, an attractive, able and fearless reporter, who has since gone on to writing books that have brought her fame and fortune. The story said, in part:

"PHILADELPHIA, Sept. 5—An appeal to the International Council of Women to call on the United Nations to 'stop the terror regime' in the Baltic states was received today from the former president of the Lithuanian Women's Council, now living in exile in Italy.

"The Dowager Lady Nunburnholme, vice president of the International Council, holding its first post-war meeting here, read the plea from Mrs. Wincente Lozoriatis. . . .

"Tears came to the eyes of some of the delegates from European nations as they listened to the letter, made public at a group meeting on 'the status of women.'

" 'Today, while the International Conference of Women is meeting under the slogan of liberty, Lithuania, as well as Latvia and Estonia, is still under Soviet occupation,' wrote Mrs. Lozoriatis.

" 'Lithuanian women and the entire Lithuanian nation enjoy neither liberty nor elementary human rights and are living under the conditions of an unbridled terror,' the letter declared.

"She wrote that in 1941 'under the first Soviet occupation' 50,000 Lithuanians were deported to concentration camps in the Arctic regions of Siberia and that since 1944, 'under the second Soviet occupation,' 100,000 more, including two-weeks-old babies as well as 90-year-old men and women, had been deported.

"She appealed to the council on five points. She asked that it call on the governments of the United Nations 'to stop the terror regime and the deportation in Lithuania, as well as in Latvia and Estonia;' that it 'use its influence to prevent the international recognition of Lithuania's incorporation into the Soviet Union, as no government body should recognize a criminal action contrary to general human rights and the international law'; that steps be initiated to return deportees to their homes; that international relief organizations assist the Baltic deportees in Siberia, and that Baltic refugees in Western Europe receive sufficient care and women refugees be represented on the International Relief Organization."

Whether The Times or the Associated Press or any other newspaper or newsgathering organization ever followed up this request is not known. Nothing was ever turned up in vigorous researches on any help given to the deportees. Whether the Soviet Government could have been persuaded under the relentless jackal Stalin to permit any assistance to the deportees is problematical. The United States Congress from time to time has adopted pious resolutions on "the captive peoples of Europe," and all the newspapers have published handwringing editorials. But no effectual help was ever given or advocated, and, indeed, no effort worthy of the name was made to determine the fate of the deportees, much less to bring them back to their native land. Nor, in the case of the Baltic nations, was any sound journalistic attempt made to cover the fate of the masses of those peoples in their native lands.

Seventeen years later a tiny, happy-ending glimpse of a terrifying situation in Lithuania was given. On Dec. 26, 1964, The New York Times printed on page 19 under a 3-column picture a story headed, "Baltic Family Reunited After 23 Years": Mrs. Stefanija Rukas of Lithuania and Siberia rejoined her husband and their daughter at the John F. Kennedy Airport in New York. She had last seen them in 1941 in Kaunas, Lithuania, where she was a teacher and her husband was the school principal. The story says:

"In June, 1940, the Soviet Army occupied the country. A reign of terror was instituted.

"The intellectuals of the country were a particular target. Often they were arrested at night and deported to Siberia.

"As a precaution, the principal, Konstantina Rukas, often took his wife and their 3-year-old daughter at night to his mother's farm on the edge of the city. But on June 13, 1941, Mrs. Rukas decided to stay behind while father and daughter went to the farm.

"At midnight the Soviet secret police arrived. They seized Mrs. Rukas and carried her off. . .

"Mrs. Rukas was sent to the village of Bakchar in Siberia, where she remained for 13 years. She would not talk of her Siberian experience yesterday. 'I worked in the woods,' was all she would say."

Meantime the husband and daughter made their way to a displaced persons camp in West Germany then to America. Mrs. Rukas was allowed to return to Kaunas in 1956. It took another eight years to get the Russians to let her join her family in the United States. Yet we may be sure that Mrs. Rukas was among the fortunate ones among the 150,000 Lithuanians who were deported. She survived.

How many Estonian and Latvian intellectuals among others in their countries paid the penalty for loving learning and hence liberty? One thing is certain: The New York Times was not quick to point out the numbers. Nor is it easy, if at all possible, to learn how many other East Europeans were sent away to death or misery in Siberia. The toll among Poles was ghastly and appalling—first from the Germans and then from the Russians. A bitter column by Jim Bishop in the New York World Journal Tribune on Sept. 23, 1966, bears recalling. First, there were the concerted German and Russian attacks in September, 1939. Caught in the vicious pincers, the Poles had no choice:

"At 2 p.m. on Sept. 27, 1939, Gen. Juliusz Rommel surrendered 140,000 soldiers and there was silence. The first blitzkrieg was over. The Germans came in cautiously.

"In six years, Warsaw dropped from 1,290,000 persons to 150,000. Snows draped the gutless walls. First, the intelligentsia was sent to Oswiecim, which the world calls Auschwitz. Then the Jews. (There were about 190,000 in Warsaw.) The Germans had them in a sealed pigsty, and removed as many as they pleased each day.

"On April 19, 1943, the ghetto began to struggle for life. The German Army required three weeks to erase it, down to the last sewer. The able-bodied were shipped to Germany as slave labor. Schools, libraries, and theatres were closed permanently. In the ruins, Warsaw still breathed.

"The Germans began to pack on Aug. 1, 1944. The Russians were coming. Warsaw arose from its deathbed to fight. Gen. Tadeusz Bor Komorowski (expecting to be joined by the Russian troops standing just outside Warsaw) led the teenage boys and girls against German armor. Within 60 days, 100,000 Poles— mostly youngsters—lay dead in the streets.

"This time the Nazis did a complete job. They examined the remaining population and shipped all healthy persons to Germany, expelled the sick and the old, and when the city was empty, blew it up. It required time to destroy churches and palaces, museums and monuments, but they had time. [Stalin had ordered that the Russians give the Nazis time.]

"On Jan. 17, 1945, Soviet Marshal K. K. Rokossovsky drove

through the cold furnace and saw snow, falling slow and fat, drape the empty city. In a pronunciamento, he said: 'I declare Warsaw liberated.' The rats running along the curb squeaked with joy."

Liberated! East Europeans came to know that word well in the hideous upside-down lexicon of the Russian Communists. The Greeks overcame the word, as did the South Koreans, the Malayans, the Filipinos, the Indonesians, the South Vietnamese and collaterally the Americans, Australians, New Zealanders, Thais, Laotians and other determined peoples. (The Filipinos are resisting Communists for the second time.) It is interesting that in the Communists' effort to take over Greece in the 1940's they followed the same pattern as they are now following in Vietnam—a National Liberation Front and a fighting force. In Greece, also, they committed assassinations and kidnapped children by the thousands, some of whom were returned to Greece years later.

Always, one returns to that conversation that Anthony Eden, who was Winston Churchill's Foreign Secretary during World War II, had with Joseph Stalin in the Kremlin. Eden and Stalin were talking about post-war problems and how to meet them. Stalin said that the trouble was that most victors had never known when to stop expanding. Eden smiled. Then Stalin said: "You think I won't know when to stop, either." Eden was so right, but he could not have guessed then how right he was.

An even more fundamental trouble, perhaps, was that the Russian attitude toward life was wholly different from the kind of freedom practised by the English-speaking peoples, who thought they were fighting to free Europe and Asia of Nazism and Fascism —totalitarianism without principles of law and freedom, with little or no regard for human life or any right to live, with a readiness to commit genocide against great sections of their own people (this was as true of Russia under Stalin as it was true of Germany under Hitler), and a systematic contempt for laws on the part of the dictators.

Soon after the Russians entered Poland it became clear that they intended to stay. Communist tactics boil down to Stalin's injunction to his interrogators seeking "confessions": "Beat. Beat. And, once again beat." When an intended victim was not pliable, such as an opposition political leader, he was marked for assassination. Stanislaw Mikolaczyk, leader of the Polish Peasant party, was deemed lucky to escape with his life to England. Jan Masaryk, the Czechoslovak Foreign Minister, was less fortunate. He was pushed from the second floor of the Foreign Ministry the day before he planned to leave the country. The rise of systematic Communist crime in Eastern Europe is described by Seymour Freidin in *The Forgotten People* thus:

"A new alphabetical language came into use. Men and women spoke the letters in whispers. They stood for police organizations, the hard-eyed security men who took people away at night. More often than not the victims never returned. It was in Rumania the Siguranza; in Czechoslovakia, the SNB; in Yugoslavia, OZNA, later the UDBA; UB, in Poland; AVH, or 'Avos,' in Hungary. The alphabet sometimes changed with shifting personnel and purges. The job was always the same—buttoning up lips and battening down criticism.

"Lawlessness and crime washed like a tidal wave over Eastern Europe in those postwar days. Red armies of occupation lived off the land. They looted and they raped. Soviet monuments to 'liberation' quickly acquired different names among the subject peoples. 'Statue to the Unknown Plunderer,' Eastern Europeans would say as they saw another concrete monument erected in a central plaza. The peasants, defending their own countryside, resisted the incursions of the commissars more violently than their city kin. . . .

"But terror only planted deeply the seeds of doubt, distrust and mass confusion in a generation the Communists set about to nurture as their own. Eastern Europe was in the throes of a revolution and didn't realize it.

" 'You can't do it the way you did in the Soviet Union,' cried Nikola Petkov.

"The Russians and their East European proconsuls paid the

warning no heed. What mattered, as Vyshinsky said, was the letter of the law. Soviet law, then, became rapidly applied the length and breadth of Eastern Europe."

And Soviet law stemmed from the barrel of a gun, the tip of a bayonet, the caterpillar treads of a tank, or any other instrument of force.

The New York Times did not always make the Russians in Eastern Europe appear so unattractive as that. The news was presented but mildly most of the time, and the Russian takeover of the region was treated as an ideological inevitability—with an irritating resignation, it seemed then, but perhaps there was more point to it than one realized. At any rate, the loss of Eastern Europe turned out to be one of the earliest victories for the balance of power theory, which has grown with the years and is now flaunted as a dire necessity for the endurance of civilization.

For instance, on March 3, 1947, The Times printed a roundup of articles under the front-page heading, "Future of Free Enterprise in World Found Uncertain—Times' Survey Shows Nationalization Trend Growing Outside Western Hemisphere—Mixed Economy in Many Lands." There was an introductory lead written by the late Russell Porter, who was an excellent reporter, a solid citizen, and a fair-minded man. Then followed a series of dispatches from Melbourne, Australia; Vienna, Brussels, London, Ottawa, Prague, Paris, Berlin; Salonika, Greece; Budapest, Rome, Tokyo, Warsaw, Moscow, Madrid, Stockholm, Istanbul, and Belgrade. The small heading over the Budapest story read, "Capitalism Lost in Hungary." The dispatch said:

"The Hungarian Government to date has been coy in responding to these (Rumanian) overtures, but few doubt that eventually Hungary will find herself in a Danubian customs union, to which Russia will also be a party.

"Meanwhile, foreign capital is being cold-shouldered out of Hungary by the same methods that are proving successful in Rumania.

"Eventually, under terms of the Hungarian peace treaty, the

Soviet Army must leave Hungary. But steps are being taken—with every prospect of success—to install a Communist-Socialist-dominated Government in office before the Russian occupation ceases. When that aim has been achieved private enterprise will have short shrift."

The author of that piece, not identified by a byline, was so right—so objective, and bloodless—and indifferent. There is a chemically pure objectivity here, without a word about what this would mean to the people or how brutally it was being accomplished. Strangely, one of the groups that suffered most of all in each of the Eastern European countries appears to have been members of the Communist party. That story was not fully told in any newspaper. Not fully told? Actually, it was scarcely told at all. And so, from time to time, we are bowled over by some book or article or perhaps a survey in The New York Times itself telling about happenings in Eastern Europe that had never been reported over the years. One instance is the appearance in January, 1965, of the book *Red Pawn,* by Flora Lewis, wife of Sydney Gruson, who was then foreign editor of The New York Times. (Miss Lewis, a columnist, is a former writer for The Times.) Another instance is the economic survey of Eastern Europe done for The Times by Max Frankel in January of 1965.

Miss Lewis's book made The Times look poor for its failure to cover the story of Noel Field and the great purge of scores of thousands of Communists in Eastern Europe. The daily review of *Red Pawn* added nothing to the stature of The Times, either. Mr. Frankel's articles on the economic mess of Eastern Europe made The Times look good until the reader reflected that the ghastly failure of Communism had been going on unreported for years. Now we have come full circle again. The inanity of some of The Times reports out of Eastern Europe in 1966-67 have to be seen.

The life of Noel Haviland Field was a shadowy and mysterious one until Miss Lewis decided to put an end to the gnawing enigma. With great diligence, courage and candor she gathered and recited the facts for all but the wilfully blind to see. In doing so she lifted a curtain behind the Curtain and showed that Joseph Stalin and his Russian henchmen were even more monstrous than Mr. Khrushchev had revealed.[1]

Gilbert Highet, distinguished professor at Columbia University, writing in the Book-of-the-Month Club News of February, 1965, reacted in the following manner to the book *Red Pawn:*

"In chess a pawn is worth little on the second or third rank. If it can move forward it becomes proportionately stronger. When it reaches the sixth rank it is as dangerous as a land mine. Noel Field was such a pawn. Born in 1904, he entered the U.S. Foreign Service in 1926, left to join the League of Nations secretariat in 1936, and worked for the Unitarian Service Committee in Europe from 1941 to 1947.

"He had been a Communist sympathizer for many years— although Hede Massing, who recruited him as a courier for a Russian spy ring, urged him not to compromise himself by joining the party and getting a card. Fluent in several languages, long experienced in international negotiations, and provided with a disarmingly humane disguise, he was a busy and effective Communist agent at a time when the party needed all the help it could get. Much of his energy was expended on rescuing and sheltering Communists, and, after the war ended, planting them in liberated countries as quickly as possible.

"He also worked with OSS: for the Communists had no hesitation in using OSS facilities, and OSS was so eager to help defeat

---

1. Stalin alone could not have accomplished all his crimes without many accessories, just as Hitler alone did not perpetrate all the terrible acts of the Nazis. Some Russians in exile want a distinction made between the Soviet Communist infamies and treachery and the essential morality and decency of the Russian people as a whole. I gladly do so, for the Russian people are one of the most likable and vital I have ever met. It has been said, however, that a people gets the government it deserves. I have heard persons of Russian origin argue that that is not true, but I believe it cannot be denied that, as the verdict of history, it is true and there can be no appeal from it—as history. The Russian people cannot escape *all* responsibility for the actions of their government, in the present or in the past.

Hitler that it would enlist virtually any anti-Nazi. In 1947 the Unitarians, apprised of his activities, closed down in Europe and invited him to return to the United States. He refused. In 1949 he went to Prague, and disappeared. His wife and his brother vanished a few months later, also in Prague. His foster daughter Erika made the mistake of going to East Berlin in 1950. She got as far as the Russian slave camp at Vorkuta in the Arctic Circle. The others were in prison cells in Budapest and Warsaw, of course unknown to one another.

"Stalin had decided, because of the OSS connection, that Field was first and foremost an American agent. Noel Field himself was never put on trial by the Russians, but many hundreds of loyal Communists in East Germany, Hungary, Poland and other satellite countries who had been helped by him were arrested, tried and imprisoned or executed for treason to the party. After Stalin's death, the Fields reappeared, pale and shattered. Field has severed his ties with the United States. He and his German-born wife live in an expropriated villa in Budapest, sustained by a salary from the Hungarian Communist government and by apparently unquenchable illusions. The story of his bizarre career has been reconstructed with keen penetration and told with clarity in a book which will be a classic among true histories of espionage."

Other reviewers of Miss Lewis's book likewise found that Noel Field was a dedicated Communist in accordance with the evidence offered in great masses by the author of *Red Pawn*. According to her findings, Noel Field boggled at betraying State Department secrets in the United States but not at murder on behalf of the Soviets in Europe. The assassination in which Noel Field claimed a key role involved Ignatz Reiss, code name Ludwig, a German Communist who was the head of a Soviet spy ring in Europe. It appears that Ludwig did not like Field and would not have him as an agent on his (Ludwig's) team. Here is how Miss Lewis tells of the murder:

"The breaking point of a disillusioned believer is a strange thing, not to be determined by any kind of measure ever invented.

It can be erasure of a name from a history book when erasure of millions of the living from the earth did not provoke a lifted eyebrow. The trial and execution of General Tukhachevsky, hero of Bolshevik battles, was Ludwig's breaking point. It was estimated that 25,000 Red Army officers were executed in connection with the Tukhachevsky trial. [Mikhail N. Tukhachevsky was a Marshal, the top general of the Soviet regime at the time of his execution. He was "rehabilitated" in the 1950's.]

"He [Ludwig] sent a defiant letter to Stalin, describing what was going on in Moscow for the insane horror he saw it to be; and he sent a copy to every one of the agents who had worked under him in Stalin's service, urging them to break their apprenticeship to the evil sorcerer. The startling declaration immediately set the vast machinery of the Soviet police in a new frenzy of motion. Ludwig had been of top importance. While agents under him and their sub-agents knew little of each other and the import of their work, Ludwig could expose and thus forever ruin whole networks. There were countless old crimes hidden by the shiny promises of Soviet propaganda and new crimes yet to be committed that he could disclose by the simple act of telling what he knew and naming names. He did not, for the enemy was still Hitler and he said he would not give the enemy aid or comfort. But his mere existence, once so valuable to Moscow, became, in the eyes of the dictator there, an affront and an intolerable danger.

"On September 4, 1937, Ludwig was mowed down by a gunner at the side of a lonely Swiss road. Stalin's GPU claimed its own. The assassination caused a major scandal in Switzerland, and eventually its immediate authors were tracked. A GPU officer named Spiegelglass had been sent to Paris expressly to arrange the murder. It was to have been done with a box of candy containing strychnine, which Gertrud Schildbach, a GPU agent in Italy who had worked closely with Ludwig, was to give the victim. She knew his wife and son and apparently had not the heart to present the candy, which could easily have caused several irrelevant deaths, for it was left behind in her Lausanne hotel room when Ludwig had been shot and the conspirators had fled. But Gertrud Schild-bach, by implying that she, too, was beginning to share Ludwig's revulsion for Stalin and his works, did succeed in luring Ludwig to a rendezvous to talk it over. He came out of hiding to have dinner with her at a restaurant near Chamblandes. Afterward they went for a walk, and he was ambushed. Ludwig tried to fight off his assassins. The police found strands of gray hair in his dead fist, but the dozen bullet holes showed he had been shot from the back.

"Obviously a large number of people were involved in making the careful plans for the murder. The police tracked down several of them and found the names of others, including a 29-year-old Swiss woman student, a White Russian who belonged to a Czarist society, a Frenchman and a Monegasque who were GPU agents in Paris. These were the direct participants. Others must have helped by following Ludwig, arranging the assassins' escape, and covering the GPU tracks. No one ever knew all the names.

"Noel Field apparently talked with Spiegelglass about it, but just what part he played, if any, has never been proved. Later he boasted to Paul Massing and to an important Swiss Communist that he had had a key role; but if he did, it was perfectly hidden."

Later Miss Lewis writes that, "whether or not he [Noel Field] helped the GPU kill Ludwig, he had been connected, however thinly, with the defector, and he knew before the Swiss police investigations made the knowledge public who had been responsible and why." Thus it is clear that Field had to be a dedicated Communist if he would boast of having taken part in a murder. Indeed, this put him, in a way, beyond Joseph Stalin, because the dictator was extremely shy about being connected personally with the killing of defectors or personal enemies on foreign soil—the murder of Leon Trotsky in Mexico, for instance. Stalin never boasted of that, but there can be no doubt that he was the author of that crime, too. Stalin said that he could go home and have a good night's sleep after having done a particularly dirty trick to some real or fancied enemy. Apparently he had few sleepless nights, especially in his later years.

Among other book reviewers who accepted the evidence compiled by Miss Lewis were Harry Altshuler in the New York World-Telegram of January 7, 1965, and William Henry Chamberlin in the Wall Street Journal of February 16, 1965. Mr. Altshuler, reporting on the findings in *Red Pawn,* wrote that "Field wept when, on release from prison (in Budapest), he learned Stalin was dead. And still believing, despite all the evidence, that Communism was what he wanted it to be, he chose to remain in the country where he had been jailed for five years." Mr. Chamberlin wrote:

"By a stroke of grim irony, at the very time when Communist inquisitors were extorting by their well-known third degree methods a 'confession' of being an American espionage agent from Noel Field, his name came up in a very different connotation in the trial of Alger Hiss. Hede Massing, an old friend of the Fields, a German woman who acted as a Soviet spy courier (she completely broke with communism in the end) testified that she and Alger Hiss, acting for rival Soviet spy rings, were competing for Noel Field as a recruit when he was employed by the State Department in the 1930's."

In this connection Miss Lewis wrote (page 257) that Endre Marton, a Hungarian newspaper man, told a United States Senate Committee, "he felt from his interview with Noel (in Budapest) that the Fields' connection with the Hiss case had been an important factor in their refusal to go home."

Quoting from Mr. Marton's testimony, Miss Lewis wrote:

" 'I don't think there is any doubt why he didn't come back,' Marton testified. 'He knew perfectly well that he was involved in the Hiss case. . . .'

"Senator Hruska asked Marton, 'In what way was he interested in the Hiss case?'

" 'He was involved in the Hiss case,' Marton answered. 'That is what he said. It wasn't apparent to me what he meant.'

"Noel admitted to Marton that he was a Communist, which he had not said to non-Communists before, but this time, at the end of 1956, he attached reservations to his credo. As Marton recounted it, Noel described himself as a Communist who 'accepts the Marxist doctrine with the exception of the theory of violence, the theory that the workers' class has to seize power by force, using force. This he does not—this theory he does not accept. Now, how can a man be a Marxist without accepting the theory in full, I do not know, but he is certainly one of them. My impression was that Mr. Field is a rather weak man. The strong character is Herta, his wife. That was my impression.'

"Although he never specifically said that he would not go home because of his Communist background, Noel made clear on more than one occasion that his deepest wish was to see his own country support his faith and join the Communist camp."

In describing the 1956 revolt in Hungary and the Fields' reaction to it, Miss Lewis stated this, pages 254-255:

"Children not yet in their teens fought street by street [in Budapest] against the crushing [Soviet] engines of modern war. Peasants, who had never thought much of city folk, brought all the produce they could into town and left it on street corners for free distribution to the fighters, their way of nourishing the struggle for liberty. The whole world caught its breath as the Hungarians fought to free themselves and, unaided, lost. Budapest was consumed with the battle; no one at the center of the eruption could fail to be shaken.

"Noel and Herta lived through it, silent and unobserved. When it was over, when the flames were doused to smoke and ruins, then Noel spoke. Endre Marton, the Hungarian newspaperman, had learned Noel's address. At the end of the year (1956), Marton and his wife, who worked for the United Press, went up the Buda hill to seek an interview from the Fields.

"Neither Noel nor Herta was pleased, but they courteously agreed to discuss their attitude to the revolution with the Hungarian couple. Janos Kadar, the new Communist leader installed by the Russians, Noel said, had saved Hungary from a 'white terror' and he denounced the 'counterrevolutionaries.' Now, more than ever, the Fields said, they had no desire to return to the United States, for they found life in Hungary after the rebellion 'so exciting.' "

So this Uriah Heap of the Communist world was at long last exposed to view through the efforts of Miss Lewis, who obviously felt the need to take the mystery out of this character. She represents the man's foolishness as boundless and not a little nauseating. His hope that the United States would join his faith in Communism and wallow in his absurd weakness was revolting. Yet Miss Lewis does far more in *Red Pawn* than merely portray the real person of Noel Field—she describes the Soviet method under Stalin of killing off the strongest and most independent of the Communists of Eastern Europe so as to ease the way for absolute domination of these countries by Russia. Miss Lewis cited Ladislav Kopria, a member of the Communist central committee of Czechoslovakia, as asserting in March, 1950, that the Czechoslovak Communist party, trade unions and nationalized enterprises had been discovered to be "teeming with Western and Titoist spies and saboteurs." By the beginning of 1951 the staggering number of 169,544 Communists, "over a tenth of the Czech party's total membership, had been purged." And this kind of thing was going on all over Eastern Europe, on top of the fact that many Eastern European Communists were killed in Russia during the war through Stalinist treachery. Miss Lewis quoted Vaclav Kopecky, the Czechoslovak Information Minister, as having said, "Let us remember how the whole international network of Anglo-American espionage was unmasked in connection with the well-known Noel Field."

And now we come to the book review of the *Red Pawn* in The New York Times of Wednesday, January 13, 1965. The word "Communists" is mentioned twice, once in speaking of Communists in Prague, the other time in connection with "conjectures" that the Fields were Communists. The review carried the heading, "The Story of a Dedicated Man." This review says:

"Noel Field came from a distinguished Quaker family. He was known as able and honest to a fault, a devoted public servant for the betterment of mankind. He had worked in the State Department for disarmament, in the League of Nations for world peace, in Spain against the Fascists. During and after World War II, he had given selfless aid to refugees as European director of the Unitarian Service Committee. If he was a little odd, a trifle earnest in his idealism—well, that came with dedication.

"The Communists knew him better, and when he arrived in Prague, they were frightened."

Imagine, the Communists were frightened. So they put him, his wife, his brother and his adopted daughter into prison for five years.

This review does, however, make several telling points. One is this: "The story of the Fields has never been fully told." Because a great institution like The New York Times permitted itself to be scooped by a determined woman bent upon giving the world the facts in this case. Another useful point made by the review is this: " 'Red Pawn' is first-class reporting, well worth the reader's time." Indeed, it is, even if the review is inadequate. The review in the Times Sunday Book Review of January 17, 1965, is a far more complete statement, although the following observation is baffling: "Boston-born Noel Field never really performed as a Communist spy or agent." That is not the impression given to other reviewers cited here or to this writer, who also reviewed the book. The Sunday Times review, however, also gives high praise to Miss Lewis for writing *Red Pawn*—"she has performed brilliantly what must be considered a public service." The daily Times reviewer took the occasion to drag in the name of Senator Joseph McCarthy, quite quixotically, since it is not at all clear where McCarthyism enters into the deadly struggle of Communist against Communist in Eastern Europe. Who are the McCarthyists today in the differences between Russian Communists and Chinese Communists? That is not an entirely pointless question, because the relevancy with which the word "McCarthyism" is used in the Western world is often dubious. There are red herrings and Red herrings.

By coincidence with the publication of *Red Pawn,* The New York Times on January 14, 1965, published a journalistic bombshell on Eastern Europe, written by Max Frankel, a most astute and capable observer, gatherer and purveyor of news. This told that Communism in Eastern Europe had been a smashing failure and that the people were restive and becoming defiant, while "losing faith in the leadership long provided or imposed by the Soviet Union and are now striking out in many political directions." (Let us accept the word "imposed." For "Soviet Union" the words "Russian Communists" would be a more accurate substitute. But after years of dearth, no one would haggle over a bargain like this.) Naturally, the conditioned reader approached this story with the same skepticism he would have for a live, unexploded bombshell. Having read the first few paragraphs once, one is apt to read them again, as a precaution. Here they are:

"From the Baltic to the Balkans, from the Berlin Wall to the Ukrainian plain, economic slump, stagnation or backwardness have shattered Communist theories and assumptions of two decades. They have also exposed the underlying political strains.

"In one way or another, nearly all the Communist governments of Eastern Europe are seeking ways to appease their populations and to rouse them to more productive labor.

"They are experimenting with the devices of free-market economies, contemplating curbs on the blind and arbitrary powers of the central bureaucracies, enlisting the services of once suspect or hostile experts and even thinking of how they might attract the favors of Western investors.

"The overwhelming impression of a two-month journey through the region is that great shifts of economic and therefore also political and diplomatic policies are in the offing, some with Soviet blessing or tolerance, some in deliberate defiance of Moscow. The entire area seems torn between its historical ties to the East and the contemporary attraction of the West."

This was indeed a promising beginning, and the large jump, or carryover, from page one also contained much interesting and even startling information. One paragraph recalled the *Red Pawn:* " 'You should see the way these youngsters go after us,' a Czech teacher remarked. 'They have dug out statements by Marx against party control of the press. They are demanding confession of guilt for the purges. They are asking why even Communists had more freedom to speak and write in the old bourgeois days.' "

This article and another by Mr. Frankel, printed on January 18, gave a wholly new view of Eastern Europe through The Times. Bloodless and aseptic, like so many Times pieces, they advocated nothing, made only long-term safe predictions, but gently revealed some feeling of discontent and desire for change from the Soviet oppression. There was no suggestion of the Russian milking process through price differentials and currency controls. There were no reports of threats or expressions of hatred. A mild nostalgia for the good old "bourgeois" days is the strongest expression one finds. "Premier Janos Kadar has gained greatly in prestige" in Hungary. "Rumania has virtually bolted out of the Soviet bloc." Nonetheless, one is deeply grateful for this paragraph in the January 14th piece:

"A decade or more of terror, dogmatism and isolation has had to be condemned [by Eastern European Communist leaders] as a terrible 'mistake'. The 'planned' but actually indiscriminate development of industry has had to be recognized as a terrible waste of resources. And agriculture has been everywhere and all too obviously a failure."

But Mr. Frankel has been away from Eastern Europe now for more than two years, and the coverage has drifted farther and farther backward. Try again, Max. That region of more than 100 million people needs another look. The Frankel prediction about Rumania is holding up but only on paper—newspaper. If Rumania has bolted out of the bloc, she has not bolted away from the Black Sea, which would seem to be the surest—and only—way for her to escape from the Soviet coils at the moment. A great newspaper cannot pretend to cover all, or half or even a tenth of the news by sending a correspondent even of Mr. Frankel's stature into a region of numerous countries for a quick survey and a quick getaway to some other post, where Eastern Europe is soon forgotten again.

While this treatment seemed to put The Times on the side of all those who want to see justice and freedom reign in those lands, it was only a token display of compassion. It vanished as quickly as it arose. Moreover, the survey appeared to be based almost exclusively on interviews with Communist officials of the various nations. What we need is a survey that touches intimately the lives of the people, that shows what the imposed Communist system has done to them and what hope they have of ever enjoying the liberty every single human being must deep within him strive for in his mature years.

It is significant that *The Forgotten People,* by Mr. Freidin, was published in the New York Herald Tribune rather than in The New York Times. For that book aims to portray the peoples of Eastern Europe, as well as their leaders, present and past, and to show with what cynicism and raw and ruthless power the Russians took over from the native leaders. For instance: "To weld a common front among Saxon, Hungarian and Rumanian [in Rumania] was a wild dream no Rumanian politician tried to translate into practical terms. Within this division, the Russians and their puppet regime moved with trial by terror. They split communities and drove one ethnic group against another. Ambuscados and resistance were easier to smash by isolating groups and factions." Also: "Everyone knew, or said he did, that the Communists and the Russians would find themselves ultimately in an impossible fix. Give them enough rope, was the cliché applied to the masters of Europe. They got it and hanged their enemies."

Then there was the young Bulgarian intellectual who said:

"We worked for a chance to have people say what might be on their minds. We wanted some genuine social justice. In the old days we were all lumped as Communists. There were quite a few Communists, and though they were not in the majority we still had plenty of opportunity to see how they tried to push us around. You can't be pushed around by both right and left indefinitely, and, after the war we thought we had a future. Now people like me know. Everyone has forgotten us except the Russians. My generation—the hopeful ones—is finished. It's up to the next, and the next."

Bitter, bitter words, but the truth, the reality. In this study the reader gets a look at the arrogance of power in action—the arrogant native Communists who tried to outdo their Russian mentors in nastiness but not, in the long run, in violence. Oh, how they were going to be suspicious of all who did not know how to mouth and holler all the Communist cliches! And how they were digging their own graves instead of building anything but an enormous mistake!

"The most vivid statement of aims I remember," wrote Mr. Freidin, "came not from any venerable statesman but from a 20-year-old boy in Budapest in 1956 who was a rifleman from the Revolutionary Students' Committee:

" 'Some day the world will realize that Eastern Europe is simply people who want to live like decent people,' he said. 'For us and for you it is a search that never ends. It is a journey without time.' "

The timeless pursuit of life, liberty and happiness is something that most Americans take for granted. Nearly every country of continental Europe has known what it is to be occupied and fought over since 1936. (Portugal, and Sweden on the continent, and the United Kingdom were not occupied, but the British Isles underwent some fearful bombing and suffered great losses in men and material during the war.) Spain had a civil war in which the fighting was fierce and the casualties were large. Then the Nazis sprawled over Europe to the Atlantic on the West and to Stalingrad on the East. After them came the insatiable Russians, hungry for victories and hell-raising after suffering from the Nazi invasion and the austerities of Stalin's rule. Who in the world believes that Communism as practiced in Russia and as imposed in Eastern Europe is as productive in goods and human happiness as the freedom, including freedom of business and professional enterprise, followed elsewhere?

Politics, economics and the world cultural hayride make the strangest bedfellows of all. For instance, Time magazine, which hardly misses a chance to lambast The New York Times for some putative shortcoming, believes wholeheartedly in Rumania's great leap out of the Soviet fold. In making a kind of fruitcake case for that view, Time on March 18, 1966, asserts that "the main reason for Western capital investment in Eastern Europe is access to a cheap labor supply." Hence Rumania's leaders "Ceausecu & Co. seem assured of a sound future." It is truly remarkable to read that the Communist countries, so called, are now being sought out as investment havens because they offer a cheap labor supply. Karl Marx would not like that, although it may be so. So we turn to that pillar of the investment world, Barron's National Business and Financial Weekly, and read an article titled, "Dangerous Bridges: Proposals for Expanded East-West Trade Rest on Shaky Ground," published Jan. 16, 1967. The article was written by Brutus Coste and Hal Lehrman. Their article pleads for, among other things, better treatment of labor in Eastern Europe! It argues against easy credit for the satellite states on the grounds that this only encourages the Communist governments (which they are) not to improve the conditions of labor. It is the kind of switch that would not be printable in the Communist world because it makes a hash out of the upside-down language. But Barron's presents Coste and Lehrman as "authorities on Communism in Europe," and their lengthy and logical piece bears that out.

" 'So naive that it borders on the grotesque,' said the official Slovak Communist newspaper Pravda, in a typical comment on the notion that the carrot of American machinery and technology might convert the Marxist donkey," the Coste-Lehrman article sets forth. "But such Communist candor failed to daunt U.S. policymakers, perhaps because the scoffing was restricted to local consumption in local languages, while Red broadcasts abroad, declarations by bloc leaders and informal talks with foreign diplomats, reporters, and stray business men hinted of native nationalism, economic liberalism, evolution toward freedom and other hopeful developments."

While hats were being thrown into the air, the authors suggested:

"Despite the near-unanimity, however, American parents, taxpayers and entrepreneurs have cogent reasons for withholding their hurrahs. One is that Moscow began pushing bridges long before Washington . . .

"A second good reason not to be over-awed by a proposition just because most policymakers and experts agree on it is that recent history bulges with consensus that went wrong. To cite a few exploded axioms: we can trust Joseph Stalin's wartime pledges on free elections in East Europe; let's let the Red Army get to Berlin first; the Chinese Reds are agrarian reformers; Fidel Castro is a patriotic anti-Communist; Arab unity and Egypt's Nasser are irresistible forces which the U.S. should appease and support.

"One way to test the bridges proposition would be to examine some of the economic 'facts' on which its widespread acceptance rests: 1) satellite defiance (especially Rumania's) has thwarted a Soviet drive for bloc integration; 2) satellite economic reforms are trending toward a Western structure; 3) another mark of the satellites' growing emancipation is their increased trade with the West; and 4) satellites have actually begun exploiting the USSR, reversing their previous condition of servitude.

"Upon examination, these assumptions look more like fiction than fact. The evidence suggests instead that Moscow is the chief beneficiary of bloc non-integration; that satellite reforms have failed to shake the basic centralism of Communist management, leaving the concept of a market-oriented economy as remote as ever; that the Soviets have upped their trade with the satellites as fast as the West; and that the USSR is getting more mileage, not less, out of East Europe since the dawn of so-called Red nationalism."

Coste and Lehrman found that Eastern Europe had relatively little to export that the United States would want or could accept in payment and that the basic issue was U.S. credit, not trade. Moreover, they held that unless the Communists gave *something* in return for credit the purpose of bridge-building would be defeated: "They must face up to decentralization, *higher rewards for labor,* greater initiatives for management, real adaptation of Western market techniques (not merely U.S. technology) and a shift from armaments to better-quality exports. But this they will not do unless compelled, because such reforms would reduce the [Communist] Party's totalitarian power."

In opposing American subsidies, or aid, to the satellite countries as they are now operated, the authors look behind the heralded burgeoning independence of the nations of Eastern Europe:

"Consider the theory that plucky Rumania prevented the Soviets from integrating the bloc's economies. A typical statement of the theory—with an air of absolute verity—is J. W. Fulbright's passing reference in a Senate speech that the Rumanians had 'defied the Russians in refusing to subordinate their economies to a Soviet-sponsored program for joint economic development of the Soviet bloc. . . . (and in) undertaking to strengthen (Rumania's) economic independence by broadening their industrial base.'

"The bridge-building chairman of the Foreign Relations Committee was saying that the Soviets had tried to impose a so-called 'socialist division of labor' on Comecon—the Council for Mutual Economic Assistance, East Europe's answer to the Marshall Plan. Each Comecon member was to specialize in what was best for the bloc rather than for itself; all the satellites obeyed—except Rumania, a 'defiance' which wrecked the Soviet design.

"But the truth is that Comecon integration was wrecked by

the region's built-in confusions, which made a 'socialist division of labor' simply impossible. Moreover, Rumania was only one of several members which insisted on 'broadening their industrial base' instead of serving as sources of raw materials. Foremost and decisive among such recalcitrant members was the USSR.

"West Europe could achieve an operating Common Market because the area possessed systems of adjustable internal tariffs, convertible currencies, an infra-structure of independent economic units competing under fairly equal terms and a reasonable free play of market forces. East Europe could not integrate because it traded inside itself by barter instead of money; had no independent economic units, no solid currencies and no internal tariffs to adjust and was entirely innocent of competition.

"Integration might still have been possible if Comecon could figure out objectively which member might produce what item at what cost for equal quality, and make an assignment of tasks accordingly. But this was unattainable in the area's accounting nightmare of artificial money rates and non-economic State-manipulated 'costs' beyond the reach of rational audit.

"Soviet economic journals have been angrily debating for three years just how production cost should be defined. Rumanian money is a normal example of the bloc's currency chaos: the lei's official rate for foreign trade is six to the dollar; for individual remittances abroad it is 12; for foreign tourists 18; for Rumanians tourists 30; official Rumanians abroad have to pay 60 lei for every unaccounted dollar; the lei's real purchasing power meanwhile is 25 to 1."

Indeed, the real nub of the matter of the Eastern European nations is: Will a single one of them dump the Communist system and its economic chaos, and institute freedom of enterprise? No. A subsidiary touchstone would be: Will any of the satellite nations vote freely in the United Nations? That would be the day. The technical dissection of Eastern Europe by Coste and Lehrman, highly recommended to readers who wish to pursue the subject further, points out that it is precisely the workers and peasants who are the principal sufferers under the irrational system imposed upon their countries by the Soviet Government in the name of a sacrosanct Communism, an international fraud of monstrous proportions.

The blind groping of the United States Government to find some kind of detente or easing of relations with the Soviet Government is not all bad, basically. It must eventually come or the world will live under the continuing possibility of being smashed to smithereens. The idea of sneaking up on the Russians, however, and handing them a basketful of credits by way of their Eastern European satellites is altogether bad because appeasement of that kind could only bring increasing demands—until war is made inevitable. That was true in the days of Hitler and it is true today, the New York Times to the contrary notwithstanding. The Times holds that appeasement of the Russians is different.

The New York Times has a tendency to throw its hat in the air for anything, anything at all that could be taken as a sign that the Russians are changing in their attitude toward the West. Agreements with Britain and France that might at best be considered Soviet moves to detach those countries from the West are hailed as signs of detente, instead of maneuvers in the Cold War. For as long as the Soviet regime continues to push the "wars of liberation"—currently the one in Vietnam—Americans will be faced with the fact that Russian imperialism is on the move and that they will have no rest and no detente. While the Russians failed in their big military gamble in the Middle East in 1967, it has to be remembered that they did make it, even while the war in Vietnam was increasing in its fury through Russian assistance. Only the lightning action and the military genius of the Israelis prevented a greater explosion with much wider consequences. The Russians for their part have given warning that they intend to seek another "balance" in the Middle East—the same old one that can hardly mean a different outcome. Other freedom-loving countries may shrug off their world responsibilities, but the United States, one of the two towering atomic giants, cannot sleep. A Times editorial on February 15, 1967, headed, "Anglo-Soviet Detente," said:

"The British-Soviet communique at the end of Premier Kosygin's visit to London suggests that something approaching a *detente* was agreed to by the Russian leader and Prime Minister Wilson. If the communique's words mature into action, there will be major increases in trade, air services, technological cooperation and cultural and other exchanges between the two countries, as well as the conclusion of a treaty of friendship and peaceful cooperation. . . .

"Even more than the earlier Soviet *rapprochement* with Gaullist France, the Kosygin-Wilson accords testify to the rapidly changing political configuration of Europe. The French have been proceeding on the assumption that a nation has to be fully divorced from and even somewhat antagonistic toward the United States to establish meaningful cooperation with Moscow. . . .

"Kosygin and Wilson provided additional proof, if any were needed, that the era of ideological war is ending in Europe, and that national interests—not propaganda shibboleths—are the chief impellers of statesmen and the nations they rule."

Soon after this was published, Americans received the news that new sophisticated Russian weapons were in action in Vietnam —heavier rockets and more MIG fighter planes. Then came the "news" * that the Russians had begun deploying an anti-missile missile system, which could result in the spending of $40 billion by the United States in the endlessly wasteful, but necessary, job of competing with the Soviet Government in defense weaponry. But perhaps that was the purpose of the Russians, since they would hardly undertake a task—or issue news—of that sort without calculating upon the effect it would have on the United States. From the very end of World War II, American statesmen have noticed steps of this kind that seemed to be designed to make the United

* Actually the fact that Russia had built an anti-missile missile system around Leningrad four years earlier was said to be well-known in Washington among reporters as well as officials. This news was printed in the magazine Tactics in 1963, and it was published elsewhere.

States spend itself into trouble. Still later: Czechoslovakia. Additional proof, if any were needed, that the Times' view of the cold war has been largely a matter of wishful thinking.

Two increasingly antagonistic schools of thought in regard to the Soviet Government have emerged in America—the school that would seek to appease the Russians (it cannot accurately be described as having any other method), and the school that would stand up to them but without seeking to engender a great military conflict. At this point, the unflinching group is becoming larger almost by the hour as it becomes clearer every day that the Communists, as Secretary of State Rusk has put it, are playing "for keeps." No doubt each school of thought hopes to prevent a great war, not to make one.

In writing about daily events, or contemporary history, one is forced to rely upon those who follow these happenings from day to day and comment upon them with the greatest force and pertinence. Historians show as much passion and division as the man in the street on such matters. Statesmen or politicians often follow their party's line. Joseph Alsop is one of the most competent, vigorous, fearless and peripatetic of the world's journalists. He has the intelligence and forensic writing ability to stand up to and rebuke bumbling professors who wander into the arena of journalism and politics and expect fighting men to be as docile as students. Once mauled by Mr. Alsop they do not tangle with him, though they rarely change. Another among many American newspaper writers and commentators of exceptional integrity is Henry J. Taylor, a former United States Ambassador to Switzerland and in recent years a columnist for the Scripps-Howard newspapers. Since contemporary human beings seeking to make up their minds about events cannot depend upon history books for decision-making answers, they must look to the student of current affairs. Mr. Taylor's comment of July 2, 1965, is worth considering:

"One of the major problems of the free world today is that the great company of wiser intellectuals nevertheless contains many who are either too civilized or too pacifistic to grasp the obvious about the Sino-Soviet menace.

"Let President Johnson show courageous leadership for a single moment and they shrink away from him like a rabbit bolting for its hole.

"Their wisdom for the West is: 'Give up.' Yet human freedom is so unmistakably the central issue of our day that accommodations with Communist imperialism seem almost like treason.

"Our pacifist intellectuals reason logically, but from a false premise.

"They are the victims of their own irrational belief that wishing well equals doing good and that doing good equals international progress and that, therefore, wishing well is the equivalent of international progress.

"Yet there is no valid foreign policy outside realities. What we are faced by is the Soviet technique of gradualism. Accustom people to retreating and you cannot only push them out of firm positions (like Cuba) but they'll even begin to believe that ducking into doorways is really much better than walking down the street.

"What the Sino-Soviet leadership wants President Johnson to do is not make peace as the pacifist intellectual understands it but to make the President stop resisting Moscow and Peking and seal the status quo, plus a great deal more. These marauders want America's slogan to be: 'Ready, aim, flee.' . . .

"Our pacifist intellectuals help to spread an international epidemic of erroneous reasoning. Their damage to the United States is great. For once a nation appears to be a coward nation the demands of the aggressors increase—and increase and increase."

A dispatch written by K. C. Thaler for the trade magazine *Editor & Publisher* and reprinted in the Bulletin of the Overseas Press Club of America on Oct. 22, 1966, gives some explanations for the scanty, foggy and irregular newspaper coverage of Eastern Europe. Obviously a correspondent cannot write freely under his byline if he intends to travel and report events behind the Iron Curtain. States Mr. Thaler:

"VIENNA—Unlike tourists, Western newsmen still have their problems when trying to visit Communist Eastern European countries.

"The tourist is welcome, especially if he carries hard currency, which makes him a distinct favorite over those coming from the socialist neighboring countries.

"But not so the Western newsman, particularly if he is American or British. His designation as journalist, reporter or commentator in his passport makes him at once a suspect who requires special attention. . . .

"The newsman from the West is tolerated when things go comparatively well in those countries. He is unwelcome when things go wrong or in the event of an internal crisis. He is always suspect and a subject for scrutiny, though once admitted he may generally move freely, except for special reserved areas of a military character. . . .

"The process of news gathering behind the Iron Curtain is no easy task for either the resident or visiting correspondent. Information in the accepted Western sense is not available. Government departments are not easy to approach, and in crucial cases are virtually impossible to contact with any hope of response.

"There are some topics which are definitely taboo virtually everywhere. Most regimes strongly dislike any probing into the top leadership, and are especially resentful of any ridicule of or disrespect for their prominent figureheads. Intra-party problems or conflicts represent another topic which is generally taboo, as are activities and policies of the secret police.

"They like foreign newsmen to deal with their economic issues, provided they are not overcritical, and above all with tourism, especially when they are pointing to the attractions . . . A recent reference by a Western newsman to bad roads resulted in his being refused a renewal of his entry visa . . .

"Another problem for newsmen is to keep themselves informed on day-to-day events outside the Iron Curtain. With only a few exceptions no Western papers are obtainable.

"In Czechoslovakia no foreign papers are obtainable, except for the Communist organs of Britain, France and Italy . . .

"Poland is more liberal. Big hotels have a room set aside where foreign papers are available for on-the-spot reading by foreign guests. Several bookshops sell Western papers only . . .

"There are no foreign papers in Rumania, except at Black Sea resorts for the benefit of tourists. In Bucharest they are not obtainable. The same applies to Bulgaria. The possession of a radio set is often the only means to overcome the stifling sensation of isolation from the stream of world events."

Beyond these problems, with their hidden persuaders, are the terror that struck whole populations, including correspondents, during the Stalinist purges.

In Moscow, I stood in the diplomatic section, quite close to Lenin's Tomb in Red Square, on May Day in 1937. Harold Denny, The New York Times correspondent in Moscow, had arranged my credentials with the Foreign Office. Harold was a great man if ever I knew one. (He was later held in the Gestapo prison in Berlin while that city was being bombed by the Western Allies. He feared nothing and came out unscathed. He told me he tried to help a Russian in the prison whom he had met in the wash room but the Russian would not talk to him, perhaps fearing that Harold was a plant. If the Russian was a secret agent he may himself have once served as a plant since it is an old Russian custom.)

In those days I handled most of the Russian news for The Times in New York, and I had always wanted to see Russia, having read many Russian books and plays, listened to much Russian music and acquainted myself with the Russian language. And so at last I found myself in the viewing stand there in Red Square. Joseph Stalin was on top of the Tomb, surrounded by members of his Cabinet, plainclothesmen and soldiers. Below and in front of him, most prominently of all, because he was in a central position in front of the Tomb, was Marshal Tukhachevsky.

The Marshal was the first soldier of Russia, the top strategist (whose strategy Stalin is said to have followed when the Germans attacked), and one would have thought that every one in Russia knew him as well as any American in the 1940's would have recognized General George C. Marshall, Chief of Staff of the United States Army during World War II. Certainly I recognized Marshal Tukhachevsky immediately from pictures of him that I had seen. Hence my surprise when Harold Denny turned to me and asked me to inquire of the Soviet Foreign Office representative who was standing at my side whether that was in fact Marshal Tukhachevsky standing there in the front of Lenin's Tomb. But I had learned long since not to show surprise, much less to question, an unusual move like that, and I straightway asked the Foreign Office man whether that was Marshal Tukhachevsky there—he was not many feet away; nor was Stalin. Now, however, I was to get a real surprise. The Foreign Office official said to me: "I don't know, but I will find out." He spoke excellent English; and he was gone.

Then I turned to Harold and said: "What's it all about? I can tell you that that is Marshal Tukhachevsky."

"I know," Harold replied, "but we [meaning the foreign correspondents in Moscow] have to have official verification from the Foreign Office, and since you are only passing through Moscow and Russia we thought you would not mind asking the question."

"Oh, I don't mind at all," I replied gaily on that beautiful, brisk, brilliant May Day. The terror had not only not touched me; it was not within a hundred miles of me. I was determined to enjoy myself on this trip through Europe, including Russia. Life is short, and misery is long. It was different with the correspondents, who lived in the nightmare of those times in Stalin's territory. At that moment it did not occur to me that the foreign correspondents wanted to be able to write about Tukhachevsky but they did not want a single statement of theirs to be linked with him, not even asking for identification. The terror had touched them, too.

Tukhachevsky himself was pale, though straight and soldierly; his eyes were red-rimmed. He looked as if he had been let out of prison merely for this occasion because Stalin did not want all those millions of people who marched through Red Square to wonder about Tukhachevsky—that's how famous he was. It was he who put down the sailors' revolt at Kronstadt in 1921. ". . . on March 7, government forces directed by Trotsky and led by Tukhachevsky began vigorous preparation for an assault which took place on March 18. Some 140 delegates to the Tenth Party Congress, which had convened on March 8, joined the soldiers in the final storming of the sailors' stronghold. The fortress fell and some fifteen thousand of its defenders who surrendered were massacred without trial." * That was in the days of Lenin. Now 25,000 Russian Army officers were to die, with their great leader Tukhachevsky.** In Russia there is a saying, "One life, one kopek." It was coined in the old Czarist days, before inflation. Life was cheaper under Stalin.

About ten minutes later the Foreign Office representative, a pleasant and cheerful man, small of stature, returned from nowhere and said, smiling: "Yes, that is Marshal Tukhachevsky." I could not resist saying: "I thought I recognized him from newspaper pictures I had seen." The Soviet official nodded and smiled but gave not the slightest sign that all this rigmarole was in any way extraordinary. In Washington, such a question in regard to the Chief of Staff would have caused laughter after some such reply as, "Oh, no, he's the head of the Boy Scouts." How many times I was to see the dead pan in Russia—the blank expression that betrayed no knowledge at all. And how sad and rather disgusted it made me feel.

I turned to Harold Denny later on and said, "Well, I have confirmation for you. That is the Marshal." Harold immediately informed other correspondents. I saw the story later in Paris.

Tukhachevsky was executed after a brief, closed trial soon

---

* *USSR: A Concise History*, Basil Dmytryshyn, page 117.

** *JUGGERNAUT: History of the Soviet Armed Forces*, by Malcolm Mackintosh (Macmillan Co., 1967) puts the figure of military officers purged at 35,000.

afterward. Stalin at that time was accusing a great segment of the Red Army of collaborating with the Germans and Japanese.* In the spring of 1937 I passed through a military center in the Ukraine at about noon, when hundreds of officers were having a smoke on the outside of the war college, and I remember how tremendously impressed I was with this fine-looking group of men, who appeared stern and grim, and all seemed taciturn—none of them seemed to be talking with others. They just smoked and looked outward. God knows how many of them were slain by the mad Stalin, who seemed to require a certain amount of blood-letting annually. At any rate, I thought then that if these fellows ever came up against the Germans they would give a good account of themselves, and they and others like them did, in spite of the incredible and ghastly bungling of Stalin. In one case, according to Khrushchev, Stalin actually lost hundreds of thousands of Russian soldiers to the German armies, although he had been told before-hand how the loss could be avoided.

On Lenin's Tomb that May Day Stalin never stood in one spot for more than a minute during the morning. He circulated all over the Tomb. I thought he looked concerned and anxious, as he had every right to be. It was in the morning when the great military display was put on, with thousands of soldiers marching through the Square, weapons exhibited and planes flying overhead in formation. In the afternoon the people walked past their leader, millions of people in drab clothes. But the youths, boys and girls, in colorful uniforms were a bright contrast. Now Stalin stood still, on top of the Tomb but at the front. He was a burly man, with a ruddy color in his cheeks, and he could smile. It could not be denied that he did not seem to fear his people. I was the only journalist left in the diplomatic section. Most of the foreign visitors

---

* Two years later—in August, 1939—Stalin concluded a nonaggression treaty with Nazi Germany. Thus he did the very thing that he was accusing the generals of seeking to do—that is, he made a deal with Hitler, and Stalin did it to avert a war in which he foresaw and feared enormous popular defections from the Communist regime. This did in fact occur. Cf. *Workers' Paradise Lost* by Eugene Lyons (Funk & Wagnalls, New York, 1967).

and correspondents had left the stands by 1 P.M. Late in the afternoon Stalin received a delegation of Spaniards. From where I stood it seemed to be an emotional and happy meeting. The Spaniards, however, fared no better than other foreign Communists —or thousands of Russian Communists—in the land of the Soviets under Stalin.

Some months later, after I had returned to New York, Harold Denny wrote a series of articles on Russia, for which he asked the most prominent location. They were put on the front page at the top under a two-column heading. In them Denny characterized Stalin as a dictator of the stripe of Genghis Khan. Nothing happened to Harold. He did not expect to return to the Soviet Union once he went out again. At any rate he did not do so. When World War II broke out he went abroad from New York as a correspondent and was captured by the Germans in the Egyptian desert. He was put into an Italian prison but the Germans demanded that he be sent to Germany as a prisoner of the Nazis, who had captured him—a good exchange prospect, perhaps. Harold Denny died in the United States after the war. He had a most winning manner, a charming smile, lots of ability and industry, endless courage and hope—he was always busy but ever ready to chat and swap yarns, of which he had an abundance. A great man.

Those were the days when The New York Times was not grinding an axe in its news and editorial columns. It was devoted to the truth. The Times printed all the texts of Hitler's speeches with all their antisemitic poison and their frightful ignorance and malevolence. Much was said against Walter Duranty both inside and outside of The New York Times, and much of the criticism of that Moscow correspondent of The Times was justified. He was frankly an apologist for the Soviet regime. He preceded Harold Denny in the Russian capital. Yet Duranty was at least open about his attitude toward the Russians, who did not always regard him without suspicion. While one would not exchange ten Durantys for one Eugene Lyons, for example, the careful reader could gather much useful information about what was going on in the Soviet

Union from Duranty's dispatches. He told of the frightful waste of lives in the Ukraine and elsewhere during the forced and ruthless farm collectivization drive of the late 1920's and the early 30's; and when the country was in the middle of another man-made disaster he wrote a veiled plea for the return of Trotsky! It sounds so utterly absurd today. Yet in those days few who pretended to be thinkers asked for the introduction of freedom. Such unthinkable thoughts were the province of the business men, who had relatively little standing immediately after 1929, which was considered the business men's Waterloo. Duranty saw that there was no movement worthy of the name—no effectual underground, if any at all—that was likely to topple the Soviet Government under Stalin.

Duranty had much of the British colonial's attitude toward the Russians. They were the burden of the Communist leadership under Stalin, the avowed and acknowledged leader of all the Russians after he had outwitted, exiled, imprisoned, or murdered his most dangerous competitors. To Duranty the Russians were "Asiatics." They were incapable of having a democratic country as matters stood, and Duranty was not going to worry much about the atrocities that they practised upon one another. Moreover, Duranty had witnessed horrors in France during the First World War that had insulted his brain and appalled his mind, after which he lost a leg and suffered more pain and anguish. But it can never be said of him that he peered out of a train window in middle Asia and, seeing no prison camps, concluded that there were none in all of Soviet Asia. Duranty knew better. He did not try to fool his readers in such matters. Over and over again he said that the Russians followed the saying, "One life, one kopek." Late in the 1930's Duranty predicted a deal between the Russian Communists and the German Nazis, a hateful and odious thing but entirely realistic from the point of view of Stalin and Hitler, neither of whom had a shred of international morals. Duranty was attacked for that forecast when in fact he was right as a newspaperman. There are times when telling the truth is a dangerous and most unpopular thing. Khrushchev said later that Stalin refused to believe that the Germans were going to attack Russia in 1941 and that he (Stalin) even barred the digging of anti-tank traps on the Soviet side of the frontier on the grounds that that might provoke the Nazis!

Edwin L. James, tough, cocky, snarling and brilliant journalist, who became managing editor of The New York Times in the 1930's, told this story about Duranty: Walter Duranty was an Englishman. He lost a leg in France in a railroad accident after the first World War. Physicians gave him considerable amounts of narcotics to reduce the pain, and he became somewhat dependent on drugs. He asked for the post in Moscow and The Times gave it to him. Here James said:

"Duranty came to like Russia because it enabled him to break his dependence on drugs. And if that is not why he likes Russia, damned if I know what it is."

Both James and Duranty were remarkable characters. James was fabulous, though little known to the average newspaper reader except through his scintillating articles in The Times. He had a tremendous following in the business and diplomatic world. He used to say, in his sandpapery voice, and with a knowing look, "There are wheels within wheels." Both men would have been aghast at the newspaper principle that news should be written on the basis of what you hope will become the truths, or failing that, that news should be evaded or ignored—or that the truth should be published only fitfully in such areas as Eastern Europe on the grounds that too much truth interferes with bridge-building.

For instance, the story from Budapest published on the front page of The Times on Oct. 23, 1966, the tenth anniversary of the Hungarian revolt, was repugnant to this reader. There was no mention whatever in The Times of a gathering of former Hungarian freedom fighters in Washington on the evening of October 22 to commemorate the bloody bid for freedom that failed, with the flower of Hungary's youth slain, maimed or exiled. The Budapest dispatch asserted that the revolt in 1956 "left almost everyone, including Hungarians, puzzled about what had happened."

"Today," the dispatch said, "in the lambent light of autumn, Budapest is glowing perhaps more beautifully than ever before. There is a shining new bridge spanning the Danube." (No doubt a very practical example of bridge-building.)

The correspondent mentions a taxi driver who refused to talk about the revolt and a Communist writer who was opposed to it, to prove that "utter confusion reigned in those days" about the insurrection. "Ten years is a short time for a nation with a history of more than a thousand years," the dispatch says. "Ten days of revolt against Communist power is shorter still." But it was not a revolt against Communist power. The revolt was against Soviet Russian power, and it was started by Communists—Hungarian Communists. Confusion reigns today as well. Two more paragraphs will suffice:

"Curiously enough, Janos Kadar, the man who was regarded a decade ago as a traitor when he was appointed Premier Nov. 4, 1956, under the protection of Soviet guns, has become a surprisingly popular leader. He is widely viewed as a Hungarian patriot . . .

"The Soviet Union remains Hungary's foremost trading partner, and will be for decades to come. The Soviet Union remains vitally involved in Hungarian affairs and keeps 50,000 troops in the country."

A solid bit of information, that, but it is about the only useful suggestion of news to be found in this thin substitute for journalism. In fact, it is an outright defense of the Soviet occupation. How does the writer know that the Soviet Union will be Hungary's foremost trading partner "for decades to come"? The writer might plead that such information as he gave is all that he was permitted to write if he intended to stay in the country. If so, it would seem to be better to have no dispatch. Unfortunately, it appears that that is the kind of reporting that The New York Times wants out of Eastern Europe today.

There is, however, as has been said, no consistency in The Times policy. An editorial, "East Germany and the U.N.," published on March 22, 1966, said:

"The puppet East German regime, which imprisons eighteen million people behind barbed-wire and denies them reunification with West Germany, has no place in the United Nations—an organization of independent states."

The Soviet Government has demonstrated beyond peradventure that it will not permit any independence of action in the United Nations by the satellite nations. The editorial continues:

"The proposal of other Communist countries (the Soviet Union, that is) that East Germany be admitted would frustrate rather than promote reunification of Germany, as the joint American-British reply has emphasized. If the Communist objective were really to achieve 'reconciliation' with West Germany and thus pave the way for reunification, as the Communists assert, something might be said for an examination of the problem in a proper form. But Europe's most unpopular Communist regime seeks precisely the opposite, an enhanced legal status that will harden the division of Germany."

If East Germany is a "puppet regime," as indeed it is, it is not East Germany that is seeking to harden the division but the nation that pulls the puppet strings, the Soviet Union. To confound the confusion absolutely, the last paragraph of the editorial says:

"The essential principle to be safeguarded is that of self-determination. Whenever the East German regime is prepared to accord that right to the people it misrules, it will have no difficulty finding a forum in which to advance the objective."

But the East German regime—that is to say, the Soviet Government—is not going to grant self-determination to the East German people. That was the principle established, positively, in June of 1953 and reinforced for all of Eastern Europe, in Poland in October of 1956, in Hungary in October of 1956, and now in Czechoslovakia in August of 1968—that there was not to be self-determination. Is there less reason why the Hungarians should have self-determination than the East Germans? The Times editorial attack was vigorous but it certainly was a tilting at windmills.

One year later—on March 16, 1967—The Times published a

story on page 3 under a four-column headline, "Poland and East Germany Sign a 20-Year Military Pact Aimed at Bonn." The dispatch out of Warsaw by the Associated Press quoted Wladyslaw Gomulka, Polish Communist leader, as saying at the signing that the positions of West Germany and the Communist states of Eastern Europe are "contradictory, never to be reconciled." Thus reconciliation goes out of the window. Yet, despite the "semi-liberation" of Poland, it is entirely possible that the whole round of treaties signed among East European states will have little validity if the Soviet Government decides to overrule them.

A few headlines will give a further idea of the character of The Times coverage of Eastern Europe:

"Anger Over Prices Wanes in Hungary" —Feb. 27, 1966
"A Sunny Budapest Casts Off Worry" —Feb. 28, 1966
"Hungarians Who Like Gambling Keep Two
State Lotteries Busy" —March 6, 1966
"Ideology Withers in Eastern Europe" —March 28, 1966
"Rumanians Practice Red Magic: Now You
See It, Now You Don't" —April 8, 1965
"Poles Remember Another October '56 Show-
down With Soviet Recalled" —Oct. 20, 1966
"East Berlin Assumes Air of Capital City Peo-
ple Display Sense of Solidity, Pride and
Comfort" —March 11, 1967
"Czech Christian Church Termed More Vital
Under Communist Regime" —Nov. 10, 1966
"Prague's Beauty Emerges Once Again" —Jan. 29, 1967

The U.S. News & World Report in an article, "Communism: World's Greatest Failure," on December 5, 1966, stated:

"A recent visitor to Cuba wrote this in the Neue Zuericher Zeitung, a Swiss newspaper:

"'While in Eastern Europe Communism prevented cities from recovering, in Cuba it has within a few years completely run down one of the most flourishing capitals of all Latin countries . . .

It is not wealth, but rather poverty, that has been distributed and equalized."

The Russians never intended that Eastern Europe should be a showcase of prosperity for the West or for the East—no doubt. But it is not at all probable that the Russians would know how to make a prosperous Eastern Europe while their own country was forced to purchase grain for itself as well as some areas of Eastern Europe, though both regions were once abundant granaries and could be so again if the farmers had greater freedom to make them so.

In The New York Times Sunday Magazine of March 12, 1967, there is an article by David Binder entitled, "The Lenin Farm is 'The Best Collective in Hungary.' " It reads like a Horatio Alger study in success until you analyze some of the figures and until you arrive at the last paragraph. After all the cognac, coffee and those dark brown Kossuth cigarettes, one could be "dizzy with success," as Joseph Stalin used to say about some of his worst mistakes. We learn that this collective wheat farm of 10,677 acres supported 948 members, of whom 700 worked. That is to say, 248 were retired, and they received $29,700 a year in pensions—about $120 each annually. Seven hundred persons working on 10,677 acres figures out to one person for 15.2 acres. The Farm Journal, an American publication not linked with the United States Government, is authority for the following comparative figures for farms and farm families and employes in this country. An 8,000-acre wheat farm in Kansas is worked by the owner and eight (repeat 8) hired men. The owner keeps the men on his payroll all-year round because good or experienced men are not always easy to find, though they are not needed in the winter. The average number of man hours per acre of wheat grown was 2.9 in 1964. For 1,000 acres that would mean about 3,000 man hours. For a modest 8-hour work day that would be 375 man days per 1,000 acres, or one (repeat one) man per 1,000 acres per year. The average size of a farm in the United States in 1964 was 351.5 acres. (The figure goes up each year.) There were 3,100,000 farms in America and 5,600,000 farm workers in 1964, so that there were fewer than two workers per farm of 351.5 acres. About 95 per cent of the farms in the United States are family-owned, rather than owned and operated by large corporations, and the ratio of family-owned farms to corporation farms is not decreasing. In the United States one farmer supplies himself and 30 (thirty) others with food. The farm population in the country is 5 per cent of the total. In Russia it is 50 per cent, and still the crops are poor by comparison with those of the United States.

If in Hungary the idea were to make work for people, that would be one thing, but the collective farm head said he felt the work could be done by half the number of the present staff. It is not much to look forward to a pension of $120 a year, on the part of the workers retired from the farm. And this is the "best collective." The others give poor reports, which figure in the total annual harvest of Hungary. Everything, including time, seems to be on the side of the wisdom of having the greatest amount of private initiative in agriculture, in industry and in every other human pursuit.

"This brings the American visitor to a vision of troubled Utopia," Mr. Binder writes, "perhaps not unlike those early Utopian Socialist experiments, the Brook Farm in Massachusetts and the Phalanx Farm in New Jersey, which foundered more than 100 years ago. The collective farm in East Europe today is also a noble experiment combining strong elements of faith and charity. Good ones, like the Lenin collective, may even provide a basis for efficient modern farming. But the evidence suggests that its very organization precludes the development of the apex of efficiency: a maximum of machines and a minimum of men."

That is the last paragraph.

It is a one-dimensional kind of piece, bloodless, with no invidious comparisons (Canada is mentioned once). It is not an uninteresting story. It is just that it is highly superficial, on the side of bridge-building perhaps. We do have to be grateful for a paragraph like this:

"In theory, all of Hungary's more than 3,000 collectives have the right to sell their products on the open market, but in practice no real market exists. Furthermore, the collectives do not possess the means or the capital to provide transport. So, in general, the collectives make contracts with state purchasing agencies for their sales. But the economic reform foresees greater contracting freedom and possibilities for the farms."

Things are always "in the future" with the Communists. Mr. Binder, however, has a right to say that he warned the reader early on in this article. For the farmer who is utterly dependent on the government for his market knows that he is in trouble, especially the farmer who has no choice at the polls—no way to throw the rascals out. No wonder stealing is rife on the collective farms of Hungary.

The reader may have noticed that Albania has hardly been mentioned in this chapter—for the reason that The New York Times almost never covers that little country on the Adriatic Sea. It plays a large newspaper role as an ally of Communist China in the great dispute between that nation and the Soviet Union over the direction Communism should take. This boils down to a quarrel between the two nations over which should lead the Communist parties of the world. "Albania"—that is, the Communist leaders of the Albanian party, formed in 1941 while the Western democracies were fighting to rid Europe of Nazi totalitarianism—Albania is with Communist China. A strange bedfellowship that could only happen in a rapidly unifying world. The courtship must have been conducted by radio. Albania's population is estimated at 1,865,-000, Communist China's at 700 million. Albania's contribution to the theory of Communism has not been extensive. No Albanian Mao Tse-tung ever said, "Let a hundred flowers bloom," only to have to take it back not many months later. The blooming flowers have been the basis of Red China's "cultural revolution," which in the Peking lexicon means "non-cultural counter-revolution," or purge and rule by thugs. Officially and journalistically, we do not even know that flowers bloom in Albania, the capital of which is Tirana. The little country has been consistently ignored by the press of the "imperialist nations", except for its gadfly aspects. Actually, there is no great desire on Albania's part to be covered by correspondents. Nonetheless, it is the duty of a great newspaper to survey the nation that plays such a large role as Communist China's chief partner in the perennial dispute with Communist Russia. Albania has been left alone even more than Bulgaria. It makes the oddity of Albania's world political position more remarkable.

One of the saddest commentaries upon the condition of the Eastern European countries is a dispatch from Warsaw written by David Halberstam for The Times of February 10, 1965. It said that lines of Polish people seeking visas to enter the United States started forming before the United States Embassy at 6 A.M., although the offices did not open until 8 o'clock. It said that 80,000 were registered for visas but that the embassy was only then processing applications made in 1959. The chief reason for these Poles' desire to emigrate to the United States seemed "to be simply a desire for a better life." This dispatch did not endear Mr. Halberstam to the Polish Communist Government, but being loved is not the function or usually the fate of an honest correspondent.

The news coverage of the Soviet Union by The New York Times is not sufficient to keep the reader abreast of Russian events without reference to other newspapers and periodicals. Of course, the Russians do not make it easy or even possible for the newspaperman to give a rather complete picture of what is going on in their country. It is convenient to have a body of doctrine handy to prove that foreign newsmen are spies—and that, even if they are not, their governments would use every item of information sent out of the Soviet Union to combat it in one way or another. Vast areas of the country are barred to correspondents except for occasional visits. You don't just get on the train or plane and go in Russia. You must have permission from the Foreign Office first. And you don't wander all over the place when you do get a chance to get out of Moscow. You are not privy to what the government leaders are thinking. Neither Communist Party Secretary Leonid I.

Brezhnev nor Premier Alexei N. Kosygin gives press conferences, at which embarrassing questions may be tossed at them. From time to time they do give interviews, which are no doubt designed to serve a special purpose. They are not granted at random or on the basis of personality or any kind of non-political favoritism. It must be evident that covering the Soviet Union is the most difficult task a newspaper can undertake. It is simply not possible for any newspaperman, no matter how good, to do the job.

The New York Times' zealous pursuit of a detente between the Soviet Government and the United States precludes anxiety on the part of the newspaper that its readers are not being fully served. Hence the necessity to present the Soviet Union in the least unfavorable light in its own territory; in that of other nations, some of them captive, or satellite, countries; and in the United Nations. Naturally, a large book could be written on this phase of Times coverage (or non-coverage). In truth, it is likely that The Times is showing somewhat more freedom in revealing Russian activities now than at the time of the Korean War, which will be dealt with separately.

The Soviet Union had a bumper grain crop in 1966. A Times dispatch from Moscow for the paper of October 9 said that the wheat harvest was expected to be around 90 million tons, setting a new record from the previous mark of 76.6 million tons in 1958 and showing a great recovery from the 1963 "crisis harvest of 49.7 million tons." Soviet annual internal wheat needs are put at 70 million tons. So the 1966 crop provided a tidy surplus. It was something to cheer about all right, but it was not going to transform the peasants overnight into rich farmers. Hence the surprise of some readers when they saw in The Times of March 16, 1967, a story bearing the headline: "Soviet Study Finds Prosperity on Farms Is Lowering Morality." It was startling to read that one good crop had introduced such prosperity that the peasantry was becoming decadent. The story said:

"MOSCOW, March 15—A new problem is arising on the Soviet Union's collective farms—the blight of prosperity.

"According to a sociological study published today, the rapid improvement in the condition of the farmers is being accomplished by a deterioration of moral integrity and work discipline and an undermining of the development of a 'Communist psychology.' "

The study centered on a single collective farm at Kazminskoye in the richly fertile Stavropol region of the North Caucasus and would be unrepresentative of the Soviet Union as a whole. This the story did not say. It continued:

"The writers noted that earnings on the farm more than doubled in the last six years [but without knowing what the original pay was, the reader cannot know what the doubled amount would be]. At the same time, the sale of vodka in the village stores also doubled. This was eloquently evident, they said, from the number of drunken people stumbling along the village streets in broad daylight. . . .

"The writers, Vladimir Logvinov and Aleksandr Yanov, protested that farm leaders were neglecting the 'moral education' urgently needed as farmers found themselves with money to burn."

Strange to say, people in the Soviet Union have had "money to burn" for years on end but that does not prove that they enjoy prosperity. Often their money would buy little but train rides or some other diversion, vodka being one of them. The correspondent sitting in Moscow picked this story out of the Komsomolskaya Pravda (Young Pravda) and sent it on, without explanations, and thus gave a false impression of general prosperity on the farms. The story said that one of the chief causes of the decline of "rectitude" on the farm was that the director ignored suggestions made by the members for improvements in the fields and barns. At that point the story went into a situation that has plagued Communist farm life in the Soviet Union from its inception:

"As a result, they (the writers) added, the farm families are giving more time to their private plots and animals and have become increasingly involved in shady manipulations to increase their wealth at the expense of the collective farm.

"An indifference to theft on the farm was assailed by the two sociologists, who described the following scene with dismay:

" 'On the farm sector operated by the fourth brigade, women were stuffing bags full of ears of corn * before our eyes and those of the director, A. I. Rudenko. They were dragging the bags home and returning for more.

" ' "You don't really think that is stealing, do you?" Rudenko said, shrugging his shoulders; "after all, a team driver will load up a whole wagon and dump it in his yard. And you should see what the tractor drivers take." ' "

It is reminiscent of a situation described by The Times writer on Hungarian collective farms. Paying too much attention to private plots, stealing and drinking on Soviet collective farms is still news but it is not novel. It does not represent a great decline in morality, nor indicate the grave inroads of prosperity. Bouncey, unconventional Mr. Khrushchev when Premier revealed a good deal more about what was going on in the Soviet Union than we learn today. In one of his outbursts he flailed at the Russian economy from stem to stern. An item on the decline of morality as seen by him is quoted on page 155 of Mr. Schwartz's book, *The Soviet Economy Since Stalin:*

"Many planners, Khrushchev complained, get their jobs through 'friendship and nepotism,' have no 'production experience, do not know management fundamentals, work organization, or the accounting system . . .'

"Finally, Khrushchev assailed different types of corruption, theft, embezzlement, and swindling in the Soviet economy. Thievery from state enterprises detected during the first half of 1962 and made the subject of court cases, he revealed, amounted to 56,000,-000 rubles. Padding of accounts and misrepresentation of different kinds were rife on Soviet farms, he declared, while bribery had penetrated Soviet institutions and had even infected executives belonging to the Communist party. As a result, he declared, 'state

* The story read "cornstalks," apparently a mistranslation.

goods are wasted, apartments assigned illegally, land plots given away, pensions granted, students allowed to enter higher educational institutions and even diplomas granted, all for bribes."

Mr. Khrushchev at that time (1962) was only confirming what was general knowledge—that the collective farms were breeders of human degradation and economic waste. Yet stories of this kind almost never get into The New York Times—that is, stories describing in detail the seamy side of Soviet life on the farms and in the factories. The average cash payment per family per year on the collectives has been about $200, and this is a big increase from the annual $60 per peasant household in 1952. If any peasants have money to burn, it is because the government is not offering them things they want—and need—to buy. And if this is happening in 1967, it is simply an extension of what has been going on for years.

Victor Riesel, labor columnist for the Hearst papers, wrote for the New York World Journal Tribune on January 5, 1967:

"WASHINGTON—From the Soviet Union, via two American labor men, comes news, buried in two unnoticed reports, that if such hardworking proletarians as steelworkers and teamsters can't eat slogans they grow lean and hungry under today's Socialism.

"One of these eyewitness reports discloses that a Soviet steelworker's average wage per week (a mighty long one) is $41. A highly skilled worker averages $68.50 a week. And that includes bonuses for those who don't get into trouble with the union-sponsored 'Comrade Courts.' This is less than a third of that being earned by an American steelworker this New Year season.

"Nor does the Soviet teamster do better. Worse, in fact. The second report now at hand discloses that a truck driver's average wage under socialism—50 years after the revolution—$38.50 a week . . .

"From Russia, without love or hate but in pure objectivity, the report on steelworkers is brought back by Meyer Bernstein, head of the United Steelworkers of America's International Affairs Dept. The trucker account comes from none other than veteran labor lawyer, one of Jimmy Hoffa's earliest counsels, David Previant. He, too, returned recently from the USSR. In his chronicle Previant discloses that truckers in the USSR earn as little as 68 rubles to drive small trucks—or about $26 a week. As for 'steel,' Bernstein's memorandum reveals that the lowest scale for a plant worker is 50 rubles a month—or about some $13.50 a week.

"But it is not merely the subsistence wage scale which appears to disturb the U.S. steel union official. This pay, though it ranges as high as $110 a week for managerial men who must belong to the Russian union, is not as disquieting to American labor as the fact that there is no such thing as a real union in the Soviet Union . . .

"Thus the low wage scales from 50 to 400 rubles a month—at an exchange rate of $1.11 a ruble—is not all that debilitates the dignity and living conditions of a USSR steelworker. The cost of living is higher than in the West (a suit of clothes costs a month's pay). Consumer goods are 'extremely short'."

There is the answer to the problem of the peasant with money that he cannot spend, assuming that the Soviet sociologists did not exaggerate the plethora of money (not a very safe assumption). Obviously, the factory worker and truck driver do not have money to burn even though their pay is higher, for most of them do not have a private garden for their vegetables and milk, although gardening by city workers is not rare. Up to now changes in the material and cultural conditions of the workers and peasants of the Soviet Union have moved with the rapidity of a glacier. It must be remembered that in 1953 the grain crop in the USSR was lower than that produced on the same acreage in 1913 in Czarist Russia (*The Soviet Economy Since Stalin,* page 62).

Sometimes The New York Times practice of neglecting some of the facts about the USSR in order to build bridges causes other publications to show irritation. For instance, The Times reported from Turin, Italy, on May 5, 1966, that the Fiat Automobile Company had signed an agreement to build in the Soviet Union an automobile factory with a daily capacity of turning out 2,000 vehicles. This caused Forbes magazine on October 1, 1966, to print a sputtery article headed: "TO RUSSIA—WITHOUT LOVE. Not many people want to talk about it, but the fact is that U.S. industry has a major role in the Soviet Union's plans for a vast new automobile industry." That story said:

"This is the story behind the story that appeared in the *New York Times* of May 5.

"It's true, as the *Times* and other newspapers reported, that Italy's Fiat automobile company has made a deal with Aleksandr M. Tarasov, the Soviet Minister for Automotive Production, to help the Soviet Union build a modern automobile plant with a capacity of about 600,000 small and medium-sized cars a year.

"What they didn't report was that Fiat will be serving as a middleman for the U.S. machine-tool industry.

"Three-quarters of the machinery that Fiat installs for the Russians will come from the U.S., either directly or indirectly through European subsidiaries and licensees of American firms. It will really be the U.S. that puts the Russians on wheels.

"Until now, the U.S. Government has refused to permit the export of U.S. machine tool technology to Iron Curtain countries on the grounds that it would help them build up their armed forces. However, this arrangement has the approval of both the State Department and the Department of Commerce."

The Forbes story went on to list American manufacturers who will take part in the deal to build the $887 million Soviet plant. The article expressed no hard feeling toward The Times but showed an eagerness to give details that The New York Times had not supplied. An odd aspect of the project was the revelation of a United States investigative arm, which seemed to be commenting on a permissive action by the State Department. Mrs. Alice Widener, the newspaper columnist, wrote early in 1967 to the chairman of the House of Representatives Subcommittee on International Trade, saying this:

"I take pen in hand to inquire whether it is true that you agreed to let the Export-Import Bank lend $50 million to an Italian credit institution to finance the sale of American machine tools for the new Fiat automobile plant at Togliatti (formerly Stavropol) on the Volga River in the Union of Soviet Socialist Republics . . . We see in the papers that the Fiat cars made in the Soviet Union won't be bought by Ivan Ivanovitch. The Central Intelligence Agency says the cars will be manufactured for the Soviet 'bureaucratic and managerial elite, not the average Russian.' Doesn't this mean that Joe Doakes will be lending his hard-earned tax money to the Ex-Im Bank to furnish American machine tools on credit via Milan to Moscow so that Kosygin, Brezhnev and the affluent clique in the Praesidium can ride around in comfort while Ivan Ivanovitch ramps to work on foot? Could you please tell us how this $50 million loan (to) Soviet Russia will help bring about a classless society there? Seems to us that what our American nieces and nephews will be doing in this deal is financing joy rides for Communist economic royalists." (The loan was subsequently voted down by the U.S. Senate.)

By the trickle-down theory of economics, the people would be able to have used cars. Still, the Russian people are less forsaken than those of the former Baltic States and others in Eastern Europe. The New York Times carried the story of the CIA. Not prominently featured, if printed at all, was a story like this one from Time magazine of Sept. 30, 1966:

"Pittsburgh Oral Surgeon Robert M. Hall was delighted by the invitation to visit Soviet hospitals. Like many Americans, he figured that Russian scientific skills in space and nuclear weaponry must reflect a similar competence in medicine. He was anxious to learn whatever he could.

"Fortnight ago Dr. Hall returned from his two-week tour in Leningrad and Moscow as a guest of the Soviet Ministry of Health. He was disappointed. 'I learned nothing,' he said. 'There is no area of equipment or research or instrumentation that comes close to that of the United States. I saw no hospital or institute as well equipped as any hospital or institute in the U.S.'

"During his visit Dr. Hall observed 15 operations and 'was

appalled by the primitive conditions.' At Moscow's Institute of Reconstructive Surgery, widely regarded as one of Russia's best, he was ushered into a small operating room without proper aseptic precautions . . .

"As far as he could determine, Russian researchers seem to go out of their way not to learn from the rest of the world; they doggedly carry on experiments already completed elsewhere. Spillover from space research has played a key role in the growth of American instrumentation, but Dr. Hall could detect no such beneficial results in the U.S.S.R. Electronic devices are so scarce, he said, that they are 'virtually unavailable. Medical technology, as we know it, is nonexistent.'

"There are, to be sure, some compensating factors. The modern drugs and vaccines familiar in the U.S. are also used by the Soviets, and no available statistics suggest that their death rate is unusually high."

Here is another item, from the U.S. News & World Report of July 11, 1966, printed as excerpts from radio broadcasts made by Hughes Rudd, CBS Moscow correspondent, during a visit home to the United States in that year:

"I've never seen any place where there were so many total drunks—drunks to the absolute extremity. They don't just have a drink. They get smashed. All over Moscow, you see people in the same condition you see among men on Skid Row in an American city.

"One school of thought in the Communist party thinks that they should open bars instead of just having liquor stores and restaurants where you've got to buy the whole bottle. You can't just buy a drink anywhere in Russia.

"The Russian expression is: 'I'm looking for a third,' because they are sensible enough to know that if one or two men cannot handle a bottle of vodka, three is just about right. So strangers on the street will approach each other and say: 'I'm looking for a third.'

"They finally pick up three men who need a drink, and then

they go and buy a bottle of vodka (there is no American whisky or Scotch, but there are wines and beer) and stand in a doorway and drink it, and fall down on the street—just crash to the street.

"Every police station in Russia has a sobering-up room in it . . .

"But the man-hours lost, of course, is not funny. Pravda and Izvestia rave about that constantly. It runs into millions of man-hours a year that are lost by drunkenness on the job or the next day's hangover, where the man just doesn't go to work . . .

"There is a lot of good food in Russia, but the problem is distribution. There are mountains of fresh vegetables and fruit in the Crimea and down in Georgia, but the system is so fouled up that they can't distribute it.

"You go for months and months in Moscow and never see a fresh cucumber or tomato, even in summertime.

"There were two (male) students from Ghana there that we became acquainted with.

"We went out to dinner one night with them, and with two [white] American girls who were in town from Paris. Every Russian man in the street insulted the girls, thinking that they were Russian girls out with two Negroes.

"Drunkards came up to the table and reeled over us, knocking over bottles and glaring at the Negroes and trying to speak, although they were so drunk they couldn't. The waiters would come up and hustle them away, and in five minutes there would be another drunk over us, glaring at the Negroes."

Here are some paragraphs from another article in U.S. News & World Report of Oct. 25, 1965, called "A LAND OF CHANGE," by Robert P. Martin, that you would hardly find in The New York Times:

"There are really two Soviet Unions.

"One you see when walking down any street in any city in this sprawling, extraordinarily complex country. The people, seen from close up, are hardy and vigorous. They have survived revolution, the Stalinist terror and the war with Nazi Germany. They find life more satisfying today than it was yesterday. They also believe that 'someday' life will be even better.

"Then there is the other Soviet Union. It is a place of surfacing discontent and rebellion against the 'establishment.' Here you find young men and women contemptuous of the party which they had been taught in school was omniscient. In them is smoldering resentment against the dead hand of entrenched bureaucracy and its resistance to change.

"It is the faces of the Russian people that you see the contrast between the past and the present and the hoped-for future.

"There is the railroad engineer, technically competent, but 'bored by this business of hauling a train a hundred miles and then turning around to haul another one back.' It is this unbroken monotony that is also driving young people from the collective farm to the cities.

"Life in the cities is more rewarding than on the farms. Even so, factory managers are plagued by absenteeism and alcoholism. The Soviet system, so far, offers few incentives for increased productivity. The unmarried worker finds his only escape from the gray drabness of labor in the plant and communal existence in the dormitory is the cigarette break and the weekend spree.

"The very old seem most contented. The men wear dreary, grimy clothes and the women their quilted jackets, high felt boots and woolen shawls wrapped around their heads. They have survived the 'knock on the door' of Stalin's day, and contact with the foreigner is no longer feared . . .

" A young teacher in Alma-Ata (Soviet Turkestan in Central Asia) glowed with pride talking about his new co-operative apartment. It had cost him 2,000 rubles, and all of his savings, but for the first time his family would have a private bathroom and kitchen.

"Is this Communism?

" 'That hardly matters,' he said. 'The point is I'm getting a new apartment.' "

It does not matter what you call it. "The good life" is how it is known the world over. That is what everybody wants. There is a temptation to write, "especially in the Soviet Union," but that might sound nasty, since, in truth, the good life is sought nearly everywhere. If it seems to be more true in the USSR, perhaps it is because the people live in a climate that invites vigor and perhaps, even more so, because they have been deprived for so long.

Professor George Lichtheim, writing in the magazine Commentary of September, 1965 offered some "reflections on The New York Times" under the heading, "All The New That's Fit To Print." While readers may differ about some of his criticisms of the paper, his views as a European used to a number of rather good newspapers are worth attention. Some of them seem to be right on target, the kind of criticism one rarely hears in America, since here the attitude is too often full acceptance or complete rejection. One or two points that Professor Lichtheim made will bear repeating:

"The fact is that the best in American journalism is very good indeed—as good as anything in Europe. It just so happens that, with few exceptions, the best American journalists do not work for The New York Times . . .

"The issue (of May 16, 1965) carried a 'human interest story' from Moscow. Nothing so dull as food prices. This one was about the behavior of young people: a typical worry, it seems, in the Soviet Union as elsewhere. 'Movie-struck youngsters are causing increasing concern for (sic) Soviet youth leaders,' cabled Mr. Theodore Shabad from the Soviet capital that day. How are they doing that? 'The youngsters flood film magazines with letters, besiege casting departments, and mob the All-Union Institute of Cinematography. The authorities are trying to deter them by painting an actor's life in blackest terms.' Clearly not a crisis dispatch— Mr. Shabad was having a day off from his usual beat. 'How to become a movie actress? That question seems to be uppermost in the minds of Soviet girls 14 to 17 years old.' And of the girls in other countries, too. The purport of this particular story (and many others like it) was that the Russians are just like you and me. This is doubtless true, except that it has absolutely no bearing upon the nature of the regime or the behavior to be apprehended from it."

This recalls a Russian play that was brought to the United States—it was presented in New York—just after World War II. The title was "The World Over," and the work depicted the trials of a Russian family that were like those of other families in other countries all over the globe. So true, but the other nations were not collecting countries as part of their foreign policy, thus increasing the problems of their own citizens and those of other nations. It is also true the world over that you have got to come into the court with clean hands.*

* Rather than pepper the pages of this chapter with suggestions that the reader compare various statements with those in Eugene Lyons's book, *Workers' Paradise Lost,* the general advice is given at this point that the reader should go to that work for more detailed enlightenment. Mr. Lyons has made the coverage of Soviet Russia by the American press as a whole look poor. His citations of various findings on the U.S.S.R. and Eastern Europe are startling as well as news.

CHAPTER III

The Times,
The United Nations,
and Stalemate in Korea

• • •

"ARTICLE I—THE PURPOSES OF THE UNITED NATIONS ARE:

"1) To maintain international peace and security, and to that end: to take effective collective measures for the prevention and removal of threats to the peace, and for the suppression of acts of aggression. . . .

"2) To develop friendly relations among nations based on respect for the principle of equal rights and self-determination of peoples. . . .

"3) To achieve international cooperation in solving international problems of an economic, social, cultural, or humanitarian character. . . .

"4) To be a center for harmonizing the actions of nations in the attainment of these common ends."—From the Charter of the United Nations, signed at San Francisco, California, on June 26, 1945.

"It's too bad the military vigor now being applied by the United States against Communist aggression in Viet Nam hasn't been matched by comparable diplomatic determination to resist Communist aggression in the United Nations.

"But it hasn't, with the result that the U.N. looks increasingly like an invalid in the final stages of starvation and paralysis . . .

"To put it more bluntly, the housewrecking hoodlums are in full charge because the appeasers don't want to offend them.

"At this rate, total demolition shouldn't take much longer."
—From an editorial in the New York World-Telegram and Sun, March 5, 1965.

BETRAYAL AT THE U.N.—The Story of Paul Bang-Jensen, *by DeWitt Copp and Marshall Peck (Devon-Adair, 1963):*

" 'The record of the press in this country is a pretty sorry story with regard to Paul's case,' Arthur McDowell said. 'The Brooklyn Tablet, *a Catholic paper, the* Indianapolis Star, *the* New Bedford Standard Times, *they backed him all the way, but aside from that, an occasional piece here and there and nothing else.' The short, peppery Union official shook his head. 'Of course, there were organizations like our own that did all they could: Brutus Coste and the Assembly of Captive European Nations, Baldwin and the International League for the Rights of Man. But I'm afraid we were small voices, very small.'*

" 'Didn't your Committee send out a petition in Bang-Jensen's behalf while his case was still before the Tribunal?'

"The Executive Secretary-Treasurer of the Council Against Communist Aggression nodded and rubbed his hand down over the silver buttons on his greenish vest."

RED SPIES IN THE U.N., *by Pierre J. Huss and George Carpozi Jr. (Coward-McCann, 1965):*

"It is the purpose of this book to focus America's and the world's attention on Soviet and satellite nation espionage as it emanates from the UN, and especially to show, by case histories obtained from the FBI, the State Department, the United Nations, and other sources, how the Russians operate this clandestine operation. These cases present documented proof that the Russians:

a) seized, with the help of the notorious Judith Coplon, a highly confidential file of FBI reports on the Red conspiracy in the U.S.;

b) launched a vast spying operation directed at gathering data and secrets of military and seaport facilities on the Atlantic coast;

c) penetrated all but invulnerable security measures in order to seize intelligence manuals at the U.S. General Staff School in Leavenworth, Kansas;

d) obtained aerial photos and maps of military installations in the Midwest where some of America's key defense bases against Soviet nuclear-missile attack are situated;

e) stole top secret information on the location of missile and rocket launching sites and bases in the U.S.;

f) plotted a master plan to blow up our eastern seaboard via a terrifying campaign of sabotage that would have destroyed much of our resources and imperiled the lives of millions.

"All of these plots and such others as we shall discuss in this book were initiated in one central location—the so-called Moscow 'high command post,' centered in a busy house not many blocks away from the United Nations: the Soviet Mission to the United Nations. Soviet nationals at the UN and staff employes from Iron Curtain satellites are part and parcel of this 'high command post' housed in that unprepossessing building just off fashionable Park Avenue at 136 East 67th Street."

MAO TSE-TUNG: Emperor of the Blue Ants, *by George Paloczi-Horvath, page 353 (Doubleday & Co., 1963):*

"In August 1949, Mao determined the basic lines of Chinese foreign policy in these words: 'It is impossible to hope that imperialists and the Chinese reactionaries can be persuaded to be good-hearted and repent. The only way is to organize strength and fight them, as for example, our people's liberation war, our agrarian revolution, our exposing of imperialism, "provoking" them, defeating them and punishing their criminal acts, and "only allowing

them to behave properly and not allowing them to talk and act wildly." Only then is there hope of dealing with foreign imperialist countries on conditions of equality and mutual benefit.'

"The method of 'provocation' was not a slip of the tongue."

MAO TSE-TUNG: Emperor of the Blue Ants, *page 256:*

"Korea was a great problem for Mao long before she became a grave international issue. The Russian troops occupying the northern half of Korea in 1945 brought with them a group of Communists from Moscow, led by Ho Kai Ye, a Soviet citizen born in Siberia. Ho Kai Ye was put into a leading position by the Soviet command in 1945.

"While the Soviet forces thoroughly crippled Manchurian industry, carting away or destroying the most important plant, North Korean industry was not harmed. *In Manchuria, an integral part of China, the pretext was that the industries there were in Japanese hands, and they constituted war booty. Yet in North Korea, where industry was completely Japanese property, the factories were left intact. If this did not make it clear to the outside world that Stalin trusted the North Korean regime more than he did Mao's in China, Mao and his colleagues had no illusions . . .*

"It is equally clear that the North Korean regime was wholly subservient to Moscow, and that it could not decide on a military campaign without getting large shipments of Soviet arms during the previous months. There was little doubt at that time that the attack against South Korea, and its exact timing, were planned and ordered by Stalin."

MAO TSE-TUNG: Emperor of the Blue Ants, *page 259:*

"The sequence of further events is also most instructive. On March 6, 1953, Stalin dies. On March 30, a diplomatic move by Chou En-lai makes the ending of the Korean War possible. This time, the Kremlin leaders, engaged in their personal struggle for power, make no more difficulties. [Previous peace moves had been blocked by Stalin, with whom warmaking was a wellspring for his

insatiable love of power. No other principle guided him.] August 1953: purge in North Korea. Nine top Korean Communists, all of them Stalinists belonging to the Ho Kai Ye group, are executed. Stalin's Number One Korean favorite, Ho Kai Ye, is said to have committed suicide. (His latest positions had been Vice Premier and head of the Secret Police.) North Korea becomes a joint Soviet-Chinese satellite. [As of 1967 North Korea is back in orbit as a Soviet satellite, quite detached from Red China.]

"In fact, the Korean war, started by Stalin's Russia, was brought to an end by Mao's China."

Barron's: "Communist ambushes south of the demilitarized zone inflicted heavy losses on American and Korean patrols, at the very time the people of Seoul gave President Johnson a rousing welcome [in 1966]. American and North Korean emissaries met in Panmunjon to discuss the 'incidents.' Prior to the Reds' denial of responsibility for the outrages, U.S. officials stated in Seoul that they could see no traces of a scheme to open a second Asian front in Korea. Though U.S. intelligence in Korea has never been distinguished by the wealth of its information or the quality of its judgment, they may well be right. In any case, Washington's studied pretense that there is a conflict between a bellicose Communist China and a 'peace-loving' Soviet Union looks less and less credible. Since North Korea is controlled by the Kremlin, the puppet's aggressive action betrays the true intentions of those who pull the strings."—Nov. 7, 1966.

"The general public in South Korea. . . . appears little concerned about the border incidents, although one of the North Korean aims is obviously to create a feeling of insecurity among the people here [in South Korea].

"Other Communist objectives are, in the opinion of military experts here, to tie down the 50,000 American troops in Korea and keep South Korea from sending more troops to Vietnam; to distract the attention of the North Korean people from the Pyong-

yang regime's economic failures, and to serve as an excuse for building up its military machinery."—From a special dispatch to The New York Times from Seoul, South Korea, on Feb. 26, 1967.

BEHIND THE U.N. FRONT, *by Alice Widener, pp. 57-58 (The Bookmailer, 1955):*

"In 1945 the United States joined the United Nations. Blind to political reality, most Americans gave the new international organization their wholehearted support.

"But in 1945, before the ink of the signatures on the U.N. Charter was dry, all disciplined Communists were fully informed about the Kremlin plan to dominate the United Nations, and all Leftists were determined to use it to establish One Marxian World.

"The entire Red scheme for the U.N. was revealed in a Communist pamphlet, 'The United Nations,' issued in September 1945 by the People's Publishing House, Bombay, India.

"Depicting the Soviet Union as the leading champion of 'equality and freedom of the peoples,' the pamphlet gloats: 'Today the socialist infant of 1919 has become the giant Soviet Union, No. 2 industrial power of the world . . .'

"According to this Communist pamphlet, the Soviet Union has three main objectives in the United Nations:

1. Use of the veto 'automatically' to prevent any restrictive or harmful action being taken against the Soviet Union.

2. To create disaffection among the peoples of the non-Communist nations, 'particularly those of Great Britain and the U.S.A.,' and thus to frustrate the foreign policy of those nations.

3. To use the U.N. Trusteeship Council and the Specialized Agencies for warping the program of national independence among the 'colonial' nations; to detach all dependent and semi-dependent areas from any foreign influence except that of the Soviet Union, and to bring about the amalgamation of all nations in a single Soviet system.

"Anyone who has studied the record of the U.N. Security

Council and of the Korean War will see that the first two Red objectives listed above have been attained."

Barron's: *"U Thant, Secretary-General of the United Nations, announced to member states that he will not serve another term. His decision came as no great surprise, having been leaked weeks ago. An eyebrow-raiser, however, was his frank disclosure of hostility to the U.S., which until last week he had sought to conceal behind cloudy verbiage. Under his guidance, the UN has been dominated by 'neutralists' generally hostile to the West; moreover, it has protected lawlessness and aggression while spending itself into bankruptcy. But for vain hopes that the UN might become an effective instrument of peace and progress, the U.S. long since would have lost patience with U Thant. Nonetheless, Washington now is trying to persuade him to stay in office rather than face a period when the world organization would lack an administrative head."—Sept. 5, 1966. As is well known, the United States succeeded and U Thant was reelected. His unskillful direction of U.N. affairs could not avert the war in the Middle East in June of 1967, and his partisan position on the Vietnam War has been no help toward peace.*

"KEPT SECRET FROM MacARTHUR," by The Insider, from an article in the magazine *TACTICS* of January 20, 1965:
"Hard intelligence had come into the [United States] government [during the Korean War] revealing that the Soviet objective was to drive the United States out of Korea by force of arms. The Soviets had trained and staffed the North Korean army and government with Russian nationals of Korean ethnic origin, and Russian officers and civilians advised and commanded these forces and the North Korean government. Gen. Vasilev, on leave from his United Nations post as head of the Military Staff Committee, commanded the entire preparatory operations in Korea and actually gave the order to cross the 38th parallel for the attack that

began the war. This shows how closely, inside a 'psywar' complex, the Soviets conduct their military movements, but theirs is a win policy. This was all known to our policy-makers at the time, but was disregarded because it ran counter to the State Department's concept of the situation.

"This concealment of Soviet intent and involvement became known in certain U.S. government circles as 'the fig leaf policy.' This policy, as textually contained in one of these N.S.C. [National Security Council] papers, reads, 'There is no reliable intelligence concerning the role of the U.S.S.R. in Korea.' Inconceivable as it appears, and as conclusive proof of the extreme to which our government officials go in not permitting facts to influence policy, the Soviet Union was actively participating at this very time in actual combat operations. They were doing so not only with arms and advisors, but with actual combat troops. Their numbers, based on a Far East intelligence estimate made in Gen. MacArthur's headquarters and accepted, were 22,000 Soviet combat troops!

"Policy papers, even while confronted by such irrefutable evidence, still continued to use such quibbling phrases as, 'that the fighting be kept confined to Korea so as to deny the Russians and their Chinese Communist allies a pretext for becoming directly involved.' At this very time, a secret document was available which proved that these Communist and Soviet forces actually had entered Korea on August 14, 1949, months before their attack on our troops.

"One of our N.S.C. papers also contains this statement: 'The U.S.S.R. is prepared to accept general war and intervene in Korea.' Policy was based upon this thesis, which paralyzed our entire activity. While this document was being read, Russian voices and Russian commands were being heard clearly by our war pilots and were being reported. The voices were those of Russian pilots in attacking MIG15's, who swooped in daily from their safe havens in Manchuria. The Washington policy makers were so intent upon maintaining their fiction, that orders were issued to the military not

to capture any Soviet Russian alive in Korea. As a matter of fact, our Korean guerrillas had Soviet officers in their possession as prisoners, and radioed headquarters asking what disposal to make of them."

REMINISCENCES, *by General of the Army Douglas Mac-Arthur, pp. 362-367 (McGraw-Hill, New York 1964):*

"Near the end of the conference [with President Truman on Wake Island in October, 1950], the possibility of Chinese intervention [in Korea] was brought up almost casually. It was the general consensus of all present that Red China had no intention of intervening. This opinion had previously been advanced by the Central Intelligence Agency and the State Department. Gen. [Omar N.] Bradley went so far as to bring up the question of transferring troops in the Far East to Europe, and said he would like to have two divisions from Korea home by Christmas for this purpose.

"My views were asked as to the chance of Red China's intervention. I replied that the answer would only be speculative; that neither the State Department through its diplomatic listening posts abroad, nor the Central Intelligence Agency to whom a field commander must look for guidance as to a foreign nation's intention to move from peace to war, reported any evidence of intent by the Peiping government to intervene with major forces; that my own local intelligence, which I regarded as unsurpassed anywhere, reported heavy concentrations near the Yalu border in Manchuria whose movements were indeterminate; that my own military estimate was that with our largely unopposed air forces, with their potential capable of destroying, at will, bases of attack and lines of supply north as well as south of the Yalu, no Chinese military commander would hazard the commitment of large forces upon the devastated Korean peninsula. Their risk of their utter destruction through lack of supply would be too great. There was no disagreement from anyone. This episode was later completely misrepresented to the public through an alleged but spurious report in

an effort to pervert the position taken by me. It was an ingeniously fostered implication that I flatly and unequivocally predicted that under no circumstances would the Chinese Communists enter the Korean War. This is a prevarication. . . .

"The conference at Wake Island made me realize that a curious, and sinister, change was taking place in Washington. The defiant, rallying figure that had been Franklin Roosevelt was gone. Instead, there was a tendency toward temporizing rather than fighting it through. The original courageous decision of Harry Truman to boldly meet and defeat Communism in Asia was apparently being chipped away by the constant pounding whispers of timidity and cynicism. The President seemed to be swayed by the blandishments of some of the more selfish politicians of the United Nations. He seemed to be in the anomalous position of openly expressing fears of over-calculated risks that he had fearlessly taken only a few months before.

"This put me as field commander in an especially difficult situation. Up to now I had been engaged in warfare as it had been conducted through the ages—to fight to win. But I could see now that the Korean War was developing into something quite different. There seemed to be a deliberate underestimating of the importance of the conflict to which the government had committed—and was expending—the lives of United States fighting men . . .

(Later in October, 1950) "We were worried . . . by the growing indication of a startling buildup of Red Chinese troops in Manchuria, just north of the Yalu.

"I was even more worried by a series of directives from Washington which were greatly decreasing the potential of my air force. First I was forbidden 'hot' pursuit of enemy planes that attacked our own. Manchuria and Siberia were sanctuaries of inviolate protection for all enemy forces and for all enemy purposes, no matter what depredations or assaults might come from there. Then I was denied the right to bomb the hydroelectric plants along the Yalu. The order was broadened to include every plant in North

Korea which was capable of furnishing electric power to Man-churia and Siberia. Most incomprehensible of all was the refusal to let me bomb the important supply center at Racin, which was not in Manchuria or Siberia, but many miles from the border, in Northeast Korea. Racin was a depot to which the Soviet Union forwarded supplies from Vladivostok for the North Korean Army. I felt that step-by-step my weapons were being taken away from me . . ."

MACARTHUR: 1941-1951, *by Major General Charles A. Willoughby and John Chamberlain, page 364 (McGraw-Hill, New York 1954):*

"The Joint Chiefs of Staff began to talk vaguely about 'the wrong war, at the wrong time, and in the wrong place.' That was the intellectual equivalent of a municipal fire chief noting calmly that a conflagration in the slums was in the 'wrong part of the city'; unchecked, the fire might spread to the business districts or the exclusive residential sections."

"One of MacArthur's old armies with a brilliant record in the Southwest Pacific, the Eighth Army, fought again [in Korea] with accustomed skill but against numerical odds at times as high as ten to one. It was severely handicapped, at various stages of the fight-ing, by a wave of distorted and unwarranted 'defeatist' publicity without parallel in the annals of this proud nation."—Page 350.

A NORTH KOREAN WAR COMMUNIQUE OF JAN. 11, 1953

"LONDON, Jan. 11 (AP)—The Moscow radio tonight broadcast the following North Korean communique:

The Supreme Command of the Korean People's Army reports today that units of the People's Army, with units of the Chinese People's Volunteers, are waging defensive battles with American-British interventionists and Syngman Rhee troops.

Today, AA units and AA sharpshooters have shot down three and damaged two enemy aircraft."

[All communiques on the North Korean side of the war were issued in this manner from the city of Moscow, picked up by radio in London and dispatched from there by the Associated Press.]

The birth of the United Nations in 1945 was greeted by people all over the world with joy, well-wishing and hope. Since then there has been a progressive disenchantment. By the end of 1966 the Soviet Government had used 104 vetoes in the Security Council, with a reckless indifference to peace, much less the well-being of the world organization. No one can know all the factors that went into the downgrading of the United Nations in the eyes of the world, because some of the machinations are hidden by the malefactors within the dark recesses of that labyrinthine organization.

Let it be said at the very start here, that from the beginning of the United Nations the Soviet Government used it as a place of treachery and espionage against other nations, but especially against the United States. The position held by the Russians in the UN during the Korean War was so fantastic as to defy description —a fact that was not made clear to the American people by their press, and especially not by The New York Times. The Russians were on both sides of the battle lines during that war and a Russian was serving in the capacity of "Minister of War, Communication, and Information" in the United Nations, according to the authors of "Red Spies in the UN"—Pierre J. Huss and George Carpozi Jr. It must be remembered too that General Vasilev of the Soviet Union took leave of the Military Committee at the United Nations in New York in 1949 to go to North Korea and stage the troops and supplies for the war, for which he gave the starting order. The Russians in Moscow then accused South Korea of invading North Korea. Really!

There are dangers in refusing to face up to the simple facts of our existence, which in this case was not (and Vietnam is not) coexistence. While the United States Government refused to recognize that the Soviet Government under the dictatorship of Joseph Stalin was conducting the war in Korea, the Russians and their agents in New York (at the U.N.) and in Washington through Communist diplomatic channels* were capturing the United Nations and United States battle plans and sending them through Moscow to North Korea. So, therefore, let us establish the basis for these charges. Sometimes it is only years later that all the facts become known—and sometimes never.

On June 22, 1950, The New York Times printed a story on its front page at the top, under a 2-column (R) head, bearing the headlines:

SOVIET AGENTS PLOTTING TO RUIN UNITY, DEFENSES OF AMERICAS

The story was a special dispatch to The Times from San Jose, Costa Rica, telling of a Russian plot for penetrating inter-American defenses in the strategic Panama Canal region and shattering continental unity. Little, if anything, was heard of this afterward. The Korean War broke out exactly three days later; so we may safely assume that the Soviet plot to shatter American intercontinental unity was a well-planted Russian feint to distract attention at the moment from the bigger and more imminent plot in Korea.

Let this much be remembered from the beginning in regard to the Korean War: North Korea was utterly incapable of mounting and carrying out the invasion that took the so-called North Koreans almost to the southern tip of the peninsula. The tanks,

---

* Guy Burgess and Douglas D. Maclean, British Communist spies, served as links between Washington and London to transmit intelligence to Moscow on the Korean War. Burgess was in the British Embassy in Washington. Maclean was in the Foreign Office in London. What part was played by Harold Philby, the top British spy, is not clear at this writing. That master of deceit actually helped to form the C.I.A. and was later briefed by Gen. Walter B. Smith, who was the first head of the C.I.A. Philby alerted Burgess and Maclean to the danger of arrest, and they fled to Russia. Philby followed them into the Soviet refuge but not before he had talked himself out of isolation and back into British counterespionage!

planes, guns, rifles, trucks and other paraphernalia had to be supplied by the Russians because North Korea does not manufacture such items of warfare. Not only were the Russians hitched to the war in Korea, but also the Poles, Czechs and other captive nations, for it is reliably reported that a considerable part of the satellite industry was harnessed to that conflict. The fact that all the war communiques from the North Korean side were issued from Moscow proves the overriding management of the Soviets. The Chinese Communists fought under the personal direction of Lin Piao, who in the "cultural revolution" of 1966-1967 in Red China was raised to the No. 2 position as Mao Tse-tung's successor.

An article of speculation but immensely important from a historical point of view is the matter of Mao Tse-tung's visit to Moscow in 1949, to negotiate with Stalin the Soviet-Chinese treaty that was signed on February 14, 1950. Professor Dmytryshyn described that treaty as follows in *USSR: A Concise History,* page 299:

"Both countries pledged to take joint action against renewed aggression by Japan 'or any other state which should unite with Japan directly or indirectly,' and promised 'in the spirit of friendship and cooperation and in conformity with the principles of equality, mutual interests, and also mutual respect for the State sovereignty and territorial integrity and noninterference in internal affairs of the other High Contracting Part—to develop and consolidate economic and cultural ties between the Soviet Union and China, to render each other every possible economic assistance, and to carry out the necessary economic cooperation.' In accordance with these high sounding principles, the USSR agreed to transfer gratis to China by the end of 1952 'all its rights in the joint administration of the Chinese Changchun Railway, with all the property belonging to the railway'; to withdraw Soviet forces from the naval base of Port Arthur not later than the end of 1952; to transfer the administration in Dalny to Chinese control; and to grant China $300,000,000 in credits, at 1 per cent interest, to pay for Soviet deliveries of industrial equipment."

Professor Dmytryshyn asserted that this "was the first major retreat of Soviet influence in the Far East." "Retreat" seems to be too strong a word. Although the ways of dictators are devious in the extreme, it seems most unlikely that Stalin failed even to mention to Mao that a Korean War was then being planned in Moscow. Some of the war materiel must have been on its way across the Trans-Siberian Railway while Mao and Stalin negotiated. It is reasonable to believe—and most probable—that Stalin plotted the entry of the Chinese Communists into the war, in case their help was needed, during these talks, which lasted for two months. The Soviets supplied the Chinese Communists with arms and materiel during the war. It would be impossible to put a half million troops into a given area of a country like China without some months of preparation—in this case a country with few transport planes and primitive transportation generally.

On page 366 of General MacArthur's *Reminiscences,* we find:

"On November 3rd (1950), I furnished Washington a (Chinese) Communist battle order, listing in complete numerical detail strength and locations in Manchuria of fifty-six regular army divisions, in sixteen corps—a total of 498,000 men. In addition there were district service forces of 370,000, or an aggregate of 868,000 in all. *This intelligence was furnished not only to Washington, but to the United Nations, either of whom could have stopped our troops at any point in North Korea if they had taken the mounting Chinese threat seriously.* (Emphasis added.) But the order I received was:

> In the event of the open or covert employment anywhere in Korea of major Chinese Communist units, without prior announcement, you should continue as long as, in your judgment, action by forces now under your control offers reasonable chance of success. In any case, prior to taking any military action against objectives in Chinese territory, you will obtain authorization from Washington.

The shattering, but not disastrous, drive by the Chinese Communists followed. In this connection General MacArthur wrote:

"That there was some leak in intelligence was evident to everyone. [General Walton] Walker [commander of the Eighth Army] continually complained to me that his operations were known to the enemy in advance through sources in Washington. I will always believe that if the United States had issued a warning to the effect that any entry of the Chinese Communists in force into Korea would be considered an act of international war against the United States, that the Korean War would have terminated with our advance to the north. I feel that the Reds would have stayed on their side of the Yalu. Instead, information must have been relayed to them, assuring that the Yalu bridges would continue to enjoy sanctuary and that their bases would be left intact. They knew they could swarm down across the Yalu River without having to worry about bombers hitting their Manchurian supply lines.

"An official leaflet by General Lin Piao published in China read:

" 'I would never have made the attack and risked my men and military reputation if I had not been assured that Washington would restrain General MacArthur from taking adequate retaliatory measures against my lines of supply and communication.' " *

General MacArthur asserted that "the order not to bomb the Yalu bridges was the most indefensible and ill-conceived decision ever forced on a field commander in our nation's history." And he added: "It is impossible to understand on a professional basis how we could have placidly accepted the disadvantages piled on the Eighth Army in Korea." At another point he wrote with some bitterness:

"Washington planning was not directed toward methods of counterattack, but rather toward the best way to run . . ."

On the subject of the Red Chinese the General wrote to Rep-

* Such assurance is reported to have been given to the Chinese Communists by the British. See U.S. News & World Report, page 28, June 28, 1965.

resentative Joseph Martin, House minority leader, with these prophetic words:

"My views and recommendations, with respect to the situation created by Red Chinese entry into war against us in Korea, have been submitted to Washington in most complete detail. Generally these views are well known and clearly understood, as they follow the conventional pattern of meeting force with maximum counter-force as we have never failed to do in the past. Your view with respect to the utilization of the Chinese forces on Formosa is in conflict with neither logic nor this tradition. It seems strangely difficult for some to realize that here in Asia is where the Communist conspirators have elected to make their play for global conquest, and that we have joined the issue thus raised on the battlefield; that here we fight Europe's war with arms while diplomats there still fight it with words; that if we lose the war to Communism in Asia the fall of Europe is inevitable; win it and Europe most probably would avoid war and yet preserve freedom. As you point out, we must win. There is no substitute for victory."

General MacArthur wanted to destroy the Chinese Communist forces in North Korea and administer such a sound defeat to the aggressive Reds that they would not soon again have attacked. Instead, the fighting was halted at the 38th Parallel, where it started, and 50,000 American troops have since been permanently stationed in South Korea. No peace treaty has been signed. A small war in Vietnam was then kindled into a flaming conflict, also fed by the Russians and the Chinese Communists, chiefly by the Soviets, and nearly 500,000 Americans, 500,000 South Vietnamese, more than 40,000 South Koreans, some thousands of Australians, about 2,000 Thais, with more coming, some hundreds of New Zealanders, and more than 1,000 Philippine supply troops are engaging the "North Vietnamese." That designation is quoted because it is said that some Russians are manning such sophisticated Soviet equipment as the SAM missiles, which are being used to bring down American planes. There are also some 50,000 Chinese Red supply troops in North Vietnam. Once again the weight of the

American press, especially The New York Times, is bearing down on the defending forces. The only effort made by The Times to discover what was going on in North Vietnam was a guided tour given to Harrison E. Salisbury, an assistant managing editor of The Times. There is no need to count dispatches by Wilfred Burchett, an Australian Communist, which The Times prints from time to time.*

In 1952, while the Korean truce negotiations were under way, although the war continued to be fought bitterly, forty Americans in the United Nations headquarters in New York were suddenly accused of espionage—*suddenly* because the press in general had given no hint that American Communists had heavily infiltrated the United Nations. (Other non-Russian, foreign Communists also infiltrated the U.N. but little has been told about them.) The American Communists, according to *Red Spies in the U.N.*,

---

* The unpleasant fact is that Wilfred Burchett is a notorious Communist with a most unsavory record, according to reports among newspapermen and also a published statement by U.S. News & World Report, which deemed it necessary to give a whole page and a third to this man on Feb. 27, 1967. That article said:

"Most American reporters who know him agree that Mr. Burchett is friendly and highly competent. But they know he has devoted years to putting the Communists' best foot forward.

"One American correspondent who knows Burchett and [Alan] Winnington [of the London Daily Worker] has described them thus:

" 'Winnington was a Communist who tried to become a newspaperman. Burchett is a newspaperman who became a Communist.'

"Mr. Burchett, who long maintained an apartment in Moscow, does not have an Australian passport any more. As long ago as the time of the Korean peace talks, Australian counterintelligence officials said he would be arrested as a traitor if he ever returned to his homeland.

"Among their charges against him then: trying to convert Australian prisoners of war to the Communist cause while acting as a bona fide war correspondent.

"So, pushing the Communist line is nothing new for Wilfred Burchett. His latest activity—telling the world North Vietnam's peace terms and inviting the President of the United States to Hanoi to talk things over—is in a pattern set many years ago."

Burchett is also said to have attempted to get American prisoners of war in North Korea to "confess" to germ warfare on the part of the United States. Mr. Burchett reported through Tass, Soviet press agency, that he accompanied Mr. Salisbury on his tour of bombed areas of North Vietnam.

worked with two Soviet United Nations officials—Konstantin E. Zinchenko, Assistant Secretary General, a Russian, who took over the reins of the U.N. in the absence of the then Secretary General, Trygve Lie; and Nicolai Skvortsov, also a Soviet citizen, one of the chief aides of Zinchenko. The latter headed the U.N. Department of Security Council Affairs, where the Americans were employed. "The probe [by the U.S. Senate Internal Security Subcommittee] led to the dismissal of twenty-nine disloyal Americans and the suspension of eleven others. Several of the latter turned in their resignations before they could be given hearings." During the height of the storm over these charges Zinchenko and Skvortsov quietly departed for the Soviet Union. Skvortsov was dismissed from his U.N. post in 1952 when the United States barred his re-entry into this country as he was charged with attempted espionage.

"In the uproar over the charges against these Americans," *Red Spies in the U.N.* revealed, page 47, "a hue and cry rose in Washington and other quarters in this country once more against the UN's Department of Security Council Affairs . . .

"There was more than a little significance in this situation because the department at the time was dealing in highly important matters pertaining to the Korean War which was then still raging.

"There was also considerable significance to the action Lie had taken against Zinchenko, in early 1952 [nearly two years after the war started!], in denying him access to any reports coming in from the Korean front. Zinchenko had been caught making unauthorized diversions of certain documents dealing with strategy, troop movements, and other military matters concerning UN forces in Korea. There can be little doubt that Zinchenko was feeding the information to Moscow which was actually directing the Red forces fighting against the UN divisions on the battle lines.

"Secretary General Lie's quarantine of Zinchenko had the effect of reducing his position on the 38th floor to that of a courier. At that same time, Zinchenko's assistant, Skvortsov, also was restricted, so that he, too, had only limited access to papers and documents dealing with Korea. To say the quarantine contributed to Zinchenko's and Skvortsov's departures would probably not be far from the truth.

"Zinchenko had come into his post in 1949 as one of the UN's eight Assistant Secretaries General. When the war broke out in 1950, Zinchenko theoretically became the UN Minister of War, Communication, and Information. That put him in charge of all operations in Korea. This prize position had been delegated to the legal, military, and judicial affairs relating to the subsequent UN operations in Korea. This prize position had been delegated to the Russians at the 1945 San Francisco Charter Conference after Molotov's threats to withdraw from further participation in the world body. Molotov then named Sobolov for the job. [Sobolov left for Russia at the time of the Judith Coplon case. He returned later to a lesser post in the UN.]

"The first weeks of fighting in Korea produced understandable confusion in the conduct of field operations and in reports on activities coming back from the front. The Security Council, which had voted UN intervention to stop the Communist North Koreans, stipulated that field commanders make frequent reports to the world organization.

"These reports went directly to Zinchenko. In time we were to learn that, in receiving this information himself, Zinchenko in effect was getting information about American and UN troops from a theatre of war where the enemy in actuality was being commanded by Zinchenko's own boss, Stalin.

"Even before Secretary General Lie suspected what was happening in his own Secretariat, the field commander, General Douglas MacArthur, who headed the U.S. forces as well as those of other nations under the UN banner on the Korean front, had begun to realize what was going on. The North Koreans seemed to have an almost uncanny ability to anticipate MacArthur's battle plans.

"The General decided on a new strategy, not on the field but in his reports to the UN. He limited information to general matters of a non-military nature and kept battlefield and logistic data down to an unenlightening minimum.

"MacArthur had a secondary reason for holding back. On more than one occasion he had found the UN Security Council censored his reports on the course of the war in the Far East. This had pulled him into a temporary feud with Trygve Lie. The General was truly on the spot. He was damned if he sent a full and accurate account of activities because he knew that, through Zinchenko, the information would go right back into the hands of the Communist Chinese and North Koreans. And he was damned if he didn't send the full report because he was committing a slur against the whole UN structure.

"It was an unfortunate position for MacArthur. And it soon made trouble for him. Zinchenko, as the UN's Minister of War, Communication, and Information, was compelled to notify Mac-Arthur that he was failing in his obligation to the UN. The complaint was certainly justified, but coming as it did from Zinchenko —he was no longer able to transmit accurate warfront information to the Kremlin because of MacArthur's holdout—the question of the General's actions became academic.

"In the exchange of messages between Zinchenko and Mac-Arthur which followed, a long-distance feud soon galvanized. Zinchenko demanded full reports; MacArthur refused to comply."

It is as if Benedict Arnold had complained, but vigorously, to General George Washington about not receiving more complete information every week about the General's battle plans. One may wonder whether in the whole world's history of international and military affairs there is another situation to match or even tie this one for gall, if not treachery. Did The New York Times print a word about this world-stirring story about an occurrence only a few blocks from Times Square? Not a word of it. On this head *Red Spies in the UN* reports on page 53:

"The public was never told that there was a direct tie between Zinchenko and Skvortsov and the forty Americans in espionage. You are reading it here for the first time.

"There is a little more to tell.

"Zinchenko's vacant chair in the Secretary General's office and in the council halls of the UN remained unoccupied through the rest of 1952 and for the first half of 1953, and the FBI always was on the wait for his return so it could see where his trail in espionage might lead."

A pretty situation, that.

How far MacArthur was able to dissemble with the U.N. is not clear, but there is plain evidence that Zinchenko was not capable of frustrating the landing at Inchon which trapped the enemy forces southward of Seoul and brought about their destruction, enabling the UN troops to start the fateful move north of the 38th parallel.*

General MacArthur was then 70 years old. He conceived and brilliantly brought off the Inchon landing, despite strong arguments against it, and he gave much credit to the United States Navy's profound knowledge and skill in executing this maneuver in an area where the tides are among the greatest in the world. The UN forces found the harbor lights still burning in the early morning when landing ships approached; the surprise was complete. The Soviet leapfrog maneuver in New York was a failure, in relation to

* Maj. Gen. Charles A. Willoughby, U.S.A. ret., who was Mac-Arthur's G-2, at his home in Washington on April 6, 1967, told Edward Hunter that General MacArthur during the Korean War used only one channel of information transmission and that was to the United States Joint Chiefs of Staff in Washington. General Willoughby added that the Joint Chiefs transmitted information to several offices, notably the White House and the State Department. He said that there was one certain method by which military information could have been sent quickly to Moscow and that was through the British Embassy in Washington via the Burgess-Maclean channel. One of those British Communist spies was in Washington and one was in the London Foreign Office. It transpired after they had fled to Russia on May 25, 1951, that this transmission line was used to send MacArthur's dispatches to Moscow. Burgess was recalled to London earlier in May, 1951.

General MacArthur said in his *Reminiscences,* page 366, as cited: "This intelligence [in regard to the Chinese Communist mobilization in Manchuria] was furnished not only to Washington, but to the United Nations, either of whom could have stopped our troops at any point . . ." Presumably, all information was cleared through Washington.

the Inchon move. But, alas, Soviet maneuvers at the UN in general have not failed—they have succeeded only too well. They were all too successful in Korea on the whole, with a fearful loss of life. Zinchenko was Acting Secretary General of the United Nations when General MacArthur visited New York in 1951, but Zinchenko was not invited to the city's reception for the General. The press did not say why.

Let it be said that General MacArthur at his advanced age gave more than any man could fairly be asked to give to his country, and yet he never complained or flinched. It was not he who turned his back upon Korea. He was turned out without a hearing, as he himself noted. No one can know *all* the facts that went into America's fighting its first no-win war. No one can doubt that the outcome of the Korean War was a partial victory for the Communists—that is to say, the Communist governmental forces in the USSR and Red China and Communist political forces in the United States and elsewhere, but especially in New York at the United Nations. Had General MacArthur's wise counsels been at least considered—had they only been presented to the people strongly by the press of America—permission might have been given him to order the bombing of all the Yalu bridges (some of them were bombed) and of air bases and supply points in Manchuria. Then, had MacArthur been allowed to carry out his plan for other landings behind enemy lines in North Korea, the Chinese Communists and Russian Communists would have learned most pointedly that aggression does not pay, and it is probable that there would have been no fighting in South Vietnam in this decade. What they learned, in fact, is that aggression does pay.

A section of the American press is committed to the view that somehow the conditions at present are different from those when part of British opinion—the controlling part—believed it was possible to placate and appease Hitler. It was wrong to appease Hitler, according to this view, but it was not wrong to appease Stalin and the Chinese Communists in Korea or Kosygin-Brezhnev in Vietnam, even when Brezhnev stamped as "a strange and persistent delusion" * a hope expressed by President Johnson that closer Soviet-American cooperation was possible despite tensions over the Vietnam War. We fed the Russian-Chinese Moloch in Korea and we feed it still in Vietnam. The Soviet ploy that the Russians are desperately afraid of the Chinese Communists has not prevented Moscow from continuing and increasing its feeding the war flames in Vietnam to keep large numbers of United States forces tied down there—and bleeding. Some of the Russian supplies are going right through Communist China.

During the Korean War the Trans-Siberian Railway was committed to its capacity in supplying the conflict. The harnessing of satellite nations, such as Poland and Czechoslovakia to the war directly, and others in Eastern Europe indirectly brought about the rise in distrust and hatred that resulted in revolts and threats of rebellion in several of those coordinated countries. Virtually nothing of these matters was printed in the American press at that time. The fiction that Red China was using only "volunteers" and that Soviet Russia was merely encouraging North Korea to fight was always an open scandal.

The aim of a journalist and a journal is to seek out and present the truth, as it must be the aim of a soldier to win in battle. When The New York Times accused President Johnson of "incitement" of American soldiers while he was in Vietnam, it demonstrated once again its inability under its present editorial leadership to distinguish one thing from another. It is possible for a general, or at any rate a President, to fight a war without having the intention of winning it. It is impossible for an individual soldier to do anything but resist with all his might the drives of the enemy and to make his own position as strong as he can by killing the enemy. Anything less than that on the part of the soldier would destroy his own and the army's morale. So also when a newspaperman does less than seek out the truth or suppresses stories because his news-

* From a New York Times dispatch of Oct. 16, 1966.

paper says, "We don't want them," the management of the news becomes far advanced like a destroying cancer. The truth, to be sure, is sometimes hard to grasp, but it is never so elusive as when it is not wanted. For example, if we continue to erect Soviet Russia as a vast and indescribable enigma, which helps to kill our men in Vietnam but honestly seeks rapprochement elsewhere—if we do this, we will eventually have to deliver to the people the fruit of this grotesque position. That fruit will be slavery. This is the cold, hard truth distilled from long observation of national power structures like the Soviet regime. It is the built-in nature of dictatorship, whether it is called "democratic centralism" or by some other euphemism.

It is wise to consider the views of one who was an aide of the United States Government and who writes under the pseudonym The Insider for the magazine *Tactics*. In the issue of Jan. 20, 1965, part of which was quoted earlier in this chapter, The Insider gave some revealing information on the Korean War. The only way one can test such news is to crosscheck it with other information and to know something about the responsibility of the magazine's editor, who is Edward Hunter. Mr. Hunter is famous for having introduced the word "brainwashing" into the languages of the world from the Chinese. He was an editor in China and Japan, and has been professionally engaged in psychological warfare for the United States Government. He is the author of a half dozen books, the latest being *Attack by Mail* (The Bookmailer, Linden, N.J.), which, the author asserts, discloses the inner working of the United States Government as illustrated by the flood of propaganda mails. The Insider's article in 1965 was news then. This specific data on National Security Council documentation has appeared only in Mr. Hunter's publication *Tactics* of limited circulation. The article is fully titled: "No-Win Policy Guidance KEPT SECRET FROM MACARTHUR." Here are some paragraphs from it:

"When the Chinese Red army, itself going under the fiction of being a volunteer force, struck at American troops, the State De-

partment no longer could maintain its make-believe as set forth in
N.S.C.-68 (National Security Council paper 68).* Therefore,
N.S.C.68/2 was written. One of its purposes was to put a halt to
Gen. MacArthur's plan to use Chinese Nationalist troops in Korea.
Again the same Washington elements revived the old scare of a
'general war' thus once more preserving the advantage for the
enemy. The document reads: 'The use of (Chinese) Nationalist
troops would create a danger of Soviet counteraction and increase
the danger of general war.'

"The new document, N.S.C.-68/2, in contrast to the original
N.S.C.-68, simply left out the reference to the Chinese Red forces,
because these were now engaged in visibly killing our men. Still
disregarded, though, was the hard intelligence that Soviet troops
actually were engaged in hostilities in Korea. Their slaughter of
our men could still, with our collaboration, be kept secret by the
Administration.

"Gen. MacArthur made his estimate that the entry of Chinese
Nationalist troops would not only save American lives, but would
be both militarily and psychologically a vital blow against the
Chinese Communists. This, for reasons of their own, the Washington policy drafters, ensconced in the middle echelons of our government, were determined would not be permitted to happen. With
all the determination with which previous Administrations had
sought victory, these government officials were determined there
would be no victory.

"The decision concerning the entry of the Chinese free forces
was so decisive in the conduct of the war that our policy-makers
showed desperation in their determination to block this at all costs.
As a result, they inserted a specific declaration into the policy
papers, which was even more definitive. It read: 'The U.S.S.R.
was prepared to accept general war and intervene.'

"We know today that the U.S.S.R. would not have intervened
in a total war engagement under practically any circumstances. In

* The National Security Council papers are fundamental policy
documents of the United States Government.

addition, their fundamental, Marxist doctrine is that war is a final step only to be taken when victory is assured. Theirs is a victory policy in every sense of the word. *Of course they want ours to be a no-victory policy.* (Emphasis added.)

"So complete was the control of the Washington policy-makers over the course of the fighting that they even hindered intelligence-gathering efforts. Pressure was put upon our intelligence sources at Taipei and in Hong Kong to avoid sending anything that might indicate Peking's preparedness to enter the Korean fighting and thus support Gen. MacArthur's position, on pain of demotion or dismissal. The specter of a general war was so strongly pressed that they inserted into our policy papers the declaration, 'aid to anti-Communist forces in China would increase the danger of a general war.'

"American intelligence efforts on the Chinese mainland would have had to cooperate with the anti-Communists in order to be productive. Certainly we could not have collaborated with the Reds in gathering honest data about their aggressive moves. Policy forbade any such working arrangement with our friends. The so-called sophisticated approach by Washington, in seeking an objective while not defining it in so many words, is demonstrated by this. Of course, without being allowed to contact Chinese anti-Reds, no American intelligence agents were able to operate on the mainland. This was intended by the Administration.

"This negative approach on our part was designed to dry up any intelligence or agent activities on the Chinese mainland, as well as to keep Chinese Nationalist commandos and troops from striking at the unprotected coastal areas and sabotaging the few railroads moving the Chinese Red armies north to Manchuria and thence into Korea. So complete was our intelligence blackout because of this specific policy that the military forces fighting in Korea were deprived of effective procedures to find out about the presence of a Chinese army which had moved thousands of miles until the American boys met them and bled at the front.

"The American public has frequently heard about the orders

that prevented MacArthur from pursuit over the Yalu River from Korea into Manchuria, and which forbade any attack by him against the combat installations just over the border. Even the bridges were immune. But the basis for these orders have not been disclosed hitherto.

"MacArthur was stopped from bombing the bridges even while our reconnaissance planes watched thousands of Chinese Red troops and tons of supplies moving across them. Numerous times, U.S. reconnaissance photographed hundreds of Russian warplanes on airfields just over the frontier. Yet we were not allowed to touch them. The policy-makers in Washington protected the enemy installation with a few words that read: 'Blockade and bombardment of ports, railroads and industry or attacks in Manchuria would carry the probability of general war developing.'

"The task of calculating the numbers of American troops who sacrificed their lives to this policy would be gruesome, indeed, although only an eye-opener.

"The same policy imposed a veto on plans for the bombardment of the Yalu River electric power plants. Military intelligence later established that these plants were supplying power to munitions, arms and repair installations directly involved in the war effort. These logistical plants were located in North Korea, Manchuria and even in the Soviet Maritime Province.

"The scandal of these orders could not be indefinitely suppressed. They were modified, therefore, in a way as to appear to meet our needs, but actually to do so very inadequately. An order was issued to bomb the power plants situated on the Korean side of the Yalu River, but to make sure that no bombs would fall on adjoining Red Chinese territory.

"Even so, this attack right at the border so startled the Chinese Communists and the Soviets that their propaganda screeched loud and long. But no general war developed. Our fear of a general war was all along fomented by the Peking-Moscow Axis as a weapon in its aggression. This is modern psychological warfare. The fact that India had an embassy in Peking with a very pro-Red

Chinese Ambassador, K.M. Pannikar, an intellectual darling of American 'liberals,' was exploited to disseminate misinformation around the world. He passed the word to Prime Minister Nehru that he had received reliable information that the U.S.S.R. was ready to intervene in the war, which Nehru rushed to receptive sources in London and Washington. Pannikar enthusiastically lent himself to this anti-U.S. gambit as part of a pro-Red Chinese policy that he had been following all along. The scare rumors were decisive. (Exact parallels to this can be found in the Vietnam War, but the Russian scare-rumors have not worked as well, though they have been by no means entirely ineffectual.)

"Even so, the fighting reached a desperate point for the Reds. They were over-committed and confronted with the probability of imminent, disastrous defeat. A new American policy was required to save them. N.S.C.-135/3 was obligingly produced, having as its basis a new twist, as follows: 'Korea is an inconclusive operation and continued maintenance of military operations would create the grave danger of general war.'

"This was designed to lead to the prolonged negotiations at Panmunjon. The truth about conditions in the Red armies in Korea at this time included:

"1. The Chinese Communist air force was almost totally Soviet-controlled and manned. Yet it was not powerful enough nor able to carry the air war much beyond the border at the Yalu River.

"2. The Chinese Communists and the Soviets realized that their armies were on the verge of collapse both logistically and militarily.

"At this propitious moment for our side, when a decisive conclusion was in our grasp, Washington gave Red Korea a life-saving truce, enabling the Reds to obtain a second wind, and to go on from there to where they are today in Southeast Asia and in Africa. (This is precisely the way the Communists in Vietnam have profited from the five pauses given to them by the United States in the bombing of the North, at this point in time.)

"The U.S. Air Force was roaming North Korea and strafing its remaining troops and those of the Chinese Communists and the Soviets at will. We possessed unchallenged air superiority. The Soviet-manned MIGs would fly high over Manchuria and then dive in on our F-86s in North Korea. They would make a fast pass, and then flee at once to sanctuary back over the river, where they knew we were forbidden by our government to follow them.

"Even against these tactics, our fliers chalked up victory after victory. They bloodied the Soviet pilots so severely that they ceased venturing beyond the Yalu River.

"Soviet bombers were never a threat, or considered a threat, nor did they ever venture into areas where our pilots could engage them in combat. They made no effort against our bases because they were not capable of doing so.

"Only a few raids on our part could have cut the two railroads leading from Manchuria into Korea. The Soviets knew that their hard-pressed Trans-Siberian Railroad was taxed to its capacity and still not able to supply the combat forces then in Korea. Even their air force was hard pressed logistically. Fuel had to be transported by the precarious sea route bordering Formosa, which was controlled by the U.S. Seventh Fleet.

"The Communists realized all these drawbacks and called for a cease-fire. The Reds view a cease-fire not as an objective but as a tactic. They sought to save their military forces from disaster. They were not unduly worried, for they knew that our policymakers would be sure to oblige them.

"A new U.S. policy was accordingly instituted which reads, 'begin talks at Panmunjon in the interests of peace,' 'the U.S. should not refer to the U.S.S.R. as an aggressor in Korea,' 'agree to the term that the Chinese Communist troops in Korea were volunteers,' 'agree to a neutral nations repatriation commission which includes Poles and Czechs,' and 'agree to a demilitarized zone which divides Korea and an inspection team which includes Czechs and Poles.'

"Even as far back as 1954, in this same basic policy, a sentence was inserted which has its effects on the present Viet Nam situation. It stated, 'The United States should not make strident statements such as, "that the U.S.S.R., Communist China and the Viet Minh are co-conspirators." '

"These were the instructions that governed our truce negotiations at Panmunjon. They were based on the policies laid down in N.S.C.-68, N.S.C.-68/2 and N.S.C. 135/3. We are still living with the effects of these policies. Even in recent months, American soldiers have been killed in the so-called demilitarized zone in Korea. [The demilitarized zone, so called, in Vietnam, also known as the DMZ, has been violated in the same manner by the Communists. American Marines in July, 1967, suffered severe losses from North Vietnam attacks through the DMZ.]

"This approach is a policy of secrecy, paralysis and diversion. As far as Korea and Vietnam are concerned, it still continues. Secrecy is for the purpose of hiding our true policy from the American people, press and Congress. Paralysis is for the purpose of halting any project that promises to be effective. Diversion is designed to turn aside any strong action long enough to allow the Communists time to consummate their sabotage and subversive activities that are aimed at achieving a Red victory.

"MacArthur was made the butt of both diversion and paralysis tactics, so as to prevent him at all costs from achieving a victory. Indeed, he never saw the policy papers that determined what he was being allowed and not allowed to do in the Korean War. He was never given the opportunity to read N.S.C.-68, N.S.C.-68/2, and N.S.C. 135/3, although his job was to implement them. He was similarly kept in the dark on fundamental decisions concerning his actions, as have been our topmost military officers generally. They have not known the policies involved and the specific reasons why their statements or speeches were censored the way they were by the State Department, as came out in lengthy Senate hearings.

"MacArthur was too keen a thinker not to know that he was fighting against a bind somewhere. He was aware of it, but he could not know, for instance, the composition of a special, combined Department of State-Joint Chiefs of Staff group sitting in Washington, deciding his day-by-day actions. At Panmunjon, for instance, there were no extemporaneous speeches, everything that was said was read. Each night, the American delegation prepared the position it would like to take at the next session of the truce talks. This was then sent to Tokyo which relayed it to this joint policy group in the nation's capital. The recommendations by men at the spot were always changed and softened. Many a morning, the head of our delegation would throw the changes on the table disgustedly, and instruct his staff, 'Do the best you can. I can't take it any longer!' ...

"MacArthur, as late as August 27, 1961, confirmed that the State Department had tied his hands in Korea, and that its officials were responsible for the no-win policy in Korea. He said so while discussing the military muzzling hearings.

"Gen. MacArthur, in spite of these obstacles, demonstrated limitless moral and personal stamina. He never compromised in his truism, 'There can be no substitute for victory,' even when the State Department, the U.N. and the British insisted on a stalemate as the national objective of the U.S. If we had been permitted, the collapse of Mao Tse-tung on the Chinese mainland and Ho Chi Minh in Viet Nam would have been sure. As the price of our no-win policy, American lives are still being sacrificed in Asia.

"The perpetrators of this secret policy remain in power and continue to lead towards disaster."

The whole truth about the Korean War and the Vietnam War must come out piecemeal. That is why the people say, "We don't know everything that is going on." It is not a compliment to our newspapers, although they continue to award themselves prizes and encomiums. That the lesson of Korea has not been learned in some quarters of the United States is well illustrated by an editorial in The New York Times of March 28, 1967:

"Renewed pressure from Senator Symington and the Senate Preparedness subcommittee to extend the bombing of North Vietnam to military airfields and Haiphong harbor is a case of exasperation overwhelming reason. Despite the natural desire to hit the enemy in so seemingly logical a place as its airfields, the risks of expanding the war and strengthening China's influence militate against such raids even if they offered important military advantages. But the military advantages are few.

"Most of the 487 American aircraft lost over North Vietnam during the past two years have been destroyed by conventional anti-aircraft weapons. Thirty of them have been shot down by surface-air missiles (SAMs). Only ten have been lost to MIG attacks. A larger number might well be destroyed in any effort to take out the four jet airfields in the Hanoi-Haiphong region, which are heavily defended.

"Destruction of those fields would very likely lead Communist China to make its airfields available to the North Vietnamese air force. The result would be to restore ground sanctuary or, if American planes were then to attack Chinese bases, virtually to assure an air war—if not a ground war—with Communist China."

Defense Secretary Robert McNamara announced on April 3, 1967, that the airfields would not be bombed. Soon afterward, the bombing of the airfields was ordered. Nothing like the predictions of The Times editorial came true. Communist China has proven that she will go to war with or without a pretext, when it suits her. Note the absence in the editorial of any mention of Soviet Russia as the donor of the SAMs and MIGs.

The New York Times is so completely committed to no victory in Vietnam, which it has specifically stated over and over again, that it unblushingly repeats the same arguments that were used during the Korean War. The Times angrily rebuked Cardinal Spellman in 1966 for urging victory in Vietnam, and sought to play him off against Pope Paul. It has never ceased asking for negotiations that would include the Vietcong, a creature of North Vietnam—an action that would almost certainly result in the defeat of the South Vietnamese, the United States and all the allies who have fought so hard against this latest Communist aggression. In view of the events since 1945, this has virtually guaranteed new acts of aggression in other areas of the world, if not in Southeast Asia itself, once Communist China had pulled itself out of its national tailspin.

That The Times played a part in the thinking of the State Department was proved by developments. The basic defect in some thinking in regard to the wars with the Communists is the view that they are just another conflict that can be settled at the peace table. The extent of Soviet indifference to peace treaties is legion. Mention only Eastern Europe, where treaties were violated and destroyed immediately after they were made, and note again that no peace treaty has ever been signed in Korea since the truce of 1953. The Times itself looks to a balance of power.

The story is told of Nikita Khrushchev that, after he had delivered his historic bridge-burning and world-shaking attack upon Joseph Stalin, a voice was heard from among the national assembly of Soviet Communists in the Kremlin. The voice asked Mr. Khrushchev: "Where were you while Stalin was perpetrating all these horrible crimes?" Mr. Khrushchev replied: "Will the person who asked that question please stand up?" Nobody stood up. Then Khrushchev remarked: "So he's nowhere to be seen. And that's where I was."

As editor of the International Edition of The New York Times from 1951 to 1960, I could only witness and raise my voice at the events as they unfolded, and I never failed to do so, loudly, for all to hear. That was equally true about my actions during the period immediately after World War II when I was associate foreign editor of The Times. My attitude and outcries may have had no effect upon the whole paper but I can say with assurance that my point of view made a difference in the International Edition.

The fundamental defect of the press coverage of the Korean War was the attitude of the United States Government, which sought not only to manage the news but to ignore the basic fact of the conflict—that it was started by the Soviet Government and was being carried on by the Soviet Government, assisted by Communist

China. The whole story is yet to be disclosed. Certain historians still insist that the Red Chinese entered the war only because the United Nations forces crossed the 38th Parallel and approached the Manchurian border. That view is not realistic in view of present knowledge of Chinese Communist behavior. No such excuse can be given for Red China's rough seizure of Tibet and her encroachment upon India's frontiers.

The Times designated the enemy forces in Korea as North Korean and Chinese Communist. It would be, similarly, a great exaggeration and almost as wrong to say that the North Carolinians and the British invaded France in 1944. North Korea was virtually a province of the Soviet Union, with a good deal less autonomy than North Carolina or North Dakota. There may have been many more North Koreans than Russians on the North Korean side, but the entire direction of the North Korean side was Russian. In February, 1953, when Stalin died, Secretary of State Dulles said that his death would hasten the end of the war. That turned out to be an accurate prophecy. And even if a Chinese Communist did make the first move for a truce in March, it was most probably done with the fullest concurrence, if not prodding, of the Russians (not North Koreans). But Gen. J. Lawton Collins' prediction in 1951 that the Korean War would probably teach the Russians a lesson against aggression was in no way fulfilled, for they immediately transferred their war-making propensities to Indo-China and have never since ceased supplying that area, now known as Vietnam, Laos and Cambodia, with weapons to invade neighboring territory. Obviously, the Chinese Communists have only vied with the Russians in helping to foster the conflict. The danger that the Red Chinese will enter it on a larger scale is always present. That will not be exorcized by any kind of timidity or useless sacrifices. Nor will Communist China escape the great dangers that will confront her if she does take any rash action.

The parallel between Vietnam and Korea was graphically drawn in a letter to The Times, printed April 20, 1965, written by Bruno Shaw, who was an Associated Press correspondent in

China, newspaper editor and publisher in Hankow, and a radio commentator in New York. Mr. Shaw wrote:

"Owen Lattimore, in his letter published April 9, accuses the United States of following in the footsteps of Japan. We are marching, he says, toward the same doom in Vietnam as Japan did in Manchuria; we will not permit union between North and South Vietnam for the same reason Japan in the 1930's did not permit the union of Manchuria with China; and China, he says, is presented as the great menace behind Vietnam as Japan once depicted Russia as the great menace looming behind China.

"Let us for a moment consider whether Russia was or was not the great menace which helped to shatter the hopes of the Chinese people for a better life. I lived in Hankow, Hupeh, in central China, for many years and published a daily English-language newspaper, The Hankow Herald, in that city. I lived through a Communist revolution there. My entire staff, editorial and mechanical, were Chinese.

"The man in charge of political affairs in Hankow at that time ordered a strike in my plant which lasted three months because I refused to print Rayna Prohme's Communist People's Tribune on my presses. That man was Michael Borodin, Moscow's top agent in China, whom I had come to know intimately during the time he was a political power in the Central Yangtse Valley.

"When I was in Korea after the cease-fire between the Chinese and North Korean Reds and the United Nations forces, I was appalled by the thousands of tiny tots, boys and girls, whose mothers and fathers had been slaughtered by the North Korean Red Army.

"The situation in 1950 when the Red armies rolled down upon Seoul was much the same as it was in Vietnam only a few years ago. The people in the north were the same kind of people as those in the south. And so, when the North Korean Reds, instigated and equipped for war by Russia, overwhelmed Seoul, the capital city, in their initial surprise attack, the people of Seoul did not run away. They welcomed them.

"And this was their reward: the Red troops savagely slaughtered Seoul's civilian men and women. They set fire to the principal buildings of the city; they left hundreds of thousands of people homeless, and they made homeless orphans of thousands upon thousands of babies and little children.

"When the North Korean Red troops, reinforced by Chinese Red 'volunteers,' made their second attack upon Seoul, after they had been driven out of the city by United Nations forces, the civilians were ready for them. They fought side by side with the United Nations soldiers against their 'brother' invaders.

"By a curious kind of inverted reasoning, Owen Lattimore compares our effort to save the people of Southeast Asia from Communism, as we did those of South Korea, to the attempt by Japan to make tributary nations of one-half of the world while Nazi Germany attempted to do the same with the other half.

"What the United States is trying to do, of course, is to act in time to help save the free nations of South Asia and the Western Pacific from onslaught and domination by Red China's puppet armies and subversive agents. If we succeed, we can hope to prevent World War III. If we do not, the outlook for freedom in the world for any free nation, our own included, will grow dim indeed."

The letter was written in New York on April 10, 1965.

Few persons in our country who did not take part in the Korean War or did not visit that country soon afterward have any idea of the enormity of that senseless conflict which was fought on the United Nations side in a manner that defied every principle of common sense. Despite superb military leadership and the great fitness and courage of the troops, including fliers and sailors as well as soldiers, the timid and divided counsels of the United Nations civilian officials were not short of disgraceful, and added to this was the treachery of the Communists, official and unofficial, in and out of the United Nations. General Vasilev was replaced by another Russian on the Military Staff Committee of the United Nations in New York, who served there during the war. Another Russian officer went to South Korea as a member of the delegation of United Nations military observers! And the Communists in the United States, together with their travellers, spread the word among the populace that Syngman Rhee, then President of South Korea, who for a generation preached the freedom of Korea, was the instigator of the war. This put the heat on South Korea, just as the bêtes noires of South Vietnam were Ngo Dinh Diem and all the Premiers who followed him, especially the latest one, whoever he might be. The Communists tried to smear De Gasperi of Italy by speaking of the "degasperization" of Italy, whatever that might mean. Actually, though it is little known, they tried to do the same thing to Churchill at the end of World War II, but the effort fell flat.

Maj. Gen. Carl von Horn of Sweden, who commanded United Nations forces in the Middle East, with headquarters in Jerusalem; in the Congo, with headquarters in Leopoldville; and in the Yemen, with headquarters in Sanaa, gained sufficient experience with UN military methods from 1958 to 1963 to give considerable authority to his words. In his book, *Soldiering for Peace,* American edition, 1967, David McKay Company, Inc., New York, page 158, he asserts that "logic, military principles—even common sense—took second place to political factors" in the Congo. And, not too strangely, the orders that came from the U.N. headquarters in New York were weighted in favor of the Communist and pro-Communist forces in the Congo; and, in any case, they promoted chaos in that country. On page 195 General von Horn states that while a certain proposed military action "might have made sense in a normal military operation it had no validity here in the steamy Congo where the United Nations had established its own conception of Alice in Wonderland." Collaterally, the Congolese military were not far behind. The General wrote, on page 212: "Passions had run high among the ANG (Congolese National Army), which now contained not a single private—every one had promoted himself one rank up."

The United Nations was being true to its policy of division, fostered by dual purposes—a policy created during the first U.N.

military operations in Korea. General von Horn also complained of a lack of supplies, just as General James A. Van Fleet, then former commander of the United States ground forces in Korea, complained on March 5, 1953, before the United States Senate Armed Services Committee. General Van Fleet asserted that during the entire 22 months he had command he suffered from shortages of manpower and ammunition.

General von Horn, a highly apolitical person, with an excellent sense of humor, did his best to get along with the U.N. "political commissioners" sent to Leopoldville to see that the pro-Lumumba and anti-Tshombe forces retained the upper hand over the U.N. military command in the Congo. The division was strikingly along Communist and non-Communist lines. The general states on page 239: "I, personally, had a great deal of admiration for Mobutu. Unlike Lumumba, he struck me as a genuine Congolese patriot with no time for playing politics with Communist theories or alliances that held no true future in the Congo. His new regime at least gave hopes of some centralized authority. He was dedicated, aloof from self-interest, essentially the soldier who had stepped in to prevent his country from disintegrating into chaos."

But General von Horn had no doubt that the general level of military and other intelligence and learning in the Congo was not sufficiently advanced to be able to provide a high order of government for the country. He asked this biting question (page 238): "Who, in the hothouse atmosphere of New York, was going to be brave enough to admit the truth—that our success in saving thousands of lives had rested exclusively on Western military discipline, training, technique, and know-how or on those same qualities the new National (Congolese) units had inherited from the old colonial armies?"

The general also felt that, with the addition of "some thirty new African states" in the United Nations, "the balance of power had been seriously upset." This, he believed, "contributed to the organization's eventual decline." (Page 306-307) Perceptively, he observed: "No great power—and fewer smaller powers—would risk their policies or aspirations being upset in the U.N. by these vociferous little countries. From now on I was sure power would inevitably escape the United Nations; the real world crises would be solved by direct negotations." Or by direct contact, in battle, he might have added. He felt it was "high time the Charter was reviewed."

It is doubtful there can be complete understanding of United Nations military actions at this point without reference to General von Horn's book. He resigned his command in the Yemen with bitterness. He leaves one in doubt, however, that he understood the fundamental political divisions that tore the U.N. apart and made any U.N. military command an impossible task.

No chapter on the United Nations would be complete without this comment: The sacrifices that have been made by men and women of many nations to help increase human dignity and freedom are not in vain. These honored persons—the dead, the wounded and those who are alive—have contributed to the sum total of such global security and individual decency and nobility on a world basis as we now have. The fact that the United Nations as an organization has been corrupted does not lessen the value of the principles for which citizens of United Nations member states have fought and died—in Korea, in the Middle East, in the Congo and in Cyprus. It will come to be seen that the South Vietnamese and their allies of many nations have equally sought in the Vietnam War to uphold the principles of liberty and the right to freedom from aggression.

The New York Times on May 30, 1967, carried its campaign against victory in war into an editorial on Decoration Day by saying, "Decoration Day would have no meaning if it celebrated a victory or if it triumphed over a fallen enemy." It concluded: "Remember the dead. Decorate their graves. Let those who send young men to die strive to end the carnage so that many more will not die in vain." This aimless outcry seems to be an attack on the

United States Administration for not striving harder "to end the carnage" so that "many more will not die in vain." But no suggestion is made on how to avoid the wars that cause carnage. Who in the world has presented a foolproof plan against war? Why wouldn't the people of the world celebrate the absolute destruction of Hitler and Nazism? What other way to get rid of them was there, besides war? It is not true that the men who died fighting Hitlerism gave their lives in vain. Such editorials do not contribute solutions, the only useful applications to problems. They only contribute to an atmosphere that invites new wars of aggression.

The discovery of a great nest of American Communists as employes of the United Nations burst like a bombshell in 1952. It may have shaken but it did not dispel the belief of the American people in the U.N., but it pointed unmistakably to the Soviet policy of using the world organization for espionage and to thwart the other powers in the Security Council in attempts to bring about peace where the Soviets wanted war. The Russians, however, missed the boat when the other powers decided to resist the Soviet invasion of South Korea through the instrumentality of the puppet North Korean regime. The Russians were at that time boycotting the Security Council and were unable therefore to use their ubiquitous veto. It would have made a fundamental difference.

Mrs. Alice Widener wrote on page 7 in her book *Behind the U.N. Front,* published in 1955, that some important diplomats at the U.N. in 1952 told her, "You Americans are responsible for much of the Marxist mischief here at the U.N." And she continued:

"Instinctively and emotionally, I rushed to the defense of 'you Americans.' But after a while, professional training made me calm down and listen carefully to what these conscientious, hardworking foreigners were trying to tell me. The sum and substance of it was: 'The U.N. Secretariat and specialized agencies are heavily infiltrated with American pro-Communists and Communists. *Some of them are in top positions and they work hand-in-glove with Soviets and with French, Canadian, British and other Communist individuals in the Secretariats.'* " (Emphasis added.)

On December 3, 1952, The New York Times printed a story on its front page under a 3-column head, reading:

CLEARING OF SPIES FOR U.N.
LAID TO STATE DEPARTMENT
BY DEFIANT U.S. JURY HERE

The story said:

"A dogged Federal Grand Jury brushed aside attempted restraints by the Department of Justice to return yesterday a presentment castigating the State Department for clearing 'disloyal Americans' for key jobs in the United Nations.

"Angrily denouncing Department of Justice representatives for trying to block publication of its findings, the panel said that within the last ten days it had received evidence that two Americans holding top-ranking positions in one of the most powerful specialized agencies of the United Nations were members of a Soviet spy ring."

The story also related:

"The jury said it was its duty to advise the court that 'startling evidence had disclosed infiltration into the United Nations of an overwhelmingly large group of disloyal United States citizens, many of whom are closely associated with the international Communist movement.

" 'We have established,' the presentment declared, 'that in some of the most flagrant and obvious cases of disloyalty, the State Department gave the disloyal officials a clean bill of health in the United Nations.

" 'Our attempt to discover the reason for these misleading evaluations made by the State Department was stymied by the position taken by the State Department that it must refuse to furnish the grand jury with the names of the State Department personnel responsible for the faulty evaluations.' "

The Times printed the text of the presentment separately. One paragraph of the document said:

"Almost without exception these same subversive employes with the United Nations were formerly employed in various departments of our own Federal Government. They were transferred from one Federal department to another, finally ending up in key positions in the United Nations. The evidence shows this is not coincidental but part of a definite, planned pattern. It appears to result from the contrivance of certain highly placed officials who have surrounded themselves in each Government agency, and then in the United Nations, with personnel who share their disloyal convictions."

On page 24 of her book Mrs. Widener states:

". . . Alger Hiss and Soviet agents in other countries lost no time in sending a stream of applicants to the U.N.

"An Associated Press report from Washington, March 23, 1953, stated:

> HISS PICKED AMERICANS FOR U.N. JOBS
>
> A State Department official testified today that Alger Hiss made unofficial reports to the United Nations in 1946 on Americans seeking U.N. jobs.
>
> William L. Franklin, special assistant to the department's security director, told a House judiciary subcommittee that department files show Hiss sent lists of names to U.N. Secretary General Trygve Lie despite a "hands off" policy adopted by then Secretary of State James F. Byrnes.
>
> In 1946 Hiss was Director of the State Department's office of Special Political Affairs . . .

"Undoubtedly, many of the Red-sponsored applicants were turned away at the U.N. door. But it appears that the cleverest of the American group not only got through, they eventually maneuvered themselves into secure positions at Lake Success, and later rode an escalator all the way to top level positions in the

U.N. Headquarters in New York City. Their efforts were twofold: 1—to undermine the morale and subvert the efforts of the Secretariat in which the majority of employees are hardworking, capable and loyal; 2—to engage in worldwide espionage, subversion and dissemination of Red propaganda."

Mrs. Widener wrote on page 22:

" 'Sometimes, when a smart lawyer wants to be really smart,' said a former U.S. Assistant Secretary of State, 'he is intentionally obscure.'

"Along with many Communists, Socialists and impractical idealists, Alger Hiss—who in 1946 acted as Principal Adviser to the U.S. Delegation at the first session of the U.N. General Assembly in London—seems to have been a master at inducing our government to go along with 'planned vagueness.'

"Certainly there does not appear to be any record of his having advised the State Department to put up a strong fight against the kind of reasoning embodied in a Secretariat personnel policy that had been decided on at meetings of the Preparatory Commission by American, British and other diplomats who evidently were in what was described as 'a London mental fog.' "

As a result the United States joined in a rule that United Nations staff members "should, as far as possible, be acceptable to the member governments. . . . but it would be extremely undesirable to write into the text anything which would give national governments particular rights in this respect."

The New York Times story of the second Hiss trial for perjury, printed on Nov. 30, 1949, reported:

"Notes on the operations of a Soviet-controlled spy ring in Washington between 1934 and 1938 were introduced by the prosecution yesterday at the second Alger Hiss perjury trial, in the form of new documentary evidence.

"Thomas F. Murphy, Assistant United States Attorney, made Government exhibits of memoranda by Adolf A. Berle Jr., Assistant Secretary of State in 1939, and by Raymond Murphy, State Department security officer. The Berle notes were based on a conversation with Whittaker Chambers in the summer of 1939. Mr. (Raymond) Murphy's memoranda recounted what Mr. Chambers had told him about spy operations on March 20, 1945, and on Aug. 28, 1946.

"Mr. Hiss, former assistant to Assistant Secretary of State Francis B. Sayre, is under indictments on two counts of perjury. The Government contends that he lied once when he told a grand jury that he had never passed State Department documents to Mr. Chambers, and again when he said he had never seen the ex-Communist after Jan. 1, 1937. The first trial ended last summer with the jury deadlocked 8 to 4 for conviction. [Hiss was convicted on both counts of perjury at his second trial.]

"Under persistent defense questioning on the seventh trial day, Mr. Chambers insisted that he received all but one of a total of 64 State Department documents from Alger Hiss. . . .

"Mr. (Raymond) Murphy's notes on his 1945 conversation with Mr. Chambers read in part:

" 'In 1934 with the establishment of the Agricultural Adjustment Administration and the introduction of much reform legislation in Washington, the Communist party decided its influence could be felt more strongly by enlisting the active support of underground workers not openly identified with the party and never previously affiliated, but whose background and training would make them possible prospects as affiliates under the guise of advancing reform legislation.

" 'The Hungarian, party name J. Peters, was selected by the Central Committee to supervise the work from New York. His Washington representative and contact man was the informant. (Chambers.)

" 'The opportunity for formation of an underground group presents itself with the appointment to a leading position in AAA in 1934 of Harold Ware. Ware had worked for years in agricultural collectivization projects in Russia. He was the son of Ella Reeves Bloor, a veteran American Communist.

" 'In being assigned to this agency Ware found a group of

very promising, amibitious young men with advanced social and political ideas. Among them were Lee Pressman, Alger Hiss, Henry Collins and Charles Kramer. (Krivitsky.) [That is the way it reads. It is not clear what it means, but it refers to General Krivitsky, a top Soviet secret police officer, who defected to the United States and died strangely in a Washington hotel room in the 1930's.]

" 'They all joined the Communist party and became leaders of cells.

" 'The top leaders of the underground were: 1. Harold Ware. 2. Lee Pressman. 3. Alger Hiss. In the order of their importance.

" 'Alger Hiss was never to make converts. His job was to mess up policy. There were other underground Communist groups in Washington, but this was the elite, policy-making, top-level group. It was not a spy ring, but one far more important and cunning because its members helped to shape policy in these departments.' "

Hiss's job "was to mess up policy." That statement rings a bell in connection with Communist policy around the world. How often we have seen Communist actions that seemed designed only to "mess up" things, rather than to have any constructive purpose. For instance, the Communist policy of assassination—this is a fixed, deep-rooted policy—is designed to spread fear and terror. The principle upon which it is based is naked power, pure and simple, exerted over the heads of the people and aimed to make them cringe into submission.

The New York Times reported the Hiss story in detail, and gave a full account of the grand jury's findings as to the subversive activities going on at the United Nations. But the fact is that there was no hint out of Washington or elsewhere beforehand in The Times as to the Communist activities in Washington and the United Nations. It is possible that most of the reporters in Washington—The Times' and others—were fooled by the Communists. It is impossible that all The Times correspondents in the United Nations were fooled. Mrs. Widener was not.

The New York Times has always taken the position that it is not a crusading or muckraking newspaper—that it prints the news as it arises. The fact is that that is no longer the policy of The Times. Witness The Times' collaboration with the scurrilous magazine Ramparts in launching muckraking stories. Said Time magazine of Jan. 6, 1967:

"A Ramparts 'expose' of the fact that Michigan State University had trained a CIA-infiltrated Vietnamese police force had already been published in book form elsewhere. But Ramparts had the savvy to release the article to The New York Times a day before the rest of the press knew about it. 'We worked very closely with the Times,' says Mander (Ramparts Promotion Director). 'The Times legitimized the story.' And The Times has legitimized other Ramparts stories that might have gone unnoticed."

And in the previous decade, the 1950's, The New York Times did a tremendous piece of crusading work in order to help the revolution of Fidel Castro and the Communists in Cuba. Positively and negatively, the weight of The Times has generally fallen on the side of the Communists since the end of World War II. Consider that throughout the Korean War, in which there were actually millions of casualties, The Times' criticism was aimed at South Korea, not at Russia and not greatly at Communist China. This is precisely what is now happening in South Vietnam. The very freedom that is permitted in South Korea and South Vietnam has been used against them to report in much detail the faults of their leaders, of their economic systems, their legal customs, treatment of prisoners—their backwardness, in a word. The real culprits—North Vietnam, Red China and, above all, Communist Russia—go unscathed. Indeed, throughout the Korean War the Russian diplomats were wined and dined in New York while they sent the U.N. Korea commander's war dispatches to Moscow. One Russian diplomat, Zinchenko, frequently presided over the United Nations in the absence of Mr. Lie. For his loyalty to the principles of the United Nations, Mr. Lie lost his job. The Russians forced him out.

It would be easy to get the impression in some quarters of New York that the real culprit in the Hiss-Chambers confrontation was Whittaker Chambers. The Communist word was out: "Smear. Smear. Smear. And smear again." Like Stalin's "Beat, Beat, Beat. And beat again." In Russia they cut down their foes with the sword. In America they do it with the word. To this day there are many otherwise intelligent persons who feel that Chambers is no better than Hiss. Quite aside from the Communists and travellers and those who would use both, there are the there-is-much-to-be-said-on-both-sides persons. Hiss was a handsome, dashing young man on the college campus. It may be that some of the sympathy he engendered grew in and was transmitted by women, whereas Chambers was a dour and rather plain man. It is not recalled that, in Hiss's protestations of innocence, he never denounced or criticized the Communists.

Neither The New York Times nor other American newspapers exposed the asserted fact that many of the foreign officials and employes of the United Nations, besides the Russians and satellite citizens, were—and no doubt still are—Communists. The United States Grand Jury in New York could only expose *disloyal Americans* in the world organization. The Times did not pursue the matter, once the forty were dealt with. Pursuit of leads on Communists is generally avoided in New York Times news practice. Mrs. Alice Widener's courageous expose of the Communists in the United Nations did not shame The Times into any action to extend her findings. Moreover, providing such information as the individual names of Communists is not done, as a general practice, by The New York Times.

CHAPTER IV

The New York Times and Cuba: Communist Castro's Rise to Power

• • •

"AT THE NOTORIOUS TRICONTINENTAL CONFERENCE (OF COM-
*munist leaders) in Havana early last year, a member of the Soviet
Politburo urged his comrades 'to unfold on a still greater scale our
common struggle against imperialism, colonialism and neo-coloni-
alism headed by U.S. capitalists.' The Reds have been as good as
their word. Bristling with Soviet arms and equipment, Cuba has
become a base of hemisphere subversion.*

"*According to James Reston in The New York Times, which
is not famous for Red-baiting: 'Last month in Mexico City I was
told that the Mexican Government had caught the Secretary of the
Cuban Embassy passing 6,000 cruzeiros to agents of the Guate-
malan Communist rebels and had intercepted shipments of arms
from Cuba to the guerrillas.' Venezuela has increased its military
budget to combat Communist insurgency. In Bolivia the Army has
been fighting a guerrilla band, led, it charges, by Ernesto (Che)
Guevara, Fidel Castro's old comrade-in-arms.*"—Barron's, April
10, 1967*

BOGOTA, Colombia, April 12 [1948]—[United States]
Secretary of State [George C.] Marshall today placed the blame

squarely on the Soviet Union for the Bogota uprising and its atten-
dant violence [in which 10,000 persons were killed]. Breaking his
silence, he permitted correspondents to quote a recent statement
he made at a meeting of senior delegates to the Inter-American
Conference, in which he said emphatically that the revolt had been
Communist-inspired and, as such, of world-wide importance.

"He added: 'This situation must not be judged on a local
basis, however tragic the immediate results may be to the Colom-
bian Government and the People. The occurrence goes far beyond
Colombia.

" 'It is of the same definite pattern as the occurrences which
provoked the strikes in France and Italy, and that are endeavoring
to prejudice the situation in Italy for the elections of April 18.

" 'In the actions we take here in regard to the present situa-
tion,' he added, 'we must have clearly in mind that this is a world
affair, and not merely Colombian or Latin American.'

"Furthermore, Secretary Marshall indicated that other dele-
gations also held the Communists responsible for the Colombian
revolt."—The New York Times, page 1, column 1, April 13,
1948.

JEFFREY ST. JOHN: "In the aftermath of the missile crisis,
the U.S. press failed to mention that the Kennedy Administration
had lost the U.S. initiative in Cuba. Proof of this loss? The fact
that the Soviets are still in Cuba and, as one Cuban underground
leader told me recently, 'Cuba today is militarily 50 times stronger
than it was at the climax of the 1962 missile crisis.'

"As this is written, reports persist that Russia has not with-
drawn its missiles from the island and that they are pointed at the
heart of the United States. Again, the U.S. Government disputes
these claims, which come from the very Cuban underground
sources that helped to reveal the existence of the missiles in 1962.

"Reports also persist that the Soviets have helped Castro
build enormous underground airplane hangers, missile sites, sub-
marine pens and other military installations. My files are bulging

with information on a progressive military buildup in Cuba by the Soviets. This information is available from the Cuban Student Directorate, the Cuban Intelligence Underground Organization, Latin American diplomats and other sources. But few of the major organs of the press in the United States bother to print this news.

"Is this the kind of free press we want in this country?" —From an article, "Is the Free Press Failing Us?" in The Catholic Layman of July, 1965

From THE CUBAN DILEMMA, *by Ruby Hart Phillips (Ivan Obolensky, Inc., New York, 1962):*

"As a child he [Fidel Castro] was belligerent, rebellious against authority, self-centered, and determined to impose his viewpoint on his companions. He fought with his father, for whom he was said to have a particular dislike, and early rejected the Catholic religion. He carried these characteristics into his high-school days, into Belen College in Havana, and into the University. Castro never achieved his ambition to be president of the University Student Federation.

"Persons who had been in the University with Castro said he belonged to one of the armed University gangs. Again and again I was told that he was connected with the killing of Manolo Castro, a student leader shot down in San Rafael Street, in Havana in 1948, but no one could prove this. The killers were never apprehended and the police shrugged it off as another student fight. The supporters of Fidel Castro indignantly denied he had anything to do with it.

"Nor have the activities of Fidel Castro in the Bogota, Colombia, uprising in 1948 ever been clarified. According to his followers, he and Rafael del Pino went to Bogota as representatives of a Havana University student organization to protest against Yankee imperialism before the Ninth Inter-American Conference. I recalled that at that time, in Havana, I had been told that the Communists intended to break up the conference and that Leftist students of various countries were gathering in Bogota to

help carry out this plan. I did not know anything about Fidel Castro then.

"Dr. Guillermo Belt, who was Ambassador to Washington during the Grau San Martin administration, headed the Cuban delegation to the conference. He told me that he arranged to get Castro and del Pino and one or two other Cuban students out of Colombia by plane to prevent their arrest by Colombian authorities. Col. Jules Dubois, of the Chicago Tribune, in his very favorable book on the Castro revolution, stated Castro and del Pino joined the Colombian insurrectionists and fought alongside them. Diaz Verson, a Cuban newspaperman, who devoted some twenty years to the study of Communism in Latin America, claims that Fidel Castro began working with the Communists long before he went to Bogota to help break up the conference.

"Those who were in the University when Castro studied there told me he was even then slovenly in appearance, that he enjoyed opposing all convention, and spent most of his time in class arguing with his teachers. One woman told me that once he stood up in class and declared, 'I am a leftist.' He reportedly read Marx, and Hitler's Mein Kampf, *during his University days and was greatly influenced by both.*

"Fidel Castro's first revolutionary experience was in 1947 when he joined the expedition being formed to invade the Dominican Republic and overthrow the dictatorship of Generalissimo Trujillo. This was broken up by the Grau San Martin administration at the insistence of the United States."

From THE FOURTH FLOOR, *by Earl E. T. Smith, former United States Ambassador to Cuba (Random House, New York, 1962):*

"I never talked to Fidel Castro. It was my intention to ask for an appointment through the Foreign Ministry shortly after his arrival in Havana. Any such thoughts on my part were quickly dispelled after his public statement to a group of reporters in the

lobby of the Havana Hilton Hotel. Castro's off-hand remarks were that if the United States intervened to protect its investments there would be 200,000 dead gringos in the streets. After such belligerent and disrespectful remarks about the United States, it was obvious that an interview between Fidel Castro and myself could serve no useful purpose. . . .

"I am convinced, I repeat, that the alternative to Batista need not have been Castro, the Communist. The United States could have been instrumental in forming a broadly-based government in Cuba without Batista and without Castro. . . . Fidel Castro was not the only alternative for Cuba, nor did Castro single-handedly conquer the island of Cuba. . . .

"My predecessor, Ambassador [Arthur] Gardner, testified that he was ignored and not even de-briefed at the end of his mission. I also was never de-briefed. [It is customary, when the man-on-the-spot returns from his post, to be questioned by the State Department as to his latest views and as to his estimate of the situation. This is what is meant by de-briefing.] This is not businesslike procedure; nevertheless, it is what happened. . . .

"Perhaps the greatest confusion in our foreign relations arises from uncertainty as to what our policy really is. As an Ambassador, I was never told. The briefings I received from Herbert Matthews and the Fourth Floor [of the State Department—Latin American affairs, lower echelon] certainly did not indicate cordiality to the government of Cuba. It seems to me that when an Ambassador is designated as Chief of Mission to a country he should be given definite briefing as to our policy, its permanent features and its flexibility—certainly about the country to which he is sent. . . .

"Surely it is difficult to understand why the higher echelon of the State Department, as late as April 1961, permitted release of the White Paper on Cuba.

"The United States cannot afford to excuse such costly mistakes by saying that the revolution was betrayed by Castro. The

United States cannot afford to risk its security by having the Fourth Floor gamble on a Leftist dictator in order to have revolutions succeed."

From a book review of The Fourth Floor *in* The New York Times Sunday Book Review, *December 9, 1962, by Adolf A. Berle:*

"Smith thinks these men [Wieland and Rubottom] knew, or should have known, that Fidel Castro was a Communist. Raul, his brother, almost certainly was. This reviewer can state that Wieland and Rubottom were not certain Fidel Castro was a Communist (most of Fidel's companions-in-arms thought he was not) though there were reports to that effect. But they were convinced he was a hopeless megalomaniac-psychopath. They did not agree with the optimistic image created by the uninformed American press, wrongly ascribing to Castro (in Smith's words) the qualities of Robin Hood, Abraham Lincoln and other heroes."

MIAMI—"The first of a new flood of Cuban refugees are reaching Florida. This incoming tide of people seeking to get away from Fidel Castro is expected to grow rapidly if the U.S. and the Red dictator agree on terms of evacuation.

"In the first wave of evacuees that came in 1962, before Castro clamped down, the number of Cubans reaching Miami and registering exceeded 180,000. The total number arriving in this city alone probably exceeded 250,000. In the wave now starting, some U.S. officials look for an inflow of 100,000 or more.

"As one just-arrived refugee put it: 'If all could leave Cuba who wanted to get out of Cuba, only Castro and a handful of aides would remain."—U.S. News & World Report, Oct. 25, 1965.

This follows the Communist pattern of killing, imprisoning or driving out unwanted citizens, as in Eastern Europe, especially Germany; in Korea and in Vietnam.

"Cuba is a tropical Siberia. The specter of forced labor camps hangs over millions of Cubans."—Marino de Medici, U.S.

and Latin American correspondent for Il Tiempo of Rome, in The Reader's Digest of July 1967.

"*WASHINGTON, Dec. 1, (1962)—Russian reconnaissance planes based in Cuba have been overflying the southeastern United States.*

"*Scripps-Howard Newspapers can report this as fact—verified from independent sources—despite Pentagon denials. The Russian planes have been spotted over Georgia and South Carolina.*

"*At one base, the Air Force commander stepped out of his headquarters building at noon and was astounded to see an easily recognizable Russian plane zoom past.*

"*The sources did not identify the type of plane used in the recent forays or the nationality of the pilots. It is known that Soviet military aid to the Cuban air force has included aircraft.*

"*The Defense Department is unwilling to tell the public about the flights, apparently for two reasons. First, it's embarrassing. Second, we'd like to wait until we shoot down one of the planes.*" *—New York World-Telegram and Sun of December 1, 1962. That story flew off into space and was never heard from again, but it was not reassuring about having a Communist neighbor, even a small one, and the worst was yet to come, with the missiles and the threat of atomic war. The World-Telegram story was on page 1 and was headed, "Cuba's Soviet Planes Openly Spying on U.S."*

HENRY J. TAYLOR: "If President Johnson's Santo Domingo action can re-establish our shattered Monroe Doctrine we'll redress one of the most dangerous collapses in American foreign policy. . . .

"*We've already paid far, far too much for blindness, or worse. And not only official blindness. For example, a New York Times editorial is utterly incomprehensible.*

"*It castigates President Johnson's 'intervention' on the basis of reports that a handful of Communists were involved in the rebellion and on flimsy evidence that they threatened to gain control of it.*

"These weren't reports. It was a plan. The Castroites didn't threaten control—they had, of course, taken it over.

"Everybody has a right to his own opinion about anything, but nobody has a right to be wrong in his facts—and certainly not The New York Times. May I respectfully ask if the Times hasn't done enough damage already in promoting this kind of anti-factual nonsense originally about Castro?

"The Times and some other voices insist that we rely on collective security. But we do not have collective security in Latin America. We have collective insecurity."—From Mr. Taylor's column, headed, "Johnson Wisely Closed The Door," in the New York World-Telegram and Sun of May 12, 1965.

"REDS ADMIT THEIR ROLE IN DOMINICAN REVOLT: The Communists themselves now say it's true: They were deeply involved in the Dominican revolt, their aim was to take over the country, and it was only armed intervention by the United States that stopped them.

"Critics of the U.S. action in the island a year ago have maintained that there was no Communist threat to justify intervention in the revolution.

"Now two Dominican Communists—J. I. Quello and N. Isa Conde—set down their versions in two articles in the authoritative Communist publication 'World Marxist Review,' These are excerpts from the articles:

> *The Dominican revolution is another contribution to the arsenal of revolutionary experience . . . it may differ from the Cuban revolution in the 'letter' but is fully in accord with it in 'spirit, meaning and lessons.'*
> *Our experience showed that the task of revolutionaries during an armed insurrection is to influence it and*

*guide it. (We) allocated armed Communists to a number
of 'commands'. . . .*

*Only by direct armed intervention was U.S. im-
perialism able . . . to check the development of the revolution.—From U.S. News & World Report of April
4, 1966.*

The evidence leaves no doubt that The New York Times was
influential in bringing Fidel Castro, a Communist, to power in
Cuba. No other Cuban was considered as the successor to President Fulgencio Batista by the chief Times editorial writer on
Cuban affairs, Herbert L. Matthews. Former President Dwight D.
Eisenhower touched upon the part played by The Times in the
overthrow of Cuba in a press conference at Grinnell College, Grinnell, Iowa, on May 13, 1965. A New York Times dispatch stated
that the former President expressed his agreement with President
Johnson on his action in the Dominican Republic at that time, and
continued:

"The situation in Cuba when Fidel Castro took power there
was entirely different, General Eisenhower said. He explained:

" 'The Cuban rebellion started about 1957 and was applauded in this country and had the support of some of our
greatest newspapers. There was a writer for The New York Times
named Herbert Matthews who almost singlehandedly made Castro
a national hero.

" 'Also, then Senator John F. Kennedy said that Castro was
following in the footsteps of Bolivar, the great liberator of South
America. Castro was then talking in 1959 about free elections. It
wasn't until December, 1961, that that man finally confessed that
he was a Marxist and always had been.

" 'I think that the United States would have been called 'in-
terventionist' and 'imperialist' of the worst degree if we had moved
quickly in that situation. It all reminds me of some of the placards

they were carrying around in Rio de Janeiro during my visit there and on which they proclaimed that "I like Ike—and Fidel, too".' "

But General Eisenhower and Senator (afterward President) Kennedy changed their opinion about Castro Cuba. The New York Times did not. It still looked upon it four years after the revolution as a nation in the middle of a new and better life and believed that somehow the United States should help it along. A Times editorial on April 22, 1963, said:

"The Soviet presence in Cuba and the dangers it represents are undeniably real and important, but the things happening inside Cuba are at least as important.

"The island is in the midst of a social revolution. Its agrarian program, industrialization, education, housing, road-building, public health and all the paraphernalia of Marxism-Leninism in the labor unions, the schools, the militia and the Government are going full blast.

". . . . Cuba is going through the agonizing process of a social revolution which, like all similar revolutions in modern history, is making a permanent imprint.

"American concern should be as much to help achieve a free, democratic, socially progressive Cuba as it is to get rid of the Soviet intrusion."

There is very little that is not wrong with that editorial. If "the things happening inside Cuba are at least as important" as the Soviet presence there, then it must be pointed out that these "things" would not be happening if the Soviet repression, effected by Soviet military forces, was not there. To say that all the paraphernalia of Communism "in the labor unions, the schools, the militia and the Government are going full blast" is no recommendation whatever to America. In this country the labor unions are free. Where Communism is "going full blast" there are no effective labor unions; the right to strike is absent; any labor leader, worker or peasant can be jailed or executed without trial as that word is understood in free countries. How does Communism at "full blast" affect the schools except to truncate education and twist the minds of the people? Communism in the militia and the Government can only mean that the people are ruled by a secret police and a succession of "plans" that fail; there are no elections. The process that Cuba is going through is "agonizing" enough. As for the "permanent imprint," it will be likened in history to the bloody excesses of the French Revolution. How the United States should help Cuba under Castro to "achieve a free, democratic, socially progressive" existence, the editorial does not say. If this means anything at all, it means that the United States should help to fasten the Soviet yoke around Cuba's neck tighter than ever, for obviously The New York Times believes that Communism at "full blast" ought not to be interfered with.

Before penetrating farther into the factitious fastnesses of Castro's career and his rise to power through the help of The New York Times, it should be made clear that Mr. Matthews does not make the policy of The New York Times. What he did and did not do had the consent of the policy-makers of the newspaper. It is inconceivable that he could have written as he did about Castro and acted as he did prior to the Castro revolution, without the agreement of The New York Times. Not only did The Times go along with Mr. Matthews before the revolution but it has permitted him to write the editorials on Cuba since. It is probable that he wrote the editorial quoted above, and that later ones supporting the revolution in Cuba also were composed by him. This is the balance-of-power philosophy in action. More than Mr. Matthews' views are involved, though it seems expedient to make an individual scapegoat of him. An article in Esquire in 1966 by Gay Talese, a former Times man, said the news department of The Times would no longer accept dispatches or articles written by Mr. Matthews. However, he continued to write editorials, on Vietnam as well as Cuba; editorial page articles, and pieces for the Sunday department in 1967. The news, editorial page and Sunday departments are separate entities in The New York Times and are tightly controlled. Once a managing editor of The Times complained that he was having a hard time getting an article accepted by—or written in acceptable form for—the Sunday department. Editorials are frequently contributed by Times writers other than editorialists, and when they are accepted they are printed exactly as written—at least that was the experience of one contributor of editorials under the very able editorship of Charles Merz.

Now we come to Fidel Castro Ruz, or, as The Times called him for some years, Dr. Castro. Where he received his doctorate and in which branch of the inhumanities is an obscure matter. More apparent, but less clear to The Times, is his title to the adjective Communist. We propose to demonstrate both a priori and a posteriori, that Castro was a Communist before he came to power in Cuba and, of course, ever since by his own acknowledgement and avowal. The political coloration of Castro and his followers in 1957, as described by Mr. Matthews and accepted without demur by The New York Times, was as follows (quotations are from three articles in The Times of February 24, 25 and 26, 1957):

"Fidel Castro and his 26th of July Movement are the flaming symbol of this opposition to the (Batista) regime. The organization, which is apart from the university students' opposition, is formed of youths of all kinds. It is a revolutionary movement that calls itself socialistic. It is also nationalistic, which generally in Latin America means anti-Yankee.

"The program is vague and couched in generalities, but it amounts to a new deal for Cuba, radical, democratic and therefore anti-Communist. . . .

". . . He (Castro) was already a hero, for on July 26, 1953, he had led a band of youths in a desperate attack on the Moncada Barracks in Santiago de Cuba. [Hence the July 26th Movement.]

These three paragraphs are from the Feb. 24 article. The story the following day included these remarks:

"The economy is good and most workers are contented. . . .

"Senor Castro's men, the student leaders who are on the run from the police, the people who are bombing and sabotaging every day, are fighting blindly, rashly, perhaps foolishly. But they are giving their lives for an ideal and for their hopes of a clean, democratic Cuba. . . .

"Communism has little to do with the opposition to the (Batista) regime. There is a well-trained hard core of Communists that is doing as much mischief as it can and that naturally bolsters all the opposition elements. But there is no communism to speak of in Castro's 26th of July movement or the disaffected elements in the Army."

On February 26, Matthews wrote:

"The directorate (of the Federation of University Students) maintains that it has the almost solid backing of the student body. The students obviously are not seeking anything for themselves. As a whole their traditions are anti-Communist and democratic. . . ."

In a review of Mr. Matthews' book, *The Cuban Story,* on October 6, 1961, Time magazine said:

"As early as 1957, plenty of evidence suggested that Matthews' admiration (for Castro) was misplaced. But the Timesman, a longtime student of Latin American affairs, apparently did not bother to examine it. 'Let us note in passing,' he writes in *The Cuban Story,*' that already in 1948, at the age of 21, Fidel Castro was anti-Yankee and agitating against "Yankee imperialism." ' But in his first story in The Times, Matthews let Castro say, without rebuttal, that 'We have no animosity toward the United States and the American people.'

"Once in power, Castro promptly confirmed the suspicions that had bothered many reporters—but not Herb Matthews. After bathing Cuba in blood—551 drumhead executions in four months —Castro edged steadily leftward, toward the shadow of Moscow. What had been a tyranny under Batista remained one under Castro. But even as other newsmen, among them Ruby Hart Phillips, the Times' Havana correspondent for 24 years, reported these facts, Matthews stuck by his adopted rebel. Castro 'insists he wants friendship' with the U.S., wrote Matthews in March, 1959. 'While welcoming American investments, he says he would prefer American loans.' Two months later Castro announced plans to expropriate 1,660,000 acres of sugar cane owned by U.S. companies. In July of the same year, Matthews wrote: 'This is not a Communist revolution in any sense of the word.'

"With little alteration, Matthews sang Fidelity for four years. His misplaced loyalty continued to color the Times's editorials on Cuba (which, curiously, still remain a Matthews responsibility). Those who saw Castro's Cuba in a harsher light he branded as 'distorted, unfair, ill-informed and intensely emotional'—accusations more accurately leveled at Matthews (who once admitted that "I would never dream of hiding my own bias or denying it").

"Intended as a ringing defense of his own reporting on Cuba, his book only demonstrates how wrong Matthews was then, and how wrong he is now."

Two years earlier, on July 27, 1959, Time magazine had expressed wonderment that Mr. Matthews could write with such scandalous superficiality about the Cuban terror under Castro. Mr. Matthews had simply said of Castro's bloodthirsty behavior: "Youth must sow its wild oats." Time commented:

"It is an explanation that rings tinnily in a reporter's accounting of desperate hours in the history of a people. And however it may fit the uses of a historical sum-up, it has even less use as an explanation of the course of seasoned Correspondent Matthews or the vagaries of the Cuba story in the seasoned (108 years) New York Times."

As recently as January 3, 1967, Mr. Matthews in a signed article at the top of the editorial page of The Times asserted:

"Castro, who became a Communist and led his revolution into the Communist camp at some period in 1960, even today, is far more of a revolutionary than he is an orthodox Communist by any European or Chinese standard."

Now it must be obvious to all that the news coverage of Cuba and the editorials on that country are exactly as The Times wants them. It will not do to blame Mr. Matthews for a condition that exists in so many regions of the world and in the United States itself. The record of The Times on the growth of Communism in the world is not confined to Cuba. It is just a little more glaring there because Cuba is only 90 miles from the Florida shores of the United States. What is more, the fact that The Times attested to the anti-Communism of Castro and his Movement when in fact he and it were Communist was a considerable disservice to the American people because they trusted The Times. Many of them to this day cannot believe that The Times would do such a thing. It is possible that the President of the United States and the Secretary of State were deprived of important knowledge largely by the State Department but also partly by The New York Times in regard to Castro. He was anything but a man of the stature and humanity of Abraham Lincoln. Castro's coming into power brought about the world's first nuclear showdown—between the United States and the U.S.S.R.

"It was not until the late spring of 1960 that the Eisenhower Administration belatedly recognized that the Castro regime was Communist-controlled and decided to take steps to destroy it," wrote Nathaniel Weyl in his book *Red Star Over Cuba* (Hillman/ MacFadden, New York, 1961). "Thus Castro had been given a breathing space of well over a year. During this time, he had moved swiftly, destroying the power of all organizations and individual leaders hostile to Communism; smashing the Cuban Army and substituting a people's militia, controlled and infiltrated by Europeans and Cuban Communist agents; organizing a ramified secret police apparatus, built on MVD (Soviet secret police) lines and bossed by Soviet-bloc specialists."

That is a somewhat different description of Communism "at full blast" from the one given in The New York Times editorial of April 22, 1963, two years *after* the Weyl book was published.

Earl E.T. Smith, who was the United States Ambassador to Cuba while Castro was in the Sierra Maestra, wrote in his book, *The Fourth Floor:*

"I knew, even before I went to Cuba, that I would have to deal with the Castro revolution. I did not know then that this was a

Communist revolution and I was informed neither by the officials of the State Department nor by Herbert Matthews of the *New York Times,* from whom I was instructed to receive a briefing, that the observation of the Castro Communist revolution would be my responsibility.

"I now know that those in charge of Cuban affairs in the State Department were advised from many other sources of the Communist infiltration of the 26th of July Movement and of the Communist sympathizers who held important positions in the Movement, especially among the troops led by Raul Castro.

"From the time Castro landed in the Province of Oriente in December 1956, the State Department received reports of probable Communist infiltration and exploitation of the 26th of July Movement. The State Department was aware of Castro's contacts with Communists in Mexico. Certain officials in the State Department were familiar with Castro's part in the bloody Communist-inspired uprising in Bogota, known as the 'Bogotazo' of 1948. [Ten thousand persons were killed in that insurrection, which "left the downtown area in ruins," according to a New York Times story from Bogota published on page 34, June 20, 1965] In addition to my reports and information from many outside sources, the State Department also had reports from its own Bureau of Research and Intelligence.

"This knowledge was not made available to the American people. (Emphasis added.) I am now convinced that neither President Eisenhower nor Secretary of State John Foster Dulles were provided with information available to officials in the State Department and the Central Intelligence Agency (CIA).

"My official briefings included a lengthy conversation in New York City with Herbert Matthews. This briefing was suggested to me by William Wieland, Director of the Office of Caribbean and Mexican Affairs, and approved by Roy C. Rubottom, Assistant Secretary of State for Latin American Affairs.

"Mr. Matthews informed me that he had very knowledgeable views of Cuba and Latin America in general. He was of the firm belief that it would be in the best interests of Cuba and the rest of the world if Batista were removed from office. Mr. Matthews had a very poor opinion of Batista. He considered him a Rightist, ruthless, and corrupt dictator.

"The significance of my briefing by Mr. Matthews is that it revealed the thinking and the aims of those influential sources in the lower echelon of the State Department at that time, for the views of the New York Times journalist on the Cuba situation were fully publicized. (Emphasis added.) . . . .

"On August 30, 1960, in reply to questioning before a subcommittee of the Judiciary Committee of the United States Senate, as to what part, if any, the United States played in Castro's and the Communist rise to power in Cuba, I testified:

" 'The United States Government agencies and the United States press played a major role in bringing Castro to power. . . .

" 'After the Matthews articles which followed an exclusive interview by the Times editorial writer in Castro's mountain hideout and which likened him to Abraham Lincoln, he (Castro) was able to get followers and funds in Cuba and in the United States. From that time on, arms, money and soldiers of fortune abounded. Much of the American press began to picture Castro as a political Robin Hood.' "

Here we see the effect of The New York Times on other sections of the American press, in a specific action.

Ambassador Smith gave a very different picture of the Cuban Federation of University Students from that given by Mr. Matthews. Mr. Smith wrote on page 40:

"Before Fidel Castro abandoned Cuba, he and many others of the 26th of July Movement leaders were active in the Federation of University Students (FEU), which was largely responsible for acts of terrorism and riots in Cuba before Fidel Castro landed in the hills of Oriente in December, 1956. The FEU since 1952 was a terroristic organization and was known to be infiltrated by the Communists. It had a history of involvement in common gangster activities and was under Communist influence. . . .

"There was a time when some authority in the United States and some newspapermen did not want Castro to fall under any circumstances. Such persons were so fanatically bound to the revolutionary concept that they were even willing to risk the prospect of Communist control of Cuba. I do not accuse anyone of deliberately falsifying the facts, but from where I sat I could see the slant of reports, and always the slanting was favorable to Castro."

The thing that pinpoints Castro as a Communist beyond anything else early in his career was the part he played in the Bogota uprising of 1948. This insurrection was arranged by the Soviet Government, according to a statement made in Bogota by the then United States Secretary of State George C. Marshall, who was there when it occurred. Mr. Smith wrote of this bloody unsuccessful upheaval, on page 67:

"Guillermo Belt (former Cuban Ambassador to the United States) was anti-Batista but had good reason to fear Castro much more. Dr. Belt was Cuba's representative at the Ninth Inter-American Conference that convened in Bogota, March 30-May 2, 1948, at the time of the 'Bogotazo' of 1948 which occurred on April 9, 1948. The 'Bogotazo' of 1948 started with the assassination of Jorge Eliecer Gaitan, Liberal leader, so as to provoke the uprising of the masses that comprised the Liberal party, since Gaitan enjoyed immense popularity. The Bogota uprising was Communist-inspired and Communist controlled by a key group of international Communist leaders and activitists who were brought to Bogota for that purpose. The effort to shatter the Ninth Inter-American Conference at Bogota and to demonstrate to the world the power of the Communist-led mob to spread havoc was part of the general anti-United States strategy."

At this point Mr. Smith adds a footnote saying, "Nathaniel Weyl gives an authentic account of the Bogota uprising in *Red Star Over Cuba*." Mr. Smith continues with these remarkable paragraphs:

"At the Bogota uprising, Fidel Castro played his first serious role as an active organizer of Communist insurrection. He was then 22 years old and a student at Havana University Law School.

It was Dr. Guillermo Belt who gave asylum to Fidel Castro in the Cuban Embassy and arranged for his safe conduct to Cuba after the Bogota uprising. Dr. Belt told me Fidel Castro was accused of committing several murders at the Bogota uprising.

"When I asked Dr. Belt why he had given asylum to Castro in the Cuban Embassy and why he had arranged for Castro's safe conduct to Cuba, he replied he was unaware at the time of Castro's crimes.

"The Department of State must have been fully informed not only of Fidel Castro's police record but also of his active participation in the Communist-inspired and Communist-controlled uprising in Bogota. Yet no one in the State Department ever mentioned the Bogota uprising to me during the briefing period in the State Department when I was being prepared to assume my new post as Chief of Mission in Havana."

Mr. Smith makes no bones about his disappointment that certain persons, including Mr. Matthews, mentioned nothing of this matter to him. He concludes with tacit asperity:

"Fidel Castro was a member of the Communist group aimed at wrecking the organization to which Secretary Rubottom served as Secretary (Ninth International Conference of American States)."

Ambassador Smith was frustrated in Cuba by a foreign policy laid down in the State Department that must have bypassed both the President and the Secretary of State. Even if the lower echelon officials believed that Castro was a "megalomaniac-psychopath," as Mr. Berle mentioned in his review of the Smith book, surely they would have had no trouble in denying him access to power in Cuba if they had gone to the Secretary of State with that information. It must be assumed that, in addition to being denied the knowledge that Castro was a Communist, President Eisenhower was influenced by the articles of Mr. Matthews in The New York Times, which every President reads. Indeed, General Eisenhower implied as much in his statement at Grinnell College. It is as clear as anything can be that many mysteries remain as to how and why Castro was pushed into power by forces inside the United States, promptly after which events the United States found itself confronted by the nuclear might of the Soviet Government on the very doorstep of this country. Why was neither Ambassador Gardner nor Ambassador Smith debriefed in the customary way? Mr. Smith implies that something was amiss in the State Department. Mr. Berle takes umbrage at this but asserts that Mr. Rubottom and Mr. Wieland felt that Castro was a megalomaniac-psychopath. That characterization, in addition to the strongest indications that Castro was a Communist—while Mr. Smith was Ambassador, and with reasonable certainty much longer—that should have been more than sufficient to block Castro.

That Castro was allowed to take over Cuba must be put down to something more positive than mere laxness in the State Department. It must be assumed—and, indeed, seen—that there were forces working very hard for Castro in the United States. One of these forces was The New York Times.

Nathaniel Weyl wrote in *Red Star Over Cuba,* page 7:

"Had American officials and publicists made a diligent and serious study of the role of Fidel Castro in the Bogota uprising, they could scarcely have escaped the conclusion that, as early as 1948, he was not merely an implacable enemy of the United States, but a trusted Soviet agent as well. In the case of at least one foreign correspondent, sympathy for Communism and Communist causes seems to have been a motivating reason for a consistent failure to report the facts with anything approximating objectivity.

"The failure to identify the Fidel Castro movement in its incipient stages as Communist helped bring oppression and terror to the Cuban people and contributed to weakening the power, prestige and security of the United States in this Hemisphere.

". . . I shall try to show that the clues to the character of Fidel Castro and his insurgent movement were clear at all times to those having eyes to see with and brains to reason with; that the development of the 26th of July movement assumed the fairly conventional pattern of a Communist cover operation; that the State Department was repeatedly warned of the Communist character of this movement, but chose to disregard such warnings; and that, once their movement triumphed, Fidel Castro and his associates followed standard Sino-Soviet operating procedures for the seizure and consolidation of power.

"There are honest and reasonably competent observers of the Cuban scene who assume that Fidel Castro is an hysteric, a paranoid personality, a cyclothyme, a psychopath, an epileptic or a drug addict, or that he suffers from some other form of mental illness. They infer from this that he cannot be taken seriously as a Communist leader and that the 'true Communists' are doubtless lurking in the background, waiting for the mountebank to fall of the stage. . . .

"However, the evidence, as I shall show, reveals Fidel Castro to be a seasoned and highly competent Soviet agent. As for many journalistic diagnoses of his mental condition, some are mutually incompatible and others are based on fragmentary evidence. It is probable, however, that Castro suffers from paranoid schizophrenia.

"The more important point is that mental illness does not necessarily prevent a man from being an efficient and ruthless dictator, a crafty politician and the incarnation of a secular ideology or religious creed. Adolf Hitler could scarcely have been described as a normal man. There is a good deal of evidence that Stalin, in his later years, suffered from a progressive paranoid condition. Andre Marty was one of the chief leaders of the French Communist party for thirty years despite the fact that he was a moral monster, a sadist and the victim of delusions of persecution.

"The political stature of Fidel Castro can be judged simply —by looking at what he has accomplished. Using brilliant public relations techniques, he managed to parlay an insignificant guerrilla operation (which had at its nadir a total effective strength of about 15 men) into a movement which made the front pages of the world's press and which eventually seized power in Cuba. . . . He successfully deceived the American government and the American people as to his true character and purposes long enough to create a mass movement, a so-called people's militia and the usual apparata of espionage and terror, all fanatically loyal to him and to his Communist program. He managed to insult the United States again and again with impunity. Within the time span of less than two years, the dictator of a tropical island of minor economic importance, inhabited by only 7 million people, succeeded in making himself one of the best known political leaders in the world."

Red Star Over Cuba was originally published in hard cover by Devin-Adair in 1960. When Mr. Weyl wrote the introduction to the paperback edition, presumably in 1961, he could not know that the Soviets would make a fortress of Cuba, though he was aware that Castro as early as 1948 was a Soviet Communist agent. Mr. Weyl found Castro's role in the Bogota outrage to have been of fundamental importance. He quotes Salvador Diaz-Verson, a Cuban journalist, to establish that Fidel Castro became a paid agent of the Soviet Union in 1943. Mr. Weyl wrote, on page 47:

"Among the Soviet functionaries brought into Cuba [in 1943 by the Soviet Ambassador, Maxim M. Litvinov, former Soviet Foreign Minister] was G. W. Bashirov, who served in Spain as an agent who recruited young Spaniards for various Soviet apparatuses. . . .

"During the first half of 1943, writes Diaz-Verson, 'young Cubans, who had already entered the service of the Soviet Union and were in receipt of monthly stipends to cover their expenses, began to visit Bashirov's house.' Diaz-Verson lists 20 persons who thus became part of the Bashirov apparatus, of whom the most important were: Fidel Castro, Antonio Nunez Jimenez, Alfredo Guevara, Luis Mas Martin and the ballet dancer, Alicia Alonso.

"Thus, if Diaz-Verson is correct, Fidel Castro was recruited into the Soviet network at the age of 17 or perhaps even earlier."

There is little doubt from the evidence presented in *Red Star Over Cuba* that Castro was a Soviet agent in his youth, as he is today without any doubt. His role in the great uprising and massacre in Bogota, Colombia, in 1948 appears to have been especially sinister and vicious. Mr. Weyl writes, page 72 and following pages:

"According to Diaz-Verson, Frances MacKinnon Damon,

Treasurer of the world Federation of Democratic Youth, a Red transmission belt, arrived in Havana on February 2, 1948, with a fund of $50,000 in her suitcases to be used for Soviet propaganda against the Pan American Conference. Continuous strategy meetings were held at Bashirov's house. . .

"(Colombian) Security Chief Nino lists the following as foreign Communists implicated in the preparations for the Bogota insurrection: Salvador Ocampo, Machado, Luis Fernadez Juan, Eugene Kerbaul, Milorad Pesic B., Frances MacKinnon Damon, Blas Roca, Rafael del Pino and Fidel Alejandro Castro.

"In terms of the Red hierarchy, Castro was in distinguished company, for most of the nine alleged agents named by Nino were veteran Communists and either responsible Party leaders or seasoned Soviet agents.

"Thus, Blas Roca was the General Secretary of the Cuban Communist Party. Machado was probably Gustavo Machado, the leader of the Venezuelan Communist Party. Salvador Ocampo was one of the top Red leaders of Chile and also Secretary General of the Chilean Labor Federation. Luis Fernandez Juan has been characterized as a former 'Red General' in the Spanish Civil War. Milorad Pesic traveled on a French passport, but was a Yugoslav agent of the Cominform (international Communist organization in Europe).

"As for Frances Damon, she was described as an American from a distinguished Honolulu family, who had lived in Moscow for years and was engaged in organizing the World Federation of Democratic Youth, a Communist-front organization. . .

"On September 22, 1949, *El Grafico* of Caracas (Venezuela) published an interesting and, for that matter, sensational report from Colombian Detective No. 6 to the 'Chief of the Intelligence Services of the Armed Forces, General Staff of the Army' entitled 'General Antecedents of the Aliens of Cuban Nationality, Messrs. Fidel Castro and Rafael del Pino.' This police report was originally published in the influential Bogota daily, El Siglo. It deals with the results of the surveillance of Fidel Castro immediately prior to and during the Bogota uprising. The report not only links Castro with

Communism, but connects him with the murder of Jorge Eliecer Gaitan!

"The authenticity of this report can scarcely be doubted. It was published in the press of three Latin American countries and has never, to my knowledge, been challenged. Moreover, it corresponds in essentials to other Colombian intelligence material, available to the writer, which has been authenticated. Nor can the report be explained away as a police fabrication designed to smear Fidel Castro, since, in 1948 and 1949, Castro was not a person of sufficient political stature to warrant such treatment."

Castro and del Pino were arrested on the night of April 3, 1948, at the Bogota Colon Theatre for showering Communist leaflets from the gallery while the Colombian President, Dr. Mariano Ospina Perez, and his wife were attending the performance. Detective No. 6 escorted the two Cubans to their lodgings in the Hotel Claridge, and he saw on their table a picture of Dr. Gaitan and found a cable message in code. At the police station Castro and del Pino could give no explanation of the cable message but seemed "extremely rattled" over it. On April 9, the day on which Dr. Gaitan was slain, the police reported they saw the assassin, identified as Roa Sierra, in the company of del Pino about an hour and a half before the murder that touched off the holocaust. Dr. Gaitan, the Liberal party leader, was most popular. Besides, passions on all sides were running high in Colombia at that time. It was a situation full of dynamite. Secretary of State Marshall had been warned in Washington of the possibility that the Communists would make trouble, but he chose to treat this lightly. Actually, there were times during the several days of rioting when the entire Western world wondered whether one of the greatest architects of victory in World War II would survive this outbreak. It was said in 1948 that the aim of the Communists was to prevent the establishment in Latin America of another Marshall Plan, such as the one that was doing so much to restore the economies of Europe. In this, despite the enormity and the depravity of the great Bogota slaughter, the Communists were successful.

The Colombian police reported that they had seized among

Castro's belongings a letter from his Cuban fiancee that said, "I remember that you told me you were going to start a revolution in Bogota." Although the letter was taken by the police on April 3, Castro was set free to work his will until the bloody "Bogotazo" April 9. Afterward he took refuge in the Cuban Embassy and got a safe conduct back to Cuba. He left almost immediately for Mexico, where he trained his cadres for the next revolution—in Cuba.

Some further items of interest are mentioned by Mr. Weyl on pages 92, 94 and 95:

"On the evening of April 13th, four days after the outbreak of the riots, Detective No. 6 was ordered to proceed to the Hotel Claridge with two associates and arrest the Cubans (Castro and del Pino). He learned from the hotel manager, however, that they had paid their bills and left for the Cuban Legation that morning. The hotel manager also told Detective No. 6:

" 'That on the night of the 9th, they had arrived armed with rifles or shotguns and revolvers and with a good haul of loot which they were hardly able to cram into their valises.' The manager added that Castro talked on the phone in English that night with various people and 'that in the last two days of his (Castro's) stay in that hotel, he was so preoccupied and nervous that he even begged the hotel manager to hide them in a secret place.'

"The detectives found a carnet (a kind of notebook) which the Office of Detectives now has in its possesson, with a photograph of the two Cubans, identifying them as first-grade agents of the Third Front of the U.S.S.R. in South America.' At that time the expression 'third front' in the vocabulary of international Communism referred to activities designed to sway governments and peoples from the Free World alliance to neutralism. In other words, it concerned action directed specifically against the foreign policy of the United States. The disruption of an Inter-American conference fell into this category. . . .

"Castro reported to Bashirov and was congratulated for having done a brilliant job. Fidel asked to be sent to Czechoslovakia for advanced training as a Soviet agent, but the request was refused by Moscow. The reason for this refusal was indicated in a letter which Castro sent his comrade in the Bashirov group, Abelardo Adam Garcia, who was being trained in Czechoslovakia. This letter was intercepted by Diaz-Verson's organization. It was written in June 1948 and reads:

" 'Our friend has told me that I am being held in reserve for bigger things and that I cannot travel now. They have a plan of which I am to be the axis and which will soon be put into effect. Accordingly, it is possible that we shall next meet without having any more reason to fear Yankee imperialism. . . .' "

After listing all the evidence that Castro was a Communist, a Soviet agent, a plotter, and connected with an assassination, Mr. Weyl writes:

"This, in substance, is the evidence that Fidel Castro was a Soviet agent as early as 1948. It is hard to see how the State Department could have ignored these facts if they were available to it. It is still harder to see how the Department could have informed Congress a decade later that Castro and his 26th of July Movement were free of the taint of Communism. . . .

"One of the American officials who witnessed the Bogotazo was Roy Rubottom, secretary to the American Embassy and to the U.S. Delegation to the Inter-American Conference. The Rubottoms took care of two of Ambassador Beaulac's children during the day of the slaughter and they are referred to in affectionate terms in the Ambassador's chatty book. . . .

"One might have imagined that the massive and savage display of Communist power which diplomat Rubottom lived through would have made an indelible impression on his mind. One might even have assumed that, while in Bogota, he would have been sufficient curious about the organization and mechanics of the uprising to read the available books and police reports and to remember the names of the principal Soviet actors in the tragedy.

"This, however, was apparently not the case. In due course, Mr. Rubottom was promoted to Assistant Secretary of State for Latin American Affairs. On December 31, 1958, a day before

Castro took power in Cuba, he reported to the Subcommittee for Inter-American Affairs of the Senate Foreign Relations Committee that 'there was no evidence of any organized Communist element within the Castro movement or that Senor Castro himself was under Communist influence.'

"In fact, throughout the period of Castro's rise to power and subsequent imposition of Communist rule upon Cuba, Rubottom's influence on American policy was enigmatic, if not unfortunate. On August 11, 1960, in an exclusive interview with the Standard-Times of New Bedford, Mass., former U.S. Ambassador to Cuba Arthur Gardner [1] revealed that his repeated warnings that Castro

---

1. Arthur Gardner died at the age of 78 at Palm Beach, Florida, on April 11, 1967. In its obituary of him on page 42 on April 12, The New York Times said Mr. Gardner "brought upon himself criticism from extremists of both sides." This would include Herbert L. Matthews, who still (April, 1967) continued to be The Times editorialist on Cuba and other Latin American countries. The Times obituary said that Mr. Gardner as Ambassador to Cuba "contended that United States security should be the basic consideration in its policy. He argued that President Batista was not only anti-Communist but a fast friend of the United States, even if he was also a dictator." The obituary added:

"Mr. Gardner based his views on information he had that Mr. Castro was courting Moscow and, once in office, would form some kind of alliance with the Soviet Union. He urged that the United States obstruct the growing Castro bid for power, as it had a previous Communist bid for control in Guatemala. Otherwise, he said, a Moscow-oriented state 90 miles from Florida was in prospect."

Mr. Gardner was so right, and for this he was rejected and, as Mr. Weyl rightly said, grossly insulted by not being de-briefed by the State Department. The fact that The New York Times correctly states his position does not mean that The Times changed its editorial position or indicated any regret for the manner in which Mr. Gardner was mistreated.

Ambassador Earl E. T. Smith, who succeeded Mr. Gardner in the Havana post, was equally badly dealt with by the State Department and was equally or perhaps even more annoyed by the actions or inactions of the department. He too was not de-briefed in the customary and sensible way by a department seeking the best information for the conduct of the foreign affairs of the United States. It is eminently clear that the State Department's Fourth Floor, handling Latin American affairs, was not interested in the views of Mr. Gardner or Mr. Smith on Cuba and Castro.

There was no Times editorial on the death of Mr. Gardner—no expression of regret that he had been mistreated, or of praise for his wisdom, good sense and patriotism in warning his country of the dangers that lay ahead in Cuba.

was Communist-dominated were disregarded by Rubottom and his cronies. The Standard-Times story read:

" '. . . Castro became Washington's knight in shining armor and Batista, now cast in the role of villain by Rubottom and company, was being eased toward the door, and not gently.

" 'Nobody listened to the pleadings of America's ambassador to Cuba, who argued in vain that "we were handling this matter in a bad and indifferent manner."

" 'It was this clique that brought about Gardner's resignation from the Cuba post—because he recognized that "Castro was no different from any other breed of Communist"—even though President Eisenhower was inclined to let Gardner serve longer.'

"As punishment for his insistent warnings that Castro's movement was Red-dominated and hostile to the United States, Ambassador Gardner was recalled in 1957. The State Department did not arrange to have the new ambassador to Cuba, Earl E. T. Smith, talk to his predecessor even though Gardner had the benefit of intimate knowledge of Cuban affairs and years of residence there. Gardner was never invited to come to Washington for 'debriefing,' a departure from precedent which can only be described as a gross and calculated insult. Instead, Rubottom and his group arranged to have Ambassador Smith briefed by *New York Times* correspondent Herbert L. Matthews, an inveterate apologist for Soviet-infiltrated movements and the American primarily responsible for the campaign of propaganda and misrepresentation which sold Fidel Castro to the people of the United States as a liberal and a democrat.

" 'It was primarily because of Rubottom's approval,' the Standard-Times stated in its interview story, 'that Castro was able to come to the United States in April 1959 to address the American Society of Newspaper Editors.' "

Mr. Rubottom was made Ambassador to Argentina in 1960.

Mr. Weyl reports further, page 97, with altogether justified excitement:

"On February 20, 1961 . . . the Senate Internal Security

Subcommittee released sensational testimony by the former U.S. Ambassador to Brazil and Peru, William D. Pawley, which cast new light on Fidel Castro's complicity in the murder of Gaitan and which made the conduct of such State Department officials as Roy Rubottom and William Arthur Wieland appear utterly inexcusable. Pawley was a delegate to the Ninth Inter-American Conference (at Bogota in 1948). In fact, President Truman or Secretary of State George C. Marshall (Pawley did not recall which) had called him to the White House and said, 'We want you to organize the Bogota conference.'

"The United States delegation had expected some trouble in Bogota, but had discounted it. Pawley testified:

" 'We had information that there was a Cuban there, a very young man who appeared to us not to be a real threat.

" 'But they organized one of the most astute pieces of skulduggery you can imagine. The Communists killed Gaitan at 1 o'clock in the afternoon—he was the most popular Liberal and was deeply loved all over the country. They told the young man who did the killing (identified as Roa Sierra) that they would be sitting in an automobile waiting to pick him up, armed with machine guns in case somebody attacked him. But the minute he did the killing, they machine-gunned him and left him there and got away.

" 'Senator McClellan: Whom do you mean by "they"?

" ' Mr. Pawley: The people who organized this killing.

" 'Senator McClellan: Do you know who they were?

" 'Mr. Pawley: We believed it to be the Fidel Castro group. I cannot testify—I am under oath—that I know positively, but this is the information that generally was considered true in Bogota and since that time.'

"Ambassador Pawley added the startling disclosure that Fidel Castro spoke over the radio less than an hour after the Gaitan assassination exhorting the people of Colombia to support the Communist insurrection. Pawley testified:

" 'The day that this happened General Marshall was at our

house. Mrs. Pawley and I had taken a house in Bogota for the conference as it was expected to last several weeks or a month. Walter Donnelly, then Ambassador to Venezuela, a close personal friend of mine and a great foreign service officer, one of the best, was also with us, and when General Marshall left, Walter and I started down to the headquarters in our car and on the radio I heard a voice say: "This is Fidel Castro from Cuba. This is a Communist revolution. The President has been killed, all of the military establishments are now in our hands. The Navy has capitulated to us, and this revolution has been a success." '

"Of course, the President had not been killed, nor had the Colombian Army betrayed their country. But, as Pawley pointed out, 'within five minutes of the time that Gaitan was killed, every one of the radio stations in Colombia was in the hands of this revolutionary group' and was being used for psychological warfare purposes.

". . . . Pawley's basic points (are) that members of the United States delegation in Bogota knew as early as 1948 that Fidel Castro was a leading Communist agent, suspected him of the double murder of Gaitan and Gaitan's killer and heard him speak on the radio as a Communist and a leader of the armed uprising. These matters should have been known to such State Department officials as Roy Rubottom and William Arthur Wieland, both of whom were physically present in the American Embassy at Bogota during the time of the upheaval and for a considerable period thereafter. Accordingly, the subsequent whitewashing of Fidel Castro by Rubottom and other State Department officials, as a man free of any taint of Communism, becomes utterly incomprehensible. . . .

"When he served as Ambassador to Brazil, Pawley had Wieland under him as press attache. His impression of Wieland was similar to that of Ambassador Gardner. Wieland's activities in Brazil gave Pawley 'a squirmy feeling.' The Ambassador 'didn't believe that Wieland was particularly useful to the U.S. Government.' After stating that he did not have reason to believe Wieland a Communist, Pawley added:

"I only know that many of these men, that get involved in this type of thing over the years that I have had any connection with, are serving the cause of our enemies, that is all.'

"(Julien G.) Sourwine, the general counsel of the Senate Subcommittee, interjected: 'You think he is doing this unwittingly, unintentionally?'

"Pawley retorted: 'I have got to say that he is either one of the most stupid men living or that he is doing it intentionally.'

"When he learned that Wieland had been promoted to serve as area officer for the Caribbean, Ambassador Pawley was so disturbed about the possible consequences to the United States that he took the matter up with President Eisenhower and Vice President Nixon. Shortly thereafter, he met with Undersecretary of State Douglas Dillon and a Foreign Service officer called Mallory who worked under Rubottom. Pawley testified:

" 'In this discussion I said, "I would like to do something that I know you people don't particularly like, but I think it is important that I do it. I have great misgivings of the wiseness to have and to continue to have William Wieland in a critical post. His close association with Herbert Matthews of the *New York Times* and the activities having to do with the whole Cuban episode in which he is in charge, and has a great deal to do with the policies that come out, this man should not be there and he should not have been there for a long time." Mallory said this to me—and this can be corroborated by Senator George Smathers who was present—he said, 'I am sorry that I am having this pressure put on me regarding Wieland because I might have changed him to some other post; but now, with this pressure, I will not change him."

" 'And I said to Mallory, "I don't understand that. I am a former U.S. Government official, I worked in this Department for five and one-half years. I was trying to be useful by pointing out something that I think is of value to the Department, and you put it on the basis that I am bringing pressure. It just doesn't make sense." '

"When this extremely damaging testimony against him was called to his attention by the press, Wieland stated that he had no comment. As for the alleged conduct of Mallory, it is perhaps pertinent to inquire whether the State Department exists to protect the security and national interest of the United States or to serve as a mutual protective association for officials whose competence, morals or loyalty have been challenged."

Since this book is primarily about the failure of a great newspaper to alert its government as well as its readers to the dangers of an expanding Communism around the world, the ramifications of the newspaper's ties with the State Department require separate treatment. It has been said by an official within the department that The Times has a deep and well-laid pipeline there. Obviously Mr. Matthews was treated as a member of the department, with authority to brief an incoming Ambassador, Mr. Smith, who, with hardly less conspicuousness, thought little of Mr. Matthews' advice.

Now Cuba is a growing cancer in the body politic and economic of the Americas. According to a procession of witnesses before the United States Senate Internal Security Subcommittee, the island ruled by Castro and Cuban Communists in condominium with the Russians is a training and exporting center for assassins and guerrillas. The aim is to spread terror throughout the Latin countries and eventually to win control of them. Above all, the Communists want to disrupt the economies and introduce sufficient instability and fear as to cause the people to export their savings. Thus poverty is insured as the birth rate rises above the creation of capital and the production of food. We have seen how this was an aim for France and Italy—which was frustrated by the Marshall Plan and the success of the Common Market. Propaganda and conspiracy find the most fertile soil among distressed people.

There are many sources of good information on Cuba. Some excerpts from testimony given before the Senate Internal Security

Subcommittee will serve. Paul Bethel testified on March 7, 1967. He is a native of Churchill, Idaho, and a graduate of Stanford University—B.A. and M.A. He entered the United States Foreign Service in 1949, served as a consular and press officer in Japan, and was assigned to Cuba as press attaché in 1958, which was just before Castro came to power. Some of the testimony follows, beginning on page 1091:

Mr. Sourwine. At the time you went to Cuba, what was Fidel Castro's situation?

Mr. Bethel. Well, the Fidel Castro situation was fairly desperate. This was right after he tried to call a general strike in April and failed to do so. So for a period, his fortunes were certainly on the ebb. And then during the summer, of course, with increased terror in the cities, that led up eventually to the end.

Mr. Sourwine. At the time you left in 1961, had his position materially improved?

Mr. Bethel. It certainly had. He was in charge and so were the Russians.

(Mr. Bethel explained at this point that he resigned from the Foreign Service after the Bay of Pigs disaster April 17, 1961; became a reporter on Cuban events to the White House for about five months, and was then, in March, 1967, executive secretary of the Citizens Committee for a Free Cuba.)

Mr. Sourwine. Mr. Bethel, have you had occasion to interview many of the refugees from Cuba?

Mr. Bethel. Well, over the past 6 years— it has been almost 6 years now—literally thousands, yes.

Mr. Sourwine. Have you any particular interest in the gradual Russian takeover of Cuba?

Mr. Bethel. Well, I have a very specific interest, yes, sir.

Mr. Sourwine. Will you give us in your own words your conclusions with respect to that situation as it has developed over the past 6 years and as it stands today?

Mr. Bethel. I would be very happy to. I have a statement, if I may read it.

Senator (Thomas J.) Dodd (Democrat of Connecticut). Go right ahead.

Mr. Bethel. For nearly 4 years now, we have engaged in intensive research on the Communist—more specifically the Russian—takeover of the strategically located island of Cuba and on the military, economic and political effect on Latin America of the lodgment of the Soviet power in the Caribbean.

First and foremost, it must be concluded that the Russians took control in Cuba for one reason: that is, for the sole, stated purpose of worldwide subversion. The Russian-managed Tricontinental (Communist) Conference on subversion, which was held in Havana in January of 1966, had as its purpose the creation of a centralized organization to explode Vietnam-type wars, not only in Latin America but in Asia and Africa as well. That conference was the culmination of 5 years of Soviet military preparations which, No. 1, have established their own military and political control of Cuba and, No. 2, converted Cuba into a forward base of subversion against the free world.

There is not much question that Moscow was the chief planner as well as the manager of that conference. Russia's preparations for the 1966 Tricontinental Conference go back to 1964 and 1965, when Communist delegates converged on Havana from all over the world and there made plans culminating in the January 1966 Tricontinental Conference. . . .

Military activities in Cuba have increased notably since the Tricontinental Conference of last year. This is so because Havana now is the site of the organization which plans, directs, and supports worldwide guerrilla wars of subversion. It should be noted that Russia and Red China both sit cheek-by-jowl on the Central Policy Planning Committee in Cuba. Armed Forces Minister Raul Castro provided some dimensions as to what is going on in Cuba when, last May 23, he said: "Don't be surprised when in the months ahead you see thousands of tons of new weapons on the highways of our country."

Soviet arms continued to pour into Cuba, the younger Castro said, "because Cuba will redouble its efforts to help all liberation movements on the three continents. We will hit them (the United States) where it hurts most—through the movements of national liberation." His belligerent speech was endorsed by none other than the Russian Ambassador in Havana, Alexander I. Alexeyev, who asserted that Russia "believes in the firm solidarity of all the revolutionary liberation forces of the world."

Raul Castro said of our intelligence community, and I think this is quite important, "They don't know the quality and quantity of the weapons we now have," adding the most arresting statement, "but we can assure them that with every passing month, we are being armed with weapons vastly superior to what we ever had before.". . . .

Mr. Bethel. Castro also bragged, and I quote again, "Every month we complete dozens of military bases in Cuba."

Now, since 1960, the Russians have literally burrowed their way through the length and breadth of the island. They have carved out a mammoth command post in Gobernadora hills of Pinar del Rio Province, and honeycombed it with hundreds of kilometers of tunnels, four of which are so large that they accommodate two-way truck traffic. . . . Now, connected as they are with cave complexes within the hills, these tunnels give the Russians the capability of moving heavy weapons, including possibly missiles, for distances up to 45 miles in any direction.

(Here Mr. Bethel described in greater detail the size and nature of the tunnels of which he had seen charts and maps.)

Mr. Bethel. Now, to continue, the tunnels of La Gobernadora connect the Russian command post to the El Rosario Mountains, which contain some of Cuba's largest caves which, together with interconnecting tunnels, all with 4 feet of reinforced concrete on the ceilings, provide the Russians with underground transit to the southern foothills of the mountain range. . . .

Mr. Bethel. It is significant that San Cristobal, one of the missile sites observed at the time of the missile crisis (October 22-28, 1962), is located near the exit of one of those tunnels, and the entrance to the vast Los Partales caves, widened and connected by tunnels, is located in those same foothills, to the west of San Cristobal. These caves were cordoned off as a military zone in 1962 and they still remain a military zone today. They are now linked to underground tunnels to a surface-to-air missile base which has been sighted and admitted publicly by our intelligence people at San Andres. It has been common for the Russians and the Cubans to protect their most important underground installations by building schools, hospitals, and even small villages above them. These telltale signs are present at the small village of San Andres, where schools were built, allegedly to house 2,000 children, way back in the mountains, which has a population of only 5,200.

(Mr. Bethel explained that Pinar del Rio, where these installations are situated, is the westernmost Cuban province, across from the Yucatan Channel, a strategic narrow stretch of sea between Cuba and Mexico—it connects the Gulf of Mexico with the Caribbean Sea.)

Mr. Bethel. In virtually all the cases dealing with tunneling, we have dealt with Cuban sources entirely, including workmen who have defected, engineers who have defected, and so on, and not certainly on Granma alone. (Granma is a Cuban newspaper.)

Now, throughout Cuba, Russian tanks, antiaircraft batteries, long-range artillery, armored personnel carriers, and every conceivable type of conventional weapon are employed tactically or are in motor pools ready for deployment. Included among this armament are hundreds of amphibious trucks and personnel carriers known by the Cuban name sapitos. These are the amphibian ducks. "Sapitos" means little frogs.

The Russians are just now completing 5 years' work at what must be stupendous cost on completely equipping Cuba with a radar system. This system scans the Straits of Florida, the Windward Passage, the Yucatan Channel, a good part of the Bahamas, and it is suspected perhaps a portion of Haiti, the Dominican Republic, and Jamaica.

In line with an announced policy of spreading terror and subversion in Latin America, Cuba has just been fitted with a 150-kilowatt television antenna, built by a Czech engineer named Bravask. This station is three times as powerful as any single radio station operating in the United States, and is obviously designed for external propaganda broadcasts.

Mr. Sourwine. Some of our stations are going to be affected (by the Russian station operating in Cuba on 600 kilocycles), but some of them are not. In their service areas, how many of them are going to have serious trouble as a result of the operation of the Cuba station?

Mr. Bethel. I think some 47 are going to have serious trouble, definitely.

Mr. Sourwine. On the other hand, there is nothing to keep that Cuba station on 600, is there? They could operate it on 780 or 900 or 1,200, by a very simple adjustment?

Mr. Bethel. Yes, they could, I assume.

Mr. Sourwine. So they are in a position to interfere with any station in our territory which is in proximity to the east coast or the Gulf coast; would that be correct?

Mr. Bethel. I think that is adequate; yes.

Mr. Sourwine. Go ahead.

Mr. Bethel. But this is only the beginning. Russia has plans to put in six such stations in Cuba. . . .

Mr. Sourwine. Is this first station a Russian station or a Cuban station?

Mr. Bethel. How do you determine?

Mr. Sourwine. I don't know. I'm asking you if you know.

Mr. Bethel. Well, let's put it this way, that, obviously, it is connected to Russia's international designs, or otherwise, it wouldn't be there. *I mean Cuba is controlled by Russia.*

[Mr. Bethel went on to describe Radio Havana, a shortwave station that broadcasts propaganda far and wide, and it can be heard more clearly in Central America than local stations. Radio Moscow, also a short-wave station, can frequently be heard with equal clarity in North America.]

Mr. Sourwine. I have thought that maybe, in response to my leading questions, you would have some testimony about the fact that there have been propaganda broadcasts to the United States over Radio Havana.

Mr. Bethel. There have.

Mr. Sourwine. Which have affected both racial disorders and student disorders in the United States and have been designed to do so.

Mr. Bethel. That is not Radio Havana. They have turned up the power of CMQ and broadcast on standard wave into this country.

Mr. Sourwine. That has also been done?

Mr. Bethel. Yes; it has been done, inciting the Negroes to burn "Charley," and go out and burn buildings and create riots in the streets, and so on. I think that—well, in fact, I know that this is perfectly a matter of record, that this has happened.

Mr. Sourwine. And it is with this background that you assume that this new station and the five others which you say will follow it in construction will be used for propaganda broadcasts to the United States as well as to Latin American countries?

Mr. Bethel. Yes, I do. I think the precedent has been established, as well as virtually all the propaganda broadcasts in English to this country have been to create disturbances among the Negroes and play upon the present problems we're having in this country.

I would like to say in this connection that Black Power Advocate Stokely Carmichael of the Student Nonviolent Coordinating Committee—SNCC—has made two trips to Puerto Rico in the last 40 days. His trips, sponsored by the Castroite Pro-Independence Movement, and the Pro-Independence Student Federation. resulted in a protocol of cooperation. This is involved with the fight which Carmichael vows to fight against imperialism, and I doubt that his enemy would be Russian imperialism.

Mr. Sourwine. What did you say about the sponsorship of his trip?

Mr. Bethel. His trip to Puerto Rico was sponsored by these two organizations I mentioned, both of whom are Communist and allied with the Fidel Castro regime.

Mr. Sourwine. They are both government-controlled organizations?

Mr. Bethel. They are funded by the Cuban government, funded and controlled in just about every sense.

For example, following the Tricontinental Conference in Havana last year, the Pro-Independence Movement in Puerto Rico opened in Havana what it called a "Free Puerto Rican Embassy." They are operating there, as they say, as a free Puerto Rico Embassy. The connection is too great to be ignored.

Now, as for the FUPI, the student organization, they are a member of Castro's CLAE, which is the Latin American continental organization of students which controls seven Communist student organizations in certain Latin American countries and even, as a matter of fact, is one of the principal means by which subversion and terror are being developed in Latin America, through students there, and I think they plan as well, through Stokely Carmichael, to do the same darned thing on campuses in this country.

I call your attention to the fact that the writer Ralph McGill has publicly written that Carmichael and his group are getting money directly from Havana. I think this is accurate, but I couldn't prove it.*

* An Associated Press dispatch from Havana, Cuba, of July 25, 1967, printed in The New York Times of July 26 on page 22, reported as follows:

"Stokely Carmichael was quoted by the Cuban news agency Prensa Latina today as saying that American Negroes were organizing urban guerrillas for 'a fight to the death.'

"The black power advocate arrived in Havana to attend a confer-

Now, to return briefly to the Russian forward military base of Cuba, this report could be expanded for 20 pages or more and barely touch on the war preparations which are under way there, such as the camouflaged airport in the tunnels of the Yumuri Valley, the Soviet base at Diego Perez Key, and many other important items of intelligence. Suffice it to say that *Russians control absolutely Cuba's three field armies, its 43 or more training camps turning out 10,000 or more trained guerrillas each year, its Ministry of Interior, together with all of its apparatus of internal terror and control.* [This goes several steps farther than Russia's methods in taking over the countries of Eastern Europe. A cardinal feature of the Soviet procedure is to get control of the Ministry of the Interior, which in most countries controls the police.] It does so, in the words of Soviet Delegate Sharaf R. Rashidov, who headed the 40-man Russian delegation to the Tricontinental Conference, because: "Our purpose is the formation of a united front against the common enemy." He defined the common enemy as, in his words, "International imperialism headed by the United States," adding: "The Soviet Union is responding to movements of national liberation."

Mr. Sourwine. A movement of national liberation has a particular meaning. That phrase has a particular meaning in the Soviet lexicon, does it not?

---

ence of the Latin-American Organization of Solidarity, opening Monday (July 31). . . .

"According to the agency's account:

"'In Newark we applied war tactics of the guerrillas,' he [Carmichael] said. 'We are preparing groups of urban guerrillas for our defense in the cities. The price of these rebellions is a high price that one must pay. This fight is not going to be a simple street meeting. It is going to be a fight to the death.'"

The Times editorial comment on the Carmichael visit to Havana says only this:

"It [Cuba] sees the United States as its greatest enemy, which is why a welcome guest for today's ceremonies is none other than Stokely Carmichael, for if it be recognized that he can do Cuba no good, it will be thought that he can do the United States some harm."

Indeed it will.

Mr. Bethel. Movements of national liberation are in fact guerrilla wars carried out in the terrain of the free world. We have a perfect example in Vietnam.

A long list of acts of terrorism by Communists in Latin America was put into the record by Mr. Bethel, who said that the consequent unrest and fear among the people were factors in the flight of capital from Latin America. He also said that he understood that Soviet intermediate ballistic missiles (IRBM's) remained in Cuba even though Khrushchev had promised President Kennedy in October, 1962, that they would be taken out. Mr. Bethel also asserted that U Thant. as Acting Secretary General of the United Nations, frustrated any on-site inspection to determine whether the missiles had been removed. Mr. Bethel said U Thant went to Cuba on October 30, 1962, "and virtually told Castro not to permit onsite inspection."

Mr. Bethel's testimony is presented in a Government publication. It is obtainable from the United States Government Printing Office, Washington, D.C. The title is "Communist Threat to the United States Through the Caribbean," Part 16, March 7, 1967.

In another Government publication, Part 17, March 7 and 8, 1967, of these hearings, the testimony of Dr. Bernardo Benes is given. He is a Cuban refugee who started work as a clerk and is now vice president of the Washington Federal Savings & Loan Association in Miami, Florida. His view of the Alliance for Progress makes sense to a student of economic affairs. Here again is shown the effect of the terrorist activities of Soviet-dominated Castro Cuba upon Latin America and, once again, we learn that a reader of The New York Times feels that something is lacking in the news columns of that paper. Some of the testimony follows:

Dr. Benes. It has become very common for unqualified sources to give opinions on the success or failure of the Alliance for Progress. If we were testifying before a subcommittee of economic development or financial affairs, or aid, foreign aid, and using firsthand information specifically related to housing, we would go into specific details to show that the Alliance for Progress has been a successful program, not only so much from the economic point of view, but also becoming a new idea or hope for Latin America.

Nevertheless, since we are testifying before a subcommittee of Internal Security we want to emphatically state that the Alliance for Progress itself cannot be the only tool to stop subversion, terrorism imposed in many different ways by the so-called national liberation movement sponsored by the Cuban regime. The sponsoring was unofficial until January 1966 but after the Tricontinental (Communist) Conference it has become an official and well-planned activity.

While we read in very reputable newspapers, and this is the most reputable newspaper in Spanish published in the United States—

Mr. Sourwine. What is the name of that?

Dr. Benes. Diario las Americas. It is published in Miami with main offices in Washington. As much as we see in this paper and I don't know why this paper gets much more coverage on what is happening in the continent—this is the paper of Sunday. I didn't bring this paper—I didn't ask them to bring this news.

Mr. Sourwine. What date?

Dr. Benes. March 5, 1967.

It says, "Commotion by the Assassination of the Brother of Foreign Relations Minister of Venezuela Iribarren."

Mr. Sourwine. That is a three-column head on the front page?

Dr. Benes. Yes. In the middle, "Government Silent About the News that Fidel Castro Ordered Assassination of President Kennedy."

Mr. Sourwine. Column 4, front page center.

Dr. Benes. "Cuba Wants to Start Guerrilla Warfare in the Mountains of Dominican Republic."

Mr. Sourwine. That is the three-column head, front page, right?

Dr. Benes. Yes sir, one column here, United Press, "Cuba Will Help Guerrillas in Rhodesia."

Mr. Sourwine. Column 8, right front page.

Dr. Benes. I have not opened this to the second page.

Mr. Sourwine. What is your point about these articles in this paper?

Dr. Benes. I am saying the Alliance for Progress by itself is not going to stop this.

Mr. Sourwine. I thought you said something about these are articles that are the news and that is not printed in the English-language newspapers.

Dr. Benes. *I read on a daily basis, I read the Miami World, Miami News, and New York Times and I rarely see any of these stories. . . .* (Italics added.)

Dr. Benes. I will continue with my statement. By no means must it be understood that the Alliance for Progress is not a success. But we very strongly feel that it would have been more successful if the Latin American private capital had not fled their respective countries. So many different aspects must be taken into consideration on this subject of the fleeing of private capital from Latin America due to the existence of the Castro regime in Cuba that much time will be needed to enumerate them all.

Since my departure from Cuba in November 1960 I have detected this phenomenon because of the following reasons:

First, I started to work for Washington Federal Savings & Loan Association 10 days after my arrival from Cuba in November 1960.

Second, I know hundreds, if not thousands of Latin Americans who all have the same fear and do not want to go through what the other Cubans have and I don't blame them.

Third, since I started to work for my present and only employer in the United States I have trained hundreds of Latin American bankers, lawyers, accountants, bureaucrats, and clerks in the concept of U.S. savings and loan association systems as a contribution to the Alliance for Progress. Most of them have the same fear, even those who cannot be considered wealthy.

Fourth, in my traveling through Latin America, as part of my work, and last year I visited—I don't know—but most of the countries of Latin America—I found that the subject of how to convert capital in Latin America into U.S. dollars and their delivery abroad is one of the favorite subjects of the people I have met and who represent the profit sector of the economic life in their respective countries.

Latin America has enough problems with lack of human resources and cannot afford depletion of local capital that should continue to be invested in the economic development of the continent. Many times I have heard discussions on the subject of how much money has the Alliance for Progress invested in Latin America compared to the private funds that have left due to Castro's existence in Cuba.

It isn't real important to determine whether the balance is in favor of one side or the other, although I have rational reasons to believe that more capital has fled Latin America since the Castro takeover since the approximately $2 billion invested until now by the Alliance for Progress.

Mr. Sourwine. You mean we have poured $2 billion in with the result that they have less available capital now than before we started?

Dr. Benes. Yes, sir.

The real issue is that this continent is badly in need of both the Alliance funds and the return of the capital that has fled, and this will only happen after the economic classes of Latin America will regain the confidence they lost because of the Communist takeover of Cuba. . . .

Mr. Sourwine. Where do you think the economy of Latin America would be today if there had not been any Castro, compared with what it is now.

Dr. Benes. I don't have a crystal ball that would have brought me back in years, but if I compare Cuba with what it was before the Castro takeover of the country I would have to say that Latin America would have been extremely rich and extremely developed from an economic point of view if this insecurity and lack of confidence of Latin American capital would (not) have existed. The only reason for the fleeing of capital is Fidel Castro and Cuba and no other.

Mr. Sourwine. You are in a position, I think, to answer this final question.

Beyond this great harm which you feel has been done to Latin America by Castro, by his existence, by his activities, by the flight of capital, the fear that Castro has engendered, has there been in your opinion also a damage to the economy of the United States and a threat to the economic security of the United States?

Dr. Benes. Logically, because Latin America has been a major market for many American exports, being as it may, that the economies of Latin America have been hit—as a consequence of Castro's Cuba, those countries haven't been able to buy from the U.S. market merchandise, merchandise from the U.S. Markets.

And so the original purpose for which Castro was used by the Russian Communists has been to a considerable extent achieved —to break up the Inter-American Conference in Bogota and to prevent the setting up of effectual economic accords and the establishment of safety for the conduct of international business. In place of such harmony, there is guerrilla warfare and a feeling of insecurity throughout Latin America that cause capital to seek havens on other continents. This is the evil fruit of Castro Cuba and international Communism in the Americas. There is no end in sight.

Chapter V

The New York Times Coverage of the Assassination of President Kennedy • • •

RICHARD M. NIXON: "Oswald, without question, was a *demented character who, according to the (FBI) reports, had also tried to kill Gen. Edwin A. Walker and had threatened to make an attempt on my life as well. What brought him to this condition is still unknown. But certainly one of the major factors which warped his mind and drove him to this terrible deed was his contact with Communism generally, and with Castro's fanatical brand of Communism in particular.*

"Fidel Castro, therefore, proved to be the most momentous figure in John F. Kennedy's life. It was Castro who provided the major foreign policy issue in Kennedy's campaign for the Presidency; it was Castro who brought him to the lowest point of his career, at the Bay of Pigs; it was Castro who supplied the opportunity for Kennedy's greatest act of leadership as President, during the blockade; and, finally, Castro was an indirect cause of the tragic snuffing out of John Kennedy's life. . . ."—From an article written by the former Vice President for Reader's Digest in November, 1964.

EDITORIAL in The New York Times, September, 1964: "The Warren Commission's report is a comprehensive and con-

vincing account of the circumstances of President Kennedy's assassination. The facts—exhaustively gathered, independently checked and cogently set forth—destroy the basis for the conspiracy theories that have grown weedlike in this country and abroad.

"Readers of the full report will find no basis for questioning the commission's conclusion that President Kennedy was killed by Lee Harvey Oswald acting alone. . . .

"Concerning the murder of Oswald, doubts have centered on the possibility that Jack Ruby was part of a conspiracy to silence the President's assassin. The report tells of the timing of Ruby's action on the day he shot Oswald, traces his and Oswald's activities in extraordinary detail during the previous two months, analyzes their respective sources of income and political ties, weighs every scrap of evidence that suggests that Ruby, Oswald and Tippit knew one another and concludes that Ruby acted entirely alone."

EDITORIAL in The New York Times November 25, 1966: "There are enough solid doubts of thoughtful citizens, among the shrill attacks on the Warren Commission, now to require answers. Further dignified silence, or merely more denials by the commission or its staff, are no longer enough.

"We have come to this conclusion not because of any of the specific charges brought by dozens of books, TV shows and articles about President Kennedy's assassination but because of the general confusion in the public mind raised by the publication of allegations and the many puzzling questions that have been raised."

NEWS ITEM in The New York Times November 23, 1963, quoting Chief Justice Earl Warren on the assassination: "A great and good President has suffered martyrdom as a result of hatred and bitterness that has been injected into the life of our nation by bigots, but his memory will always be an inspiration of good will everywhere. The entire world is poorer because of his passing. May God protect our nation in this hour of crisis."

NEWS ITEM in *The New York Times* January 3, 1967: "The Saturday Evening Post publishes in its Jan. 14 (cq) issue, distributed today, a review of the assassination of President Kennedy and of the findings of the Warren Commission and its critics. The author concludes that circumstantial evidence supports the theory of a second assassin.

"The magazine's cover article is by Richard J. Whalen, author of 'The Founding Father: The Story of Joseph P. Kennedy.' Mr. Whalen proposes that President Johnson appoint a special joint committee of Congress or a citizen's panel of independent investigators to 'weigh every shred of evidence, old and new.'

"The magazine, in an editorial, called for a new inquiry into the commission's disputed findings. 'The possibility of a conspiracy,' it said, 'is too ugly and too important to be left to gossip and speculation.' . . .

"The call for a new inquiry was the second such stand by one of the big mass circulation magazines. Life magazine called for a new official inquiry on Nov. 21 (1966)."

SENATOR RICHARD B. RUSSELL, Democrat of Georgia, a member of the Warren Commission, issued a statement at Winder, Georgia, on November 22, 1966, saying: "The Commission pursued every clue and piece of evidence of any significance, but it must be borne in mind that access to some evidence dealing with oft-repeated questions was barred either by the Iron Curtain or Fidel Castro, or perished with Oswald."—Quoted from a story in U.S. News & World Report of December 5, 1966, which added:

"In an interview published in 'The Atlanta Journal' on November 20, Senator Russell disclosed that there had been friction in preparation of the Commission's report.

"Senator Russell said that he had refused to sign the report as *long as it contained a categorical statement that no conspiracy was involved in the assassination. [It is interesting that the draft report included such a statement of no conspiracy.—H.H.D.]*

"The Senator said he felt that it had been impossible to obtain sufficient information about Oswald's stay in the Soviet Union in 1959-1962 and on Oswald's activities that were related to Red Cuba."

HARRIET VAN HORNE: "It has always seemed to me that the conspiracy theory of history makes its strongest appeal to the weakminded. I refuse to believe that some plumed and belted earl wrote Shakespeare's plays. I decline to accept the gypsy crone, who calls herself Anastasia, as the daughter of the Czar.

"Such notions are, of course, revealed truth to people who know there are hordes of Communists in the State Department and armadas of flying saucers Out There. I sit in the skeptic's corner. That's why I am astonished to find myself somewhat troubled by the recent spate of writings, here and abroad, suggesting that Lee Harvey Oswald may not have been the assassin of President Kennedy.

"These writings, let me say quickly, are not conclusive in any sense. But they do cast doubts on the official case against Oswald."
—From her column in the New York World Telegram & Sun of May 26, 1964.

HENRY J. TAYLOR: "DALLAS—The articles I wrote from New Orleans, detailing Lee Harvey Oswald's career there, reveal a self-portrait of a Red. His New Orleans Communist record continues to the end here, equally documented not by opinion, not by debatable testimony, but by Oswald himself. . . .

"The failure to unmask and sufficiently publicize the truth about Oswald is important, and the more it persists the more vital it is to spotlight it. For that failure compounds the distraction technique always adopted by the Communist communication ap-

paratus whenever a Communist policy, or individual Red, looks bad.

". . . . this man (Oswald) was a drilled, dedicated, obedient, cool and canny Communist.

"On July 26, 1963, and again September 8, Castro had casti-gated the President of the United States over Radio Havana as a 'ruffian,' 'liar,' 'imperialist,' 'my enemy,' etc. It is essential to point out again and again that surely Oswald knew that, whether Castro ordered it or not, if he killed the President of the United States (a secret the Reds most certainly would keep) he would be an inside hero in Castro's Havana hierarchy, and a hero for the first time in his life.

"Oswald's undated letter to his wife, written here and found secreted in his personal effects by the Dallas police, includes: 'Cer-tain of my documents are in the small blue valise. . . . The Em-bassy (i.e., Soviet Embassy) will come quickly to your assistance on learning everything. . . . The 'Red Cross' will also help you. . . . We have friends here.'

"Trapped by her own coverups, Marina Oswald finally stated that Oswald had, in fact, laid plans to reach Cuba by returning to New Orleans and hijacking an airliner flying to Havana from there. But he abandoned this exit method. Instead, Oswald prepared the way by going (September 25) to Castro's Embassy in Mexico City. U.S. State Department and Warren Commission investi-gators, in turn, found that 'he intended to remain in Cuba.' "
—From Mr. Taylor's column in the New York World Journal Tribune on December 30, 1966.

NEWS DISPATCH in The New York Times: "LONDON, March 13 (1965)—The suspicion of conspiracy in President Ken-nedy's assassination persists in Europe, even as the whole subject fades out of current attention and into history."

JOSIAH THOMPSON in his book Six Seconds in Dallas, *Bernard Geis Associates, 1967, suggests that three assassins took* part in the murder of President Kennedy and that Lee Harvey Oswald may not have been one of them. He writes:

"What does this collection of new evidence prove? It does not prove that the assassination was a conspiracy, and that two men were together on the sixth floor of the depository at the time the shots were fired. Nor does it prove Oswald's innocence. What it does suggest is that there are threads in this case that should have been unraveled long ago instead of being swept under the Archives' rug. It also shows that the question of Oswald's guilt must remain—four years after the event—still unanswered.

"With few exceptions, all the evidence discussed in this study was available to the Warren Commission. But the commission, in its haste, its uncritical evaluation of the facts, and its predisposition to prove Lee Harvey Oswald the lone assassin, overlooked much of it.

"Who did kill President Kennedy? This question also remains unanswered. It is beyond the scope of this examination. The purpose of this study was to perform a task of archaeology, to lay bare a whole level of contradictory evidence (much of it never published) that lay buried beneath the facile conclusions of the Warren Report. Now it has been brought to light. If its introduction makes necessary the emergence of new conclusions, then so be it."
—Quotation from the excerpt printed in The Saturday Evening Post of December 2, 1967.

FRED GRAHAM, in reviewing INQUEST, by Edward Jay Epstein (Viking Press, New York, 1966), and WHITEWASH, by Harold Weisburg (published by Harold Weisberg, Hyattstown, Md.), writes in The New York Times Book Review of July 3, 1966: "Finally, Mr. Epstein found evidence that led him to doubt the essential premise of the Warren report—that Oswald acted alone. On Jan. 27 (1964) the (Warren Commission) had seen for the first time the remarkable color film sequence of the assassination taken by an amateur photographer. It showed that the maximum time that could have elapsed between the first hits of Presi-

dent Kennedy and Governor Connally was only 1.8 seconds. Tests showed that Oswald's bolt-action rifle could not fire two rounds in less than 2.3 seconds, not including aiming time.

"This necessitated the 'single bullet' theory, because, as one staff lawyer told Mr. Epstein, 'To say that they were hit by separate bullets is synonymous with saying that there were two assassins.' (Here Mr. Graham discussed two F.B.I. reports that Mr. Epstein found to conflict with the autopsy report, and continues:) He (Mr. Epstein) views the contradictory autopsy report in the Warren Report, as 'political truth'—a deliberate fraud, although he does not use the word—to conform to the single-assassin hypothesis to which the Commission had somehow become inextricably committed.

"This point is also made in his own book by Harold Weisberg, a painstaking investigator who formerly worked for the Senate Civil Liberties Subcommittee. But Mr. Weisberg cites so many flaws in the Warren Report that the impact of the F.B.I. contradiction is lost. In fact, Mr. Weisberg questions so many points made by the report that the effect is blunted—it is difficult to believe that any institution could be as inept, careless, wrong or venal as he implies. Rather, the reader is impressed with the elusiveness of truth and the possibility that the assassination, given Oswald's death, may be inexplicable."

As the preceding paragraphs suggest, the chapter in the history of American journalism in general and The New York Times in particular, relating to the assassination of President Kennedy, is not a brilliant one. There seems to be a fairly clear feeling in the item from Richard M. Nixon's Reader's Digest article that Castro might be related to the assassination. This idea seems to be carried a small step farther by Henry J. Taylor in the piece cited in which he implies that Castro's hatred for President Kennedy, as stated by the Cuban dictator on the radio, perhaps was intended and certainly could have been taken as a sign that he would welcome the murder of the President. Preparations by Oswald to get to Cuba were additional circumstances in the chain of evidence for this theory.

The reader will have noted something else. Recall, in Chapter 4, the testimony of Dr. Benes, banker and economist who fled from Cuba, about an item in the Miami (Florida) Spanish-language newspaper Diario las Americas—an item which, he said, he did not see in any English-language newspaper in the United States. It was headed: "Government Silent About the News That Fidel Castro Ordered Assassination of President Kennedy," printed on March 5, 1967. I came upon a similar story nearly three years earlier entirely by accident. I was listening in New York City to the Randi conversation show, broadcast by radio station WOR, early in the morning of August 26, 1964, when I heard an assertion by Stanley Ross, editor of another Spanish-language newspaper, El Tiempo of New York. Those broadcasts reached into 38 states, so that it is fair to suppose that this statement reached a large audience. Yet, so far as I can tell, it didn't cause any stir.

In the course of the show, Ross startled listeners by recalling that a man had been arrested in New York by United States Immigration authorities a week or so before President Kennedy was assassinated. This man, Ross went on, asserted under interrogation that he had been sent by Castro from Cuba to the United States, along with several other men, to assassinate President Kennedy.

I was so startled to hear this that I called the radio station on the spot and tried (vainly) to talk with Mr. Ross. The following morning I reached him at the office of El Tiempo. He readily agreed that the story he told over the radio was as stated above and added that he was a consultant to the United States Immigration Bureau. He said the story of the arrest had been printed fully in El Tiempo and that a briefer account had appeared in the New York Journal American (later merged into the World Journal Tribune, now defunct). I was able to confirm that the story had indeed run in the Journal American. Ross said that the arrested man had been deported by the United States to Spain, where he was put into prison—I did not learn what the charge against him was.

In October, 1964 I again phoned Ross to re-check the story. He said he had just returned from Spain, where he had seen the imprisoned man and talked with him. I asked Ross whether he believed the man was sane and whether he thought the man's story to be true. "Well, he's not crazy," Ross replied, "and I can't imagine a sane man telling a story like that if it were not true." We cannot, of course, know whether this man told the truth. But the fact remains that there are certain phases of this matter that we cannot ignore. When two New York newspapers print a story of this sort, and it is also carried over the radio, there is bound to be discussion. Indeed, the matter was even mentioned before a Senate investigating body and duly printed in its proceedings and distributed to the public.* Could this fail to enhance the feeling of the public that it had not received the whole truth about the assassination of their President?

There arises the question as to what motive Castro could possibly have to kill President Kennedy. I learned during my inquiries in connection with the assassination that Castro had said on one of his marathon radio talks some time before November 22, 1963, that he was concerned over the murder of Premier Diem of South Vietnam on November 2, 1963. Castro is reported to have said that President Kennedy should know that two could play at that game. (The implication that President Kennedy specifically ordered the assassination of Premier Diem is baseless, despite Castro's fears. The South Vietnamese leader was slain by his own generals in an uprising against his regime. Sanctuary was offered to Premier Diem by the then United States Ambassador, Henry Cabot Lodge. Credible accounts report that Premier Diem need not have died had he chosen to accept refuge in the United States

---

* Communist Threat To U.S. Through The Caribbean, page 1195, Part 17. U.S. Government Printing Office, Washington, D.C.

Embassy.) Fear, then, could have been a motive for Castro, Communist purposes might also have been involved. This is not to say that Castro was necessarily the mastermind, but he did have motive and certainly displayed the habits of mind of an assassin dealing with dissent in Cuba.

There are parallels between the murder of President Kennedy at Dallas and the murder of Dr. Gaitan, Colombian Liberal leader, at Bogota in 1948 that are of interest, though not conclusive. The killer of President Kennedy was slain soon afterward by Jack Ruby, who is not known to have had any ties with Oswald. Nonetheless, the assassin of the President was removed and forever silenced. There are unanswered questions about Ruby. The killer of Dr. Gaitan was immediately slain in Bogota, thus removing and silencing the assassin who succeeded in the plan to incite the bloody disorders—10,000 persons died—that followed in the capital of Colombia while a vitally important inter-American conference was being held there. *Fidel Castro was implicated in the conspiracy to murder Dr. Gaitan.* The method of killing the killer has been practiced over the years by many tyrants, not least Joseph Stalin.

A story published on the front page of the New York Herald Tribune on May 19, 1964, gave an important clue to the basis for the many distortions and omissions in the American press and the Warren Commission Report in connection with the assassination of President Kennedy. That story, written by its correspondent, Dom Bonafede, in Dallas, Texas, said:

"Plans by Dallas police to link the Nov. 22 assassination of President Kennedy with an international conspiracy were headed off by Washington officials a few hours before the arraignment of Lee Harvey Oswald, the suspected assassin, the New York Herald Tribune has learned.

"The disclosure was made by a high-ranking law official here and confirmed by David Johnston, the Justice of the Peace before whom Oswald was arraigned.

" 'Washington was anxious not to have the assassination tied in with an international plot because of the harm it would do to U.S. foreign relations,' the official commented.

"He said that after the arrest of Oswald, Dallas County District Attorney Henry Wade received an urgent telephone call from Washington requesting him to make certain that the charge was one of straight murder—avoiding the mention of possible foreign implications.

"Mr. Johnston reported that Mr. Wade informed him prior to writing the complaint against Oswald that the call came from the State Department following consultation with the Justice Department.

"Speculation that Oswald may have been the trigger man in an ideological conspiracy has raged almost from the moment of his arrest and the revelation of his Marxist background. The debate continues notwithstanding contention by the FBI that evidence uncovered by that agency shows that Oswald acted on his own."

The testimony of J. Edgar Hoover, the FBI director, before the Warren Commission was first revealed in an article published in the Washington Star on October 2, 1964, five months after the publication of the story quoted above. Mr. Hoover told the commission:

"I can assure you, so far as the FBI is concerned, the case will be continued in an open classification for all time. . . . I think this will be a matter of controversy for years to come, just like the Lincoln assassination. . . ."

Representative Hale Boggs, a member of the Warren Commission, asked Mr. Hoover:

"You have spent your life studying criminology and violence and subversion. Would you care to speculate on what may have motivated the man (Oswald)?"

"My speculation, Mr. Boggs," the FBI director replied, "is the fact that this man was no doubt a dedicated Communist. He preferred to call himself a Marxist but there you get into the field of semantics. He was a Communist, he sympathized thoroughly with the Communist cause.

"I don't believe now, as I look back on it, that he ever changed his views when he asked to come back to this country. I personally feel that when he went to the American Embassy in Moscow originally to renounce his citizenship he should have been able right then and there to sign the renouncement."

Then J. Lee Rankin, counsel for the commission, said to Mr. Hoover:

"I think the commission would desire to have your comments or whatever you care to tell them, concerning the reasons why you did not furnish the information you had concerning Lee Harvey Oswald to the Secret Service prior to the time of the President's assassination."

"Well," Mr. Hoover replied, "I have gone into that very thoroughly because that was obviously one of the questions that I had in mind when the tragedy occurred in Dallas.

"In going back over the record, and I have each one of the reports of Mr. Hosty (James Hosty, FBI agent in Dallas) who dealt with the Oswald situation largely in Dallas, we had the matter that I had previously referred to, the report of the State Department that indicated this man (Oswald) was a thoroughly safe risk, (that) he had changed his views, (that) he was a loyal man now and had seen the light of day, so to speak.

"How intensive or how extensive that interview in Moscow was, I don't know. But, nevertheless, it was in a State Department document that was furnished to us."

The New York Times on October 3, 1964—that is, the next day—reported:

"The State Department issued a statement this evening (Oct. 2) saying that a thorough search of its files disclosed no document that had made or implied any such finding on Oswald."

That is a time-honored method of issuing what appears to be a denial but is nothing of the sort. It simply says that the department made a search but could not find the document that Mr. Hoover referred to. Mr. Hoover is a trustworthy man, and there is no reason to believe that he did not tell the truth about having been shown the document mentioned. The State Department does not deny that there was such a document; much less does it accuse Mr. Hoover of failing to speak the truth.

The New York Times story has this paragraph about Mr. Hoover's testimony:

"Asked for his estimate of Oswald's motives, he replied that Oswald was 'no doubt a dedicated Communist.' But Mr. Hoover discounted any claim that Oswald was a Soviet agent or had been acting on behalf of the U.S.S.R."

That is accurate as far as it goes, but there is a different quality about Mr. Hoover's testimony on this point, and a Times reader would fail to get some significant information if he did not read the original text. Mr.Hoover said:

"We had interviewed him (Oswald), I think, three times. Of course, our interviews were predicated to find out whether he had been recruited by the Russian intelligence service, because they frequently do that."

Then Mr. Boggs asked: "And had he been?"

"He had not been, so he said," Mr. Hoover continued, "and we have no proof that he was.

"He had been over long enough but they never gave him citizenship in Russia at all. I think they probably looked upon him more as a kind of queer sort of individual and they didn't trust him too strongly.

"They do have espionage and sabotage schools in Russia and they do have an assassination squad that is used by them but there is no indication he had any association with anything."

Thus it is learned from Mr.Hoover that the Russians have not only schools of espionage and sabotage but an assassination squad that is actually put to work from time to time, although the FBI does not have any information to the effect that Oswald was directly or indirectly recruited by the Soviets. As Henry J. Taylor, knowledgeable former United States Ambassador to Switzerland and now a Scripps-Howard columnist, has well said:

"Lack of evidence that Marxist Lee Harvey Oswald was linked to a Castro or Kremlin conspiracy is not pertinent." (From New York World-Telegram & Sun of December 6, 1963.)

The important thing about Mr. Hoover's testimony is that he tells of the existence of an assassination squad in one Communist regime. It is a certainty that such squads are part of the structure of every Communist government, for we encounter assassination as a Communist method in all parts of the world—specifically, in Cuba, Venezuela, Colombia, Peru, Bolivia, Laos, Cambodia, Vietnam North and South, but especially South; Switzerland, Germany, Algeria, many countries of Eastern Europe, in the Soviet Union itself, and—in the United States (one victim: Juliet Stuart Poyntz).

On the same day that the Warren Commission Report was made public, September 27, 1964, former President Eisenhower said that "America cannot use Communist methods" to defeat the efforts of Communists. He added: "Instead, to combat their insidious and dangerous tactics, we must use truth incessantly and vigorously as our mightiest weapon to defeat them."

The New York Times, which led the chorus in the nation that sang that Oswald was a loner, published an editorial on October 2, 1963, which was headed, "The Public's Right to Know." That editorial was addressed to the right of grand juries to make reports on conditions detrimental to the community. In a larger sense the public has a right to know every detail essential to the well-being of the community—a large order, perhaps, but surely it has a right to know all details in connection with the assassination of a President of the United States.

Another dispatch written by Dom Bonafede for the New York Herald Tribune of December 18, 1964, reported that "evidence and investigating reports used by the Warren Commission have been stored in a special vault in the National Archives Building and will remain inaccessible to the public for 75 years."

"As a result," the dispatch from Washington said, "much of what was said off the record by some of the 552 witnesses during the investigation of President Kennedy's assassination 'may not be known in our lifetime.'

"Only under extraordinary circumstances will parts of the historic material be made available to scholars and writers at an earlier date. . .

"Dr. (Robert) Bahmer (deputy archivist) said that barring any grants of special permission the National Archives will follow its policy of keeping the material classified for 75 years. This, he observed, is the policy concerning all historic investigations."

This recalls a statement made by Chief Justice Warren on Feb. 3, 1964, as reported by The New York Times:

"Chief Justice Warren, in discussing a general question on whether testimony taken by the commission would be made public, responded:

" 'Yes, there will come a time. But it might not be in your lifetime. I am not referring to anything especially, but there may be some things that would involve security. This would be preserved but not made public."

The following day the Chief Justice threw some doubt upon this statement but opened another door to speculation. Here Justice Warren is quoted from a story that appeared in the New York Herald Tribune of February 5, 1964:

" 'I was being a little facetious, but this man (Oswald) was over in Russia. He went down to Mexico. But we don't know yet what this will involve. There may be security aspects.' "

At the time of the assassination there was considerable, and somewhat hysterical, talk that "Right-wing" fanatics might have somehow engineered the murder. The Chief Justice's slip, however, made it very clear that the security matters would not involve any domestic organization of a "Rightist" complexion. Murders have been committed in the South by various groups, but none of them had any known or reported foreign links. In any case, with the passage of time it is Oswald's foreign associations and foreign-linked domestic associations that intrigue students of his monstrous crime.

The newspapers, almost unanimously, followed the line from one or two days after the assassination that Oswald acted alone with well nigh superhuman skill as a marksman amid a series of coincidences that rarely happens outside of fiction. The press and the investigating commission showed the same solicitude for coincidence, rather than solid information, in the findings in regard to Jack Ruby. And Ruby's action by coincidence robbed the world of Oswald's story. By another coincidence the notes made by the Dallas Police Chief, J. W. Fritz, during two days of interviewing of Oswald were destroyed. There is not a written line available on what Oswald said after his arrest.

Sylvan Fox, while City Editor of the New York World-Telegram & Sun, wrote a book titled *The Unanswered Questions About President Kennedy's Assassination,* which was published by Award Books in 1965. Mr. Fox later became Deputy Police Commissioner of New York City. He is now a member of the reportorial staff of The New York Times. *The Unanswered Questions* suggested the possible existence of a second assassin, and it questioned whether the Warren Commission had sought all the information that seemed readily available to it. Mr. Fox's book made this report, which at that time was not widely known:

"During the autopsy, X-rays and photographs were made of the President's body and its wounds. These vital medical records were turned over to the Secret Service by the Bethesda (Md.) doctors and have never been shown to the public. Not even the members of the Warren Commission have seen these invaluable records.

"Instead of studying these photographs and X-rays, the Commission relied heavily on two sources of information to determine the location of the President's wounds: The testimony of the doctors who performed the autopsy, and some rough though informative drawings made by a medical illustrator who had not seen the X-rays either, but who drew the sketches at the direction of the Bethesda doctors.

"No original notes on the autopsy survive. In an act reminiscent of Capt. J. W. Fritz's destruction of his notes on Oswald's interrogation, they were burned by the doctor who made them."

Dr. James J. Humes made the admission in a sworn statement. No reason was given for his action. He has since been allowed to view the X-rays and pictures. He said his findings in regard to the wounds were not changed.

The Commission's procedures seem, at the least, to be calculated to insure that its evidence would not inspire confidence in its conclusions.

The most unpractised eye could detect glaring omissions in the Warren Report; yet the newspapers almost without exception embraced it in some of the most glowing words ever bestowed upon a Federal document. The New York Times' comprehensive endorsement of the Report has been cited in the paragraphs that precede this chapter, together with The Times' later call to the Warren Commission to reply to the unanswered questions. The New York Herald Tribune's editorial on the Report was headed, "Beyond a Reasonable Doubt." It said:

"The report of the Warren Commission, clear, detailed, conscientious, judicial, demonstrates beyond a reasonable doubt that President John F. Kennedy was assassinated by a disturbed individual, Lee Harvey Oswald, who in turn was slain by another individual, Jack Ruby. To the extent that painstaking police work, on the broadest scale, and sober evaluation of the resulting evidence can do so, the report proves that no conspiracy, no calculated perversion of justice, no hidden forces, were involved in the tragic events of last November."

It would be hard to write more positively than that.

The New York World-Telegram's editorial was relatively mild:

"In the report of the Warren Commission on the assassination of President Kennedy there is no new fact of substance, but an infinite amount of detail which could have been gathered only by months of intensive investigation.

"The report is a model of thoroughness. It is objective, meticulous and conclusive. . . .

"The Warren Commission has done a superlative job—and all Americans are in its debt."

In the following year, 1965, the New York World-Telegram published the book written by its City Editor, Mr. Fox, *The Unanswered Questions,* which contains some blistering criticism of the commission. The publication caused not a ripple in the public's equanimity. Obviously, the public is capable of ingesting a large amount of journalistic contradiction.

Many persons felt, without knowing, from the day of the assassination, that one man acting entirely alone could not carry out the highly complicated, split-second maneuvers required to kill the President. Logically, the deed seemed to require the coordination of confederates, *physical or mental,* acting in a close conspiracy. Some of the individual investigators suggest that more than one assassin fired shots and that the Warren Commission did not pursue leads that might have revealed this, as well as possible links between Ruby and Oswald.

If some of the ideas that Mr. Fox followed could have been used by Scripps-Howard reporters during the time the commission was making its investigation, the public might have had a very different report. But the fact that the commission was in existence made it impossible for the newspapers to carry on their normal investigative function. The Leftist magazine Liberation in its issue of March, 1965, made this statement:

". . . the Warren Commission turned out a superficially plausible report and 26 volumes of evidence, which, since it is much too long for most people to read, let alone assimilate, was at first assumed to back up the Commission's conclusions. Now that the deed has been done. . . it seems impossible that the Commission could have expected to get away with it in the long run, but the same could be said in retrospect of most of the egregious miscalculations of history.

"One hesitates to speculate whether the Commission found itself trapped and saw no other way out, or whether it was content to perform a mere holding operation, convinced that time was of the essence and that most Americans would judge charitably on the theory that the Commission's actions helped save American prestige and preserve American morale during an emergency. . .

"In any event, it is already a not very well kept secret that the Warren Report will not stand up to scientific analysis and objective inquiry, and the process of exposing its failings is well under way."

In *The Unanswered Questions,* page 52, Mr. Fox writes:

"Seth Kantor, a Scripps-Howard reporter who worked in Dallas before being assigned to the Scripps-Howard bureau in Washington, had known Jack Ruby casually for five years.

"In the course of his work on Nov. 22 (1963), Kantor was at Parkland Hospital at 1:30 p.m. when Malcolm Kilduff, a Presidential press secretary, announced that Mr. Kennedy was dead. Kantor told the Warren Commission that he saw Jack Ruby at the hospital at that time.

"Kantor is an experienced and reliable reporter. He gave a coherent account of his meeting with Ruby at the hospital. But the Commission decided that 'Kantor probably did not see Ruby at Parkland Hospital in the few minutes before or after 1:30 p.m., the only time it would have been possible for Kantor to have done so.'

"Once again, the Commission simply discounts testimony, even from so good a source as this, if such testimony does not fit its conception of the events that took place."

Another point brought out by Fox (p. 167) is even more damaging:

"It (the Commission) accepted without question Ruby's explanation of his motive for killing Oswald [Ruby said he wanted to spare Mrs. Kennedy the ordeal of appearing at a trial of

Oswald], and it accepted equally without question Ruby's description of how he accomplished the murder.

"When Police Sergt. Dean suggested that Ruby had offered a somewhat different version right after the killing of Oswald, Dean ran into some rough treatment by Burt Griffin, an assistant counsel to the Commission.

"Dean told the Commission that he had been questioned for two hours by Griffin when the lawyer decided that their conversation should continue unrecorded. 'He advised the court reporter that he would be off the record and he could go smoke a cigarette or get a Coke, and he would let him know when he wanted him to get back to the record,' Dean said.

" 'Well,' Dean continued, 'after the court reporter left, Mr. Griffin started talking to me in a manner of gaining my confidence in that he would help and that he felt I would probably need some help in the future.

" 'My not knowing what he was building up to, I asked Mr. Griffin to go ahead and ask me what he was going to ask me. He continued to advise me that he wanted me to listen to what he had to say before he asked me whatever question he was going to ask me. I finally told him that whatever he wanted to ask me he could just ask me, and if I knew, I would tell him the truth or if I didn't know, I would tell him I didn't know.'

"Dean said Griffin began talking about two reports Dean had filed after the assassination. One dealt with his interview with Jack Ruby right after the Oswald murder, the second covered Dean's activities in the basement (of the police jail) at the time of the murder.

" 'He said (the police sergeant related) there were things in these statements which were not true, and, in fact, he said both these statements, he said there were particular things in there that were not true, and I asked him what portions did he consider not true, and then very dogmatically he said that "Jack Ruby didn't tell you that he entered the basement via the Main Street ramp."

" 'And of course I was shocked at this. This is what I testified to; in fact, I was cross-examined on this, and he, Mr. Griffin, further said, "Jack Ruby did not tell you that he had thought or planned to kill Oswald two nights prior."

" 'And he said, "Your testimony was false, and these reports to your chief of police are false.'

"Dean said he insisted his statements were true and asked Griffin why he was accusing him of giving false testimony, and Griffin replied to Dean, that he was not at liberty to discuss his reasons with Dean.

"Before recalling the court stenographer and resuming the recorded portion of Dean's interrogation, Griffin told Dean, according to the police sergeant, 'I respect you as a witness, I respect you in your profession, but I have offered my help and assistance, and I again will offer you my assistance, and I don't feel you will be subjecting yourself to loss of your job if you will go ahead and tell me the truth about it.'

" 'I again told Mr. Griffin that these were the facts and that I couldn't change them,' Dean informed the Warren Commission. 'So with that we got back on the record.'

"The Warren Commission eventually agreed with Dean that Ruby must have entered Police Headquarters through the Main Street ramp, but it never agreed that Ruby planned the Oswald murder before Sunday morning (when it was actually done)."

Here the curtain is drawn aside, and one of the methods of the commission is exposed to the public gaze. How *did* the Commission expect to get away with it? After all, it is on the Commission's record.

Fox raised the possibility of a second assassin, on pages 92 and 93 of his book:

"Mrs. Jean Hill was standing on a grassy incline directly across Elm Street from the book depository (where Oswald did his firing)—in other words, south of the building and grassy knoll to its west. Like every other witness who commented on the question, she said she was certain (Governor) Connally (of Texas) 'wasn't hit when the first shot hit.'

"Mrs. Hill, a school teacher, said she thought at least some of the shots came from the grassy knoll across the street from where she was standing. And she was convinced there were more than three shots. A few hours after the assassination, she informed a Secret Service man of her belief.

" 'Am I a kook or what's wrong with me?' she asked the unidentified Secret Service man. 'They keep saying three shots. I know I heard more. I heard from four to six shots anyway.'

"Mrs. Hill said the Secret Service man told her: 'Mrs. Hill, we were standing at the window and we heard more shots also, but we have three wounds and three bullets, three shots is all we are willing to say right now.'

"With Mrs. Hill at the time of the shooting was a friend of hers, Mary Moorman. Mrs. Moorman was in the same place at the same time. But she was never summoned to testify before the Warren Commission.

"Nor was Charles Drehm, a Dallas carpet salesman, who told the Dallas Times Herald he was about 10 feet from the President's car at the moment of the shooting. Drehm, the Times Herald said, 'seemed to think the shots came from in front of or beside the President.'

"Nor did the Commission call O. V. Campbell, the vice president of the book depository, who was standing in front of the building with Roy Truly, the depository superintendent, at the time of the assassination. Campbell was quoted in the Dallas Morning News as saying he 'ran toward a grassy knoll west of the building' because he thought the shots were coming from there.

"Nor did the Commission call four women employed by the Dallas Morning News who were on the grassy knoll itself. One of the four, Mary Woodward, wrote an eyewitness account of the assassination for the Morning News. She said she and her three companions were sitting on the knoll overlooking Elm Street when they heard 'a terrific, ear-shattering noise coming from behind us and a little to the right.'

"If the sound came from behind the four women, it couldn't

have come from a gun on the sixth floor of the book depository, which was to their left. Did the Commission question Mary Woodward or any of her three companions about this 'ear-shattering' noise they heard coming from behind them. It did not.

"The Commission tells us that it relied upon 'the consensus among the witnesses at the scene' to reach its conclusion that three shots were fired. Such a consensus, which overlooks or ignores many actual witnesses, can hardly be considered reliable."

The Commission offered as proof that only three shots were fired the three empty shells found on the sixth floor of the book depository. There is no doubt that the Commission proves Oswald fired from a window of that floor, but a profound and well-earned suspicion lingers after encountering this haphazard kind of investigating at many other points in the Report. For instance, the Report itself speaks of the testimony of Roy Kellerman, Secret Service man who was sitting in the front seat of the President's car with the driver, as saying that he had heard "a flurry of shots" after the first shot. A "flurry" is defined in Webster's New International Dictionary as "a light shower or snowfall accompanied by wind." In other words, a flurry suggests at least several shots in quick succession—three or four or more, certainly not just two, evenly spaced. But once you establish that there were more than three shots you destroy the theory that only Oswald fired shots, for from his rifle only three shells had been fired—in the rapid time of 5.2 seconds at a moving and changing target. Two of the three shells had to be ejected and three sightings had to be made through the telescopic sight, which, when found, was defective. The Commission produced experts to prove that this was possible. Others point out that Oswald was unable from a short distance away to hit Major General Edwin A. Walker as he sat in his home, and claim, less convincingly, that crack marksmen in Europe were not able to duplicate the alleged Dallas feat in point of time.

The Columbia Broadcasting System devoted four one-hour programs on successive nights—June 25-28, 1967—to the Warren Commission Report. The CBS presentation of studies and opinion, the latter heavily weighted in favor of the Report, compiled over nine months, found that Oswald and Ruby had acted alone, without confederates and without a conspiracy. There was, however, a suggestion of the possibility of a conspiracy between Oswald and the CIA or the FBI or maybe both. The word "Communist" was not mentioned by any of the CBS investigators.

John J. McCloy, a member of the Warren Commission, appearing on one of the CBS programs, smiled at the idea of any conspiracy on the part of members of the Commission or of Oswald but allowed that the Commission might have made some errors, such as the failure to make public the X-rays and color pictures showing the President's wounds. He also regretted the rush to go to press with the report but denied that the Commission itself was in any way hurried into its conclusions. He pointed to the high quality of the Commission members not only for their places in the nation's life but for their proven investigative abilities. He remarked that in universities he had visited he had found a disinclination on the part of professors to accept the idea that a "Communist-inclined" person had been the assassin of the President because they wanted to believe that the murder somehow had been contrived by the Right. That was as close as the CBS study came to looking for ideological causes. The New York Times story June 29, 1967, on Mr. McCloy's appearance, did not mention that phase of his remarks. Neither did the New York Post of July 1, 1967, cover that part of Mr. McCloy's views in its excerpts of the CBS broadcasts.

Eric Sevareid, with the menacing mien of a cornered Viking, asserted that "the notion" that there might have been a conspiracy to hide the whole truth about the assassination was "idiotic." He was preceded by Professor Henry Steele Commager, who managed to work in the words "McCarthy era" by asserting that *some* persons *wanted* to believe in conspiracies. That, the New York Post reported fully. The opinions of Mr. Sevareid and Professor Commager were hardly of value in clearing up what continue to be the mysteries of this case, but perhaps their views served to mollify the professorial element who might have been offended by Mr. McCloy's use of the words "Communist-inclined." (Anything that tends to disclose the existence of Communists among us is resented in some academic quarters.) CBS appeared to have satisfied itself with the thrust of the three speakers, who left no doubt at all that they took a dim view of any one who suspected conspiracies might have been involved in the assassination.

More convincing were the CBS pictures showing rifle tests made to prove that it was possible to fire three shots with a rifle identical (or at least very similar) to that used by Oswald, within the time limit of 5.2 seconds, from a sixth-floor height at a moving target. There seemed to be two weaknesses to these tests. One was that the telescopic sight used by Oswald was defective and could not be fired by United States test experts after the murder until the scope had been adjusted.* The second weak point is that the moving target in the CBS tests remained upright and did not slump as President Kennedy is said to have done after he had been hit by the first bullet. This means that a new sight had to be taken by Oswald. The first point might be explained on the theory that the telescopic sight was knocked askew when Oswald threw the rifle into a hiding place on the sixth floor of the Book Depository. The second would surely make a difference in the CBS marksmanship scores recorded.

The possibility of foreign links, such as those considered in this chapter, was entirely ignored. The reign of impulse and coincidence was extended from the press to the television screen, with the addition of some name-calling for those who did not accept the CBS conclusions. Even the American people did not come off unscathed in this series of didactic but highly superficial studies. The CBS case left the viewer with the feeling that the healthy skepticism of the people (about two-thirds say they have doubts) will not easily be submerged. There are still unanswered questions.

The late Robert C. Ruark, novelist, columnist and big game

---

* This matter is explained in the Warren Report and is cited in the book *Whitewash* by Harold Weisberg, page 26.

hunter, wrote in the New York World-Telegram of October 9, 1964, that "the ballistic end [of the Warren Report] makes no sense." Neither bullet angles nor timing of the shots satisfied him. Mr. Ruark gave various techincal reasons for his views.

Oswald called himself a Marxist, a euphemism for "Communist." Fidel Castro also designated himself as a Marxist. That Oswald associated with Communists is noted in the Commission's Report, which plays down his overwhelming preference for Communist countries, whether the Soviet Union or Castro Cuba, and such pro-Communist activity as the Fair Play for Cuba Committee. After his arrest as an assassin in Dallas, Oswald repeatedly called for the legal services of a lawyer named John Abt. Mr. Abt is simply designated in the Report as "a New York lawyer." Apparently it would not do to reveal to the public at large that Mr. Abt is one of the top legal defenders of Communists in the United States. Mr. Abt was himself identified as far back as the 1930's as a Communist, and has been implicated with a Soviet espionage ring in sworn testimony. The prisoner Oswald was never able to get into touch with him before Ruby halted all need for legal assistance.

On this point the following under statement in the Report is of interest: "His (Oswald's) commitment to Marxism and communism appears to have been another important factor in his motivation [for the assassination]." The word "appears" is bothersome here, for Oswald is shown in the Report to be murderously intent upon being a Communist. He is said to have asserted once that he would like to kill President Eisenhower "because he was exploiting the working class." Obviously Oswald believed it was possible to solve large social problems by killing somebody. Murdering people in behalf of the party is a regular Communist practice. But one would not expect to read anything so forthright as that in the Commission's Report. (A news dispatch over the radio on April 18, 1967, said that about 60,000 persons, mostly civic and religious leaders, had been murdered in South Vietnam by the Communists since they began their efforts to seize control of the country. That dispatch referred to individual executions, not battlefield deaths. The murdered were village chiefs, school teachers and others who helped to guide their fellow countrymen.) The Communist resort to killing as an instrument of political control is something that democratic and humane persons find hard to grasp.

The Commission failed to satisfy the public curiosity about Oswald's connections. On the day before the assassination he left his wallet at his wife's home—a wallet that contained about $150. For a poor man with no associations he always managed to have money—to print pamphlets for the Fair Play for Cuba Committee, to go to Mexico City, and to buy weapons. And despite an amazing record of defection and dubious activities, he was able to get a second passport in June, 1963, only a few days after applying for it. Somehow he is never connected with anybody except his wife, from whom he was practically estranged. The Commission gives glimpses of Oswald's associations with inchoate characters in New Orleans. This picture is quite inadequate. The public shares this view.

Yet the newspapers generally and now one television network have sought to foist the findings of the Warren Commission upon the public. The New York World-Telegram was the first to recover from this unfavorable position by publishing the withering attack by Mr. Fox in its news columns. His book was printed in daily installments. It is not an accident that *The Unanswered Questions* was not written by a New York Times man (Mr. Fox was not then a New York Times man) or published in the columns of that newspaper, just as it is not without significance that none of the books written to expose the espionage and sabotage of the Russians in the United Nations was done by a Times man. Nor is it accidental that *Red Star Over Cuba* was not written by a Times man or sponsored by The Times. It is significant, too, that Mrs. Ruby Hart Phillips, who for nearly 25 years was Havana correspondent of The New York Times, is no longer on the staff of that newspaper. It did not enhance her future there to be so strongly anti-Castro and anti-Communist. Neither did Mrs. Phillips accept the findings of the Warren Commission.

Atlas magazine of May, 1967, printed an article headed, "Why Was JFK Shot?" Although short on credibility, it tells an interesting story, concerning the alleged statement of a Russian merchant marine officer to a Belgian sailor in a Belgian port on September 4, 1963, less than three months before the assassination. The Russian carried a passport identifying him as Ivan Kutscharenko of Kiev, and boasted of speaking several languages. Kutscharenko became quite drunk in a bar where five Russians had joined a German and the Belgian. Now:

"At a certain moment, floating deep in drunkenness, he decided that the Belgian sailor had become his 'number one friend' and, consequently, told the latter how much it hurt him to have to leave in the morning for the United States. Peeters (the Belgian) had responded with a remark about Russian-American relations, and Ivan Kutscharenko had launched into a tirade about the dirty war in Vietnam.

"Ivan had smiled mysteriously: 'This is 1963 and you think, my dear fellow, that the war in Vietnam is coming to an end. That's completely stupid! Do you want me to tell you something? The Vietnamese war is only a beginning, a prologue. It will become even dirtier and more vicious, not just in Vietnam, but in China and America as well.'

" 'Why "in China and America as well"?'

" 'There are three big powers in the world today: Russia, the United States and the Chinese People's Republic. We Russians have decided to become the new and first world power, but we don't wish to get involved in war. We want to get China and the United States to destroy each other. If our plan is to succeed, the Vietnamese conflict must degenerate into an open war between Peking and Washington . . .'

"Peeters nodded his agreement while the Russian carried on in this way, but his mind was elsewhere. Peeters didn't have the slightest interest in politics. The Belgian seaman finally replied:

"You're boring me . . . you've drunk enough. Just forget it. Besides, Kennedy is a peaceful man. He'll never let himself be dragged into a hopeless war with Red China.'

"Ivan lapsed into silence for several minutes, then he looked Peeters straight in the eyes and murmured: 'I'm going to tell you something, comrade, and it's not a joke. *There will be no Christmas 1963 for John Kennedy* . . . By Christmas he will have been buried a long time . . .' Ivan continued in an even lower voice: 'And his successor will do exactly what John Kennedy doesn't want to do: he will expand the war in Vietnam . . . he will increase the number of Americans in Saigon . . . he will have Hanoi bombed . . . Johnson and his friends are looking for war, and that's what we desire. Kennedy must disappear from the stage . . .'

" 'That's sheer nonsense, Ivan!'

" 'Well, you can believe me. Everything has been set up, every step has been taken to silence the assassin. . . .'

"At this point Ivan Kutscharenko tore a button from his uniform and gave it to Peeters, saying: 'A souvenir from me. A sign of our friendship . . .' "

Peeters has a letter from J. Edgar Hoover, dated Oct. 30, 1964, to give credence to the assertion by Peeters that he wrote to the White House on November 19, 1963, to warn President Kennedy, in vain.

The New York Times dispatch from London on March 13, 1965, that the "suspicion of conspiracy in President Kennedy's assassination persists in Europe, even as the whole subject fades out of current attention and into history," could hardly have been more wrong. Nothing is more alive today than the assassination of President Kennedy, because that act of violence in 1963 is part of the continuing violence of the present. The public is still looking for clues. More than mere restless curiosity is at work to find all the elements that went into the killing of the American President. The sense of insecurity that all persons feel in a world that is at once integrating and disintegrating is the most deeply moving factor. Eventually the world will know all the facts. Already a great surge is under way toward discovering them.

CHAPTER VI

The New York Times and the Vietnam War

• • •

FREDERICK E. NOLTING JR., FORMER UNITED STATES Ambassador to South Vietnam: *"Why does the (New York) Times continue to distort the record on Vietnam? The reason, I think, is clear. The overthrow of Diem—which left a vacuum so great that 300,000 Americans and 2 billion a month seem insufficient to fill it—was due in no small part to the influence of The Times!"— From a letter originally written to and published in The New York Times and reprinted in Time magazine on Nov. 4, 1966.*

GEN. HAROLD K. JOHNSON, CHIEF OF STAFF, U.S. ARMY: *"With regard to the press:*

"There are not many experienced reporters who are out there [in Vietnam] all the time. When the reporter with experience does go out there and spends some time—three months or four months, or even six—and does some stories in depth, you find pretty balanced coverage. But, over all, an honest question can be raised whether the reporting from Vietnam is really accurate and balanced."—From an interview with the general in U.S. News & World Report of Sept. 11, 1967.

DAVID LAWRENCE, editor of U.S. News & World Report: *"We are being deluged with lectures and speeches in the Senate and elsewhere which keep telling the American people, in effect, that they had better run up the white flag in Vietnam."—From Mr. Lawrence's editorial in U.S. News & World Report on May 16, 1966.*

BRIG. GEN. S. L. A. MARSHALL: "The national press as a whole—with a very few individual and institutional exceptions—is doing a poor job of reporting the military aspects of the Vietnam War."—From an article by General Marshall in The New Leader on Nov. 21, 1966.

JOSEPH ALSOP: "Nhatrang, Viet Nam—Every so often an itinerant American goes to Cambodia to investigate. He is known, or at least thought, to be sympathetic; else he could hardly have obtained a visa. Prince Sihanouk grandly offers his permission to go anywhere he pleases in the country, or even gives him a guided tour of bits of the border area.

"The American does not pause to reflect that our troops have a pretty hard time finding Viet Cong units in Viet Nam, with the whole vast apparatus of American and Vietnamese intelligence to aid them. He does not bear in mind, or perhaps has never heard about the sordid results of Stalin's guided tours for people like Beatrice and Sidney Webb in the time of Russia's agony.

"So he brings back word that there are no Viet Cong or North Vietnamese anywhere in Cambodia, with all the sublime assurance of the Webbs' bringing back the word that Russia of the bloodbaths was the workers' paradise.

"And there are people at home, God help us all, who prefer this sort of evidence to the hard evidence of American troops in combat, who had engaged V.C. regiments and have actually seen them take refuge across the Cambodian border."—From a column by Mr. Alsop in the New York World Journal Tribune on Sept. 19, 1966.

JOSEPH ALSOP: "At least one enemy divisional head- quarters is permanently established in Cambodia; and either one or

*two additional North Vietnamese regiments are also based there."
From column in New York World Journal Tribune on Oct. 17,
1966.*

*COL. R. L. HOUSTON, retired, former Canadian member of
the International Control Commission: "I should say at this point
that there should be no doubt in anybody's mind that the so-called
National Liberation Front—the Viet Cong—are nothing but out-
and-out renegades, representing the North Vietnamese and the
Chinese Communists. And the mere thought of bringing such a
gang of cutthroats to the conference table is, to my thinking, the
utmost folly."—From an interview in U.S. News & World Report
on Oct. 17, 1966.*

*PRESIDENT LYNDON B. JOHNSON: "The central fact is
that this is really war. It is guided by North Vietnam and it is
spurred by Communist China. Its goal is to conquer the South, to
defeat American power, and to extend the Asiatic dominion of
Communism."—From a statement at a news conference on July
28, 1965.*

*EDITORIAL in The New York Times: "Communist politics
and the possibility—however faint—of approaching a negotiated
end to the war in Vietnam suggest that this would be a good
moment to have a long pause in the bombing of North Vietnam. . . .
The two previous bombing pauses—five days in May 1965, and
37 days as 1965 ended and this year (1966) began—evoked no
positive response from Hanoi whatsoever. But the climate has
changed."—October 4, 1966*

*JOAN BAEZ, folksinger: "I make one request to the men in
the audience—don't cooperate with the draft."—At a "Sing-In for
Peace in Vietnam," in Carnegie Hall, New York, as quoted by the
New York Post on Sept. 26, 1965.*

*BARRON'S: National Business and Financial Weekly: "The
Unified Buddhist Church, representing less than one-tenth of the*

(South Vietnam) population, is riven by factions; its moderate wing called off all demonstrations in return for a pledge that civilians will be added to the government.. . . . Probably no one is as surprised at the survival of President Thieu and Premier Ky as the average reader of American newspapers." From page 7, June 6, 1966.

CARL T. ROWAN: "This will not be the last terror tactic [the assassination of Tran Van Van] designed to discredit Ky and Thieu, because the thing the VC must fear more than American firepower is the establishment of a reasonably democratic, constitutional government. For that is what will put the VC into the posture it deserves: as a group of murderous outside rebels." —From Mr. Rowan's column in New York World Journal Tribune Dec. 23, 1966.

"MOSCOW, Jan. 4—The Soviet Government has assured the Communist regime of North Vietnam of its support and complete solidarity in the face of 'aggressive actions' by the United States." —From special dispatch to The New York Times of Jan. 5, 1965

EDITORIAL in The New York Times: "Cardinal Spellman has every right as an American citizen to express his feeling that anything 'less than victory is inconceivable' in Vietnam. When President Johnson was in South Vietnam briefly after the Manila conference last October, he put somewhat the same tough sentiment into equally unfortunate if more homely language in his now famous incitement to the American soldiers to 'be sure to come home with that coonskin on the wall.' "—December 29, 1966.

EDITORIAL in The New York Times: "The day is long past when the United States could muster big majorities at will for its policies and proposals in the United Nations General Assembly. It was passing even while Henry Cabot Lodge was ramming through the 'victories' over Russia of which the Republicans boasted in the 1960 elections."—December 26, 1966.

EDITORIAL in *The New York Times:* "The enthusiastic reception Soviet Premier Kosygin received in Hanoi yesterday contrasted sharply with the chilly atmosphere that surrounded his stopover in Peking. Taken together with yesterday's endorsement of Soviet foreign policy by North Vietnam's chief Communist newspaper, this contrast must strengthen suspicion that the Kosygin mission aims primarily at counterposing Russian influence to that of China in Hanoi. As one inducement, of course, Moscow can offer the North Vietnamese much more economic and military aid than China can, and this apparently is being done."—*February 7, 1965.*

EDITORIAL in *The New York Times:* "The latest coup d'etat in Vietnam is one more blow at the United States. It is a defeat. It is not a lost war but it certainly is a lost battle. There was nothing the Americans could do to stop this coup, which could be seen coming, and no visible choice except to go along with it and hope for the best.

"The Richard Nixon alternative can and should be disposed of swiftly. Mr. Nixon wants to 'end the war' by using the United States Navy and Air Force to cut Communist supply lines to South Vietnam and destroy Communist staging areas in North Vietnam and Laos. But the bulk of the Vietcong's forces are from South Vietnam; and a recent news dispatch to The Times reported that United States officials rate the support that the Vietcong is getting from Hanoi as amounting to only 20 per cent of the total weight of the enemy's effective strength."—*January 28, 1965.*

WHITE PAPER of United States State Department: "South Vietnam is fighting for its life against a brutal campaign of terror and armed attack inspired, directed, supplied and controlled by the Communist regime in Hanoi. This flagrant aggression has been going on for years, but recently the pace has quickened and the threat has now become acute."—*Printed in The Times Feb. 28, 1965.*

EDITORIAL in The New York Times: "The United States' reputation as a militant crusader against Communism everywhere, whatever the cost, is proving too dangerous as other nations see it. The United States also has a sometimes deserved reputation as a defender of the status quo, *of capitalism as we interpret it, of democracy only in our form, of opposing social reform if it comes from the left and of complacently accepting* coups d'etat *from the right."—July 3, 1965.*

"THANT ASKS VIETNAM TALKS LEADING TO A U.S. PULLOUT. U.N. Chief Reports He Has Offered Some Proposals —Says that If Americans Had Facts They Would Back Him." —A 2-column (R) head on page one of The New York Times of Feb. 25, 1965.

PROF. GEORGE LICHTHEIM, Visiting Professor at Stanford University: ". . . one day is pretty much like the next, so far as the handling of foreign news by the [New York] Times is concerned. The overall impression—a compound of ignorance, provincialism, and plain incompetence—remains the same year after year. Others may have a different picture. I shall be told that the Times has virtues unsuspected by foreigners. That is doubtless true; it must be true, seeing that the paper takes itself so seriously. I merely register a dissent from the seemingly widespread notion that it is an inexhaustible source of relevant information about what passes abroad. Inexhaustible it may be, but the relevance of its coverage leaves something to be desired."—From Professor Lichtheim's article, "All The News That's Fit to Print," in magazine Commentary, September, 1965.

EDWARD HUNTER: "Pierre Salinger, for years a reporter and an editor, who was press secretary for both Presidents Kennedy and Johnson, has come forth with an authoritative accusation that the press has been manipulating foreign affairs. He made his charge in a television discussion with Sander Vanocur, a National

Broadcasting Company correspondent who covered the White House for years . . .

"The extraordinary revealing dialogue developed during Salinger's and Vanocur's appearance in the 'Today' show, over the N.B.C.'s national hookup on Sept. 13 (1966), with Hugh Downs presiding. The occasion was a discussion of Salinger's new book, With Kennedy, *on behalf of which the author made a barnstorming trip across the nation . . . Salinger made the following statement, of momentous significance. He was referring to the 'mission,' as he called it, of today's newsman, as exemplified by the coverage of the Vietnamese scene:*

" 'I think insofar as their dedication to bringing down the Diem government, which they announced to one and all in Saigon as one of the aims of the stories they were writing, they went beyond the—really what I call—the guidelines of journalistic reporting.

" 'I think a reporter should report the events and not try to create them. And I think that in this particular case, Mr. [David] Halberstam, Mr. [Malcolm] Browne and Mr. [Neil] Sheehan determined that one of the objectives of their reporting should be to bring down the Diem government.' "—From the magazine Tactics *of October 20, 1966.*

BARRON'S: *"Soviet foreign policy, while always unprincipled and sometimes enigmatic, is rarely inconsistent. President Johnson, therefore, invited last week's rebuff when he urged Moscow to join the U.S. in 'rational acts of common endeavor' regardless of differences over Vietnam. Said Pravda: 'It is difficult to imagine that Washington should be so poorly informed of the foundations of Soviet foreign policy as to proceed seriously from such a premise.' As last winter's Tricontinental conference in Havana frankly proclaimed, wars of liberation are the means by which the Communists hope to destroy the U.S. Aggression against South Vietnam being the first large-scale test of that prescription, U.S. diplomacy is indeed naive in assuming that Soviet aid to*

Hanoi is a peripheral affair and that, in other matters, Soviet-U.S. cooperation might be feasible. Since the illusion has been nurtured in the diplomatic establishment, on university campuses and among all sorts of Kremlinologists, America for once owes a debt of gratitude to the editors of Pravda, who set out to destroy it."
—*Sept. 5, 1966.*

WILLIAM S. WHITE: *"Washington—The long nightmare of Viet Nam is lifting at last, and though the way to final victory over the Communist assailants from without and within still stretches out long and forbidding, a true pre-dawn does now loom faintly ahead."—From his column in New York World Journal Tribune of Sept. 16, 1966.*

JOSEPH ALSOP: *"Nhatrang, Vietnam—The chances are that the success of the Vietnamese election is being underrated at home. Any success here falsifies predictions and flouts the present prejudice of too many people at home, and in Vietnam too. So any success, however solid, tends to be denigrated by those same people.*

"Hence the first thing to note is that last Sunday's election was brilliantly, even startlingly, successful. The turnout of voters, so far surpassing the normal American percentage, was far greater than any one could have forecast.

"Furthermore, all those who voted did so in the face of the grimmest warnings by the Viet Cong. Voting was made a heinous crime by the Communist pre-election propaganda. This should be noted by the opponents of the President's policy at home, who have a way of hinting that the majority of Vietnamese secretly support the so-called National Liberation Front. The election instead proves that the Viet Cong are exactly what they appear—a small, armed minority, seeking to seize control by naked force of a people who want no part of them."—From his column, New York World Journal Tribune, Sept. 1, 1966.

SAIGON, South Vietnam, Sept. 15 (UPI)—Militant Buddhist leaders charged today that Sunday's nationwide election was 'completely crooked' and that the Government had inflated the figures on the number of Vietnamese who cast ballots for delegates to the Constituent Assembly. The Buddhists contended that only a minority of the people had participated and the assembly therefore did not truly represent them."—The New York Times, page 21, Sept. 16, 1966.

The approach of The New York Times to the war in Vietnam and to the increasing participation of the United States in that conflict has been broadly negative and carping—entirely unhelpful to the United States. This position is in line with previous attitudes of the paper toward Communist actions around the world—specifically, in Eastern Europe, in Cuba and the Dominican Republic, in its miscoverage of events in the Soviet Union and in Indonesia, and in its contradictory coverage of Cambodia as a staging area and avenue for North Vietnamese troops to enter South Vietnam and to flee back into Cambodia. The New York Times has been a depressant and a harmful factor in the Vietnam foreign policy of the United States, a policy that is not Democratic or Republican but bipartisan, with the backing of great majorities not only of both parties in the two houses of Congress but most of the public, if we may accept most of the polls. A vote of the people in a regular election in Dearborn, Michigan, in November, 1966, overwhelmingly endorsed the United States' remaining in Vietnam.

The New York Times' attitude stems from its belief in a world balance of power. The Times does, however, make use of any help it can get, including that of dissident intellectuals and others who would not ordinarily be regarded as Times bedfellows. In this balance, Communist power, including the Communist parties, serves as a counterweight to Western arms progress and Western combativeness and resistance to Communist expansion.

The limit to which this balance of power theory could be stretched by Soviet-dominated or Soviet-fostered forces without meeting the disapproval of the Times was finally reached in the Middle East in June, 1967. That was too much, and The Times demanded United States resistance. But The Times opposed defense of the Dominican Republic against a Communist move to take over that country in 1965. It denied, of course, that the Communists posed a threat there.

Adolph S. Ochs, who led the paper to greatness earlier in the century, is said to have believed that the editorial page should be quiet, if firm and strong, rather than shrill. He felt that a raucous editorial page would transfer unseemly qualities to the news pages. As the Vietnam war progressed, The Times editorials, having achieved an abnormal harvest of frustration and defeat, became strident, painfully repetitious and often one-sidedly against the policy of the United States. This had to be done by ignoring the vast and unspeakable atrocities committed by the aggressive enemy and by concentrating upon failures of the United States to protect civilians in North and South Vietnam alike. Indeed The Times has often failed to reveal details of Vietcong murders and tortures and has rarely printed a picture of these horrendous actions. General William C. Westmoreland, commander of United States forces in Vietnam, said on a visit to the United States in April, 1967, that "during the past nine years, 53,000 Vietnamese— a large share of them teachers, policemen and elected or natural leaders—have been killed or kidnapped" by the Communists.

The thing that Mr. Ochs feared has happened. The upside-down language of the editorial page appears to have governed a considerable amount of the coverage of Vietnam by correspondents. Not only are there strange defects of enormous importance in the news dispatches but The Times policy has precluded the presentation of news that might have seemed calculated to bring about a victorious conclusion of the conflict. The Times editorially even went so far as to accuse the President of the United States of "incitement to the American soldiers" fighting in Vietnam. This is carrying upside-down language to an extremity hardly known even in Orwell's 1984. Apparently The Times believes that even the individual soldier can be taught to fight a no-win war and that in such a contest the President has no right to urge the servicemen on. If this view appeared in any other paper it would cause laughter or ridicule. In The New York Times, moving on a reputation built by greater men, it is merely puzzling to readers who are willing to give the paper the benefit of the doubt that it has more than average reasoning powers.

For instance, The Times abhors and loathes the word "victory" in connection with this war, but The Times has not even begun to think this attitude through to all its logical conclusions. First of all, it specifically means that The Times is opposed to a war settlement for the Government of South Vietnam without the inclusion of the enemy National Liberation Front, the so-called political organization of which the Vietcong is the fighting arm. The National Liberation Front was set up by North Vietnam to conquer and unify all of Vietnam under the Communists. The withdrawal of American, South Korean, Australian, New Zealand, Thai and Philippine troops would guarantee a Communist victory in South Vietnam because there would then be too few forces left to prevent it. The New York Times could then say it did not realize that this would be the result of its attitude but that, as in Cuba, after all it was a social revolution.

That the denial of victory to the forces fighting for freedom is the intention of The New York Times cannot be doubted. And that adds up to victory for the other side, not a workable coalition —a result it would accept with the equanimity with which it views Communist Cuba, enslaved Hungary, and "semi-liberated" Poland and Rumania, and the thoroughness with which it has forgotten other captive nations of Eastern Europe. Unworthy as it may seem of so prominent a newspaper as The New York Times, it seeks to cloak this aspect of its editorial goal for South Vietnam. And the editorial goal seemed also to be the news goal until sometime during the year 1966, when a quality that recalled the coverage of the Allied armies in Europe during World War II began to appear in The Times news columns, though the placing of the Vietnam news frequently was still inferior to that of the news of New York City.

The highlight of the war news coverage of 1966 was the great fiasco of Harrison E. Salisbury's trip to the environs of Hanoi to "cover" the alleged U.S. bombing of civilians and non-military buildings. This transparent attempt to push the war onus upon America backfired. Mr. Salisbury, however, asserted on his return from North Vietnam that it was the Defense Department's policy that had "backfired." This was audacious of Mr. Salisbury but not convincing. The reason Mr. Salisbury's coverage backfired is easily shown. Under a two-column headline on page one Dec. 27, 1966, reading: "U.S. RAIDS BATTER 2 TOWNS; SUPPLY ROUTE IS LITTLE HURT," two dispatches by Mr. Salisbury were presented. In one he reported:

"The cathedral tower of Namdinh (50 miles southeast of Hanoi) looks out on block after block of utter desolation; the city's population of 90,000 has been reduced to less than 20,000 because of evacuation; 13 per cent of the city's housing, including homes of 12,464 people, have been destroyed; 89 people have been killed and 405 wounded.

"No American communique has asserted that Namdinh contains some facility that the United States regards as a military objective. It is apparent, on personal inspection, that block after block of ordinary housing, particularly surrounding a textile plant, has been smashed to rubble by repeated attacks by Seventh Fleet planes. . . .

"Whatever the explanation, one can see that United States planes are dropping an enormous weight of explosives on purely civilian targets. Whatever else there may be or might have been in Namdinh, it is civilians who have taken the punishment.

"A brief tour of Namha Province, in which Namdinh lies, shows Namdinh is far from being exceptional.

"President Johnson's announced policy that American targets

in North Vietnam are steel and concrete rather than human lives seems to have little connection with the reality of attacks carried out by United States planes.*

"A notable example is Chuly, a town of about 35 miles south of Hanoi on Route 1. The town had a population of about 10,000. In attacks on Oct. 1, 2 and 9, every house and building was destroyed. Only 40 were killed and wounded because many people had left town and because an excellent manhole-shelter system was available.

"The community had no industry, but lay astride a highway and a railroad line running from Hanoi, which had a couple of sidings in town."

No authority was given by Mr. Salisbury for the alleged facts and figures he offered, though he took the occasion to suggest that the announced policy of the President of the United States had no relationship to the reality. Mr. Salisbury made no mention of the possibility that some of the lives might have been taken and damage done by North Vietnamese anti-aircraft shells and missiles falling back upon populated places.

The other dispatch by Mr. Salisbury is even more remarkable:

"The railroad and highway [running from Hanoi toward Saigon] have been bombed again and again and again, but it is doubtful that rail traffic has ever been held up more than a few

---

* American fliers on bombing missions near Hanoi reported on September 3, 1967, that they had dodged two North Vietnamese missiles aimed at them. Then, they said, they watched the missiles fall upon a village about 20 miles north of Hanoi. They said the missiles made large explosions as they landed in the village.

Here is an American confirmation that at least some of the devastation reported wreaked upon North Vietnamese villages is done by North Vietnamese missiles, not American bombs. This information was given in a report heard over the New York City radio station, WNYC. It may well be that many anti-aircraft shells as well as missiles have fallen upon towns and villages in other areas of North Vietnam.

This radio item may well have appeared in the newspapers of September 3 or 4, but it was not played up as an instance of recklessness concerning the lives of North Vietnamese people as displayed by missiles falling wide of their mark.

hours, and the highway seems capable of operating almost continuously regardless of how many bombs are dropped.

"The secret of the railroad is simple and it lies beyond the ability of air power to interdict.

"If the track uses small, light equipment when a bomb smashes the rails or overturns a car, removal and repair problems are simple. Gangs of workmen can easily clear the lines. Moreover, repair materials probably sufficient to construct two or three additional railroads are kept on hand, seldom more than a few hundred yards from any possible break."

But while American bombs could do very little to damage the railroad and highway, the villages and hamlets along the route have "suffered severely." Mr. Salisbury's dispatch goes on to assert that North Vietnamese supply routes cannot be interdicted by bombing. He concludes:

"It is the conviction of the North Vietnamese that the United States is deliberately directing bombs against the civilian population, although ostensibly contending that 'military objectives' are the target."

It is hard to believe that American bombs cannot destroy a railroad or a road but can do enormous damage to civilian areas. The author of this book was not the only one to have trouble swallowing after reading the Salisbury dispatches.

Time magazine went into a high flight that required two full pages (its first two) on Jan. 6, 1967, to give its view of the Salisbury reports:

"U.S. officials by no means accepted Salisbury's overall picture of the bombing war. Iowa's Republican Senator Bourke Hickenlooper pointed out (and the Times dutifully reported) that the paper has been a consistent critic of the U.S. role in Vietnam; he complained that Hanoi would 'let a New York Times reporter in but not objective reporters.' Others speculated that Salisbury may have fallen into the same trap in Hanoi as he did in Pnompenh (Cambodia) last June. At that time, he accepted at face value assurances from Cambodian officials that there was 'probably' no such thing as a 'Sihanouk trail' along which Hanoi was trucking supplies into South Vietnam. Eight days later, Times Chief Far East Correspondent Seymour Topping, now the paper's foreign editor, reported that Hanoi was indeed using a Sihanouk trail and that 'the movement of trucks on the route has been confirmed by American and other foreign observers.' " (Prince Norodom Sihanouk is Chief of State of Cambodia. The 'Sihanouk trail' has been responsible for heavy fighting along the Cambodian-South Vietnam border over the years in which many American lives have been lost.) *

"Salisbury also failed to emphasize that his casualty and damage statistics came, unverified, from Hanoi. Only near the end of his fifth dispatch did he casually write: 'It should be noted, incidentally, that all casualty estimates and statistics are those of North Vietnamese officials.' He also gave the impression that some

---

* U.S. News & World Report of Aug. 28, 1967, made the flat news statement:

"The U.S. may soon find itself forced to carry the war into Cambodian territory—from which the Communists have been operating against South Vietnam since the late 1950's. . . .

"American troops in the field have long had proof that the Vietnamese Communists were using Cambodia as a springboard for attacks . . .

"In the highlands, where frontiers of Cambodia, Laos and South Vietnam converge, there is what amounts to a North Vietnamese Army group consisting of two divisions—possibly four. . . .

"Now there is a more ominous development: growing evidence of Russian and Chinese arms reaching Vietnamese Communists through Cambodia's international ports. Despite camouflage and denials by Prince Norodom Sihanouk, Cambodia's erratic leader, Americans say there is no doubt now that the volume has reached such proportions as to pose a new threat to the whole American strategy of winning the war . . ."

Heavy fighting between Allied forces and North Vietnamese took place in South Vietnam along the Cambodian and Laotian borders soon after the publication of that report. In the Locninh fighting it seemed obvious that the enemy forces were coming from Cambodia and re-turning thereto when defeated. The New York Times stories did not report where the enemy troops came from. The casualties in that fighting were heavy on both sides. On the Allied side, chiefly American and South Vietnamese troops were involved.

Thus the Communist forces were using the same Manchurian-Korean tactics that had worked so well 15 years earlier. They counted upon the United States to treat the situation as if it did not exist. The ostrich, un-like the elephant, has nothing to forget.

of the most heavily bombed areas were of no military significance. Yet the Pentagon pointed out that Nam Dinh, for example, has four major targets: a big transshipment area for war materiel, a thermal power plant, petroleum-storage facilities and key rail links to the South. Even if Salisbury's report of 89 civilian deaths there is true, said the Defense Department's Arthur Sylvester, that would mean 'rather precise bombing,' considering that the U.S. has made 64 raids on the city.

"Salisbury also claimed that incessant bombing of Highway 1 and the rail line running parallel to it had scarcely interrupted traffic. A British newsman recently back from North Viet Nam reached just the opposite conclusion. 'Heavy American bombing has reduced all travel—road, rail and river—to a crawl, and then only by night,' wrote Norman Barrymaine in a recent *Look* article reprinted in Aviation Week. 'Highway 1 is so badly battered that peasants call it the 'Road of Bygone Days.' The 100-kilometer (62-mile) road journey from Haiphong to Hanoi can take three or even four days.'

"Perhaps the most stinging criticism of all came from Navy Commander Robert C. Mandeville, who recently returned to the U.S. after leading a squadron of Intruder jet attack bombers in frequent raids on Nam Dinh. 'Simply unbelievable,' he said of Salisbury's conclusion that the town had no really valuable military targets. For one thing, Mandeville pointed out, 100 antiaircraft batteries protect Nam Dinh, and 'the North Vietnamese don't waste their AA batteries—they only put them around stuff they want to protect.' The town, he said, was so 'ringed with fire' that 'nobody wanted to go to that place.'

"Salisbury's series also came under attack at the Times. In a 2,000-word front-page story at week's end, Military Editor Hanson Baldwin quoted U.S. military men as saying that Salisbury's estimates of civilian damage appeared to be 'grossly exaggerated.' Some casualties, they noted, are inevitable. Said one: 'You can't fight an immaculate war.' Defending Salisbury, Managing Editor Clifton Daniel said that 'in a place like that, you test the water with your toe. Obviously, where he has been permitted to go so far is to look at the bomb damage.'

"The implication was that Salisbury was getting little more than a guided—or misguided—tour. . . .

"Why did Hanoi open its doors to selected visitors? It obviously hoped that by controlling their movements they would get a view of U.S. bombing as inffectual against military targets and brutal against civilians."

Precisely. In other words, this was a propaganda move on the part of North Vietnam. The New York Times through its assistant managing editor, Mr. Salisbury, consciously or unconsciously found itself being used to arrange a fine mix of news, editorialism, propaganda and arm-twisting of President Johnson and/or other officials of the United States Government. It was a bold move both on the part of Hanoi and on the side of The Times, but it backfired. More persons than ever in the United States came to know what kind of foe the Americans and others are helping the South Vietnamese to fight. And more came to understand the lengths to which The New York Times management group is willing to go in order to retreat to a stalemate in the war.

Time magazine was not the only periodical to show irritation at The New York Times over this ploy. U.S. News & World Report and Barron's were among the weeklies to bristle at the Times reports. The Washington-based publication (U.S. News) carried a news report similar to that of Time. Barron's commented on the Salisbury dispatches:

"The widespread presumption that such military targets as rail lines, roads, bridges, truck terminals, and oil storage plants could be attacked without risk to civilians is simply naive. Harrison E. Salisbury of The New York Times, reporting from Hanoi that any such presumption was wrong, belabors the obvious. Another fact is that by locating anti-aircraft artillery and missile launchers in or near populated centers, the North Vietnamese government made these fortresses; gun emplacements are fair targets anywhere. . . . Bombing in North Vietnam differs little * from that in Europe and Asia during World War II. But history is easily forgotten, even by newspapers that helped record it a quarter-century ago."

The Washington Evening Star commented editorially:

"To suggest, as some appear to be doing, that the civilian casualties amount to a systematic slaughter of the innocents by the barbarous United States Government is to abandon fact and good faith and to embrace Hanoi's propaganda line with a passion that defies reason."

Two paragraphs on the "Washington Whispers" page of U.S. News & World Report of Jan. 9, 1967, are of interest:

"Bertrand Russell's 'Try the American War Criminals' group in London is 'clearing' American newspapermen who are getting visas to visit North Vietnam and describe bombing damage. Mr. Russell is one of the world's leading anti-Americans.

"Wilfred Burchett, Australian Communist newspaperman and leading Communist propagandist in Asia, is guiding and 'filling in' American newsmen being admitted to North Vietnam to tell the Communist story of destruction by American air power in war. The 'Burchett line,' appearing earlier in European papers for which he reports, is showing up in the American dispatches."

One of the most vigorous reactions to the Salisbury reports was that of Joseph Alsop, writing in his column in the New York World Journal Tribune of Jan. 9, 1967, under the heading: "STOP BOMBING TO GET TALKS . . . AND GET CLOBBERED." Mr. Alsop is forthright in his statement:

"The right way to look at the so-called mission of Harrison Salisbury is very simple indeed. Salisbury was invited to Hanoi to make propaganda for a proposal long pressed by the Soviets, and he accepted with apparent alacrity.

"As reported long ago in this space, an extraordinary campaign to persuade the U.S. Government to 'stop the bombing and

---

* Military men disagree. The pinpoint bombing against military targets in North Vietnam has no resemblance to the saturation bombing of civilian targets used by all sides in World War II.

get talks' was launched by Moscow late last summer. It was well orchestrated effort, participated in by just about every Soviet Ambassador all over the world, conspicuously including Anatoly Dobrynin here in Washington. Eastern European diplomats also joined in, en masse.

"The President and his advisers had the good sense to see this campaign for what it was—a blatant attempt to get something for nothing. They did not budge. The campaign petered out. Whereupon, by some strange chance, Hanoi made available to Salisbury the visa that had been refused before; and as the Hanoi leaders no doubt foresaw, the country was soon ringing with propaganda for 'stopping the bombing to get talks.'

"What Salisbury has seen on his guided tours; the propaganda figures (very belatedly acknowledged as such) that have been given him in Hanoi; even his interviews with Hanoi leaders—all this is of very little real interest. Whether an American reporter ought to go to an enemy capital to give the authority of his byline to enemy propaganda is indeed an interesting question."

It is, indeed, a question that ought not to arise, much less have to be answered. Yet unless the nation, the United States of America, becomes enlightened so as to understand the forces at work within and outside the country, much more embarrassing situations will arise.

One of the most astonishing things about the reactions abroad was the apparent unanimity of the thinking among British journalists that the American bombing was wrong and should be stopped. This recalls once again the simplicity of some American thinking before the first World War. The people of the Middle West, many of whom deemed themselves immune to—or at least far removed from—foreign problems, were believed to be rather largely opposed to American involvement in European wars. (There were no opinion polls in those days.) This feeling was greatly dissipated by the events of the Second World War, and especially with the invention of the atomic bomb and the development of supersonic jet planes and missiles that could cover the distance from Moscow to St. Louis in about 15 minutes. It was surprising to find the British so isolationist about the Vietnam War in view of their normal relationship with global matters and the fact that members of the Commonwealth, Australia and New Zealand, are fighting beside South Vietnam, the United States, South Korea, the Philippines and Thailand. No doubt there is a war-weariness in Britain caused by World War II and the enervating events that followed; they may also have some guilty feelings about their habitual night (blind) bombing of German cities during the war.

Actually there has been no end to the wars this generation has had to endure since 1939 and earlier. The Vietnam war is only a continuation of the Korean War by the same forces that carried it on—the Russians and the Chinese Communists. And before the Korean conflagration the Russians tested Europe for easy victories in Greece, Turkey and Iran, but finding the pickings rather tough the Soviet regime turned to Korea. Then came Lebanon and the Middle East, and all the while Indochina, where the war is now mostly narrowed to the region of North and South Vietnam, with part of the territories of Laos and Cambodia being used by the North Vietnamese aggressors, while Thailand is lending some of her territory for aerial operations and is also sending some troops to South Vietnam. Thailand makes no secret of the fact that she considers South Vietnam's war her own. Obviously, in the face of Red aggression, it would not do to follow the advice of timid British journalists, but rather that of the British Government, which supports the United States position in Vietnam.

Walter Lippmann entered the field involving the Salisbury articles when on Jan. 10, 1967, he defended the Times writer. Mr. Lippmann asserted in a column in the New York World Journal Tribune that Mr. Salisbury had done in North Vietnam exactly what other reporters do in Washington. Mr. Lippmann discounted the idea that this was a propaganda move by North Vietnam but suggested the Hanoi leaders now had peace talks in mind. All that was necessary to obtain peace was for the United States to remove its military positions on the mainland of Southeast Asia, including

Thailand as well as South Vietnam. Otherwise, he said, "the Asians will fight on." This is consistent with Mr. Lippmann's view that the war in Vietnam is a conflict between whites and Asians. He ignores the fact that more than 600,000 South Vietnamese, more than 40,000 South Koreans, and also Thais and Filipinos are ranged on the side of Saigon.

When Mr. Salisbury returned from North Vietnam he was wined and dined, put on numerous television shows, crowded with speaking engagements, awarded newspaper prizes and generally lionized. Later he was sent on assignment to Moscow.

The New York Times distinguished itself further in 1966 by publishing a sharp editorial attack upon Francis Cardinal Spellman, Archbishop of New York, who spent Christmas with the American troops in Vietnam, where he said:

"We do hope and pray we shall soon have the victory for which all of us in Vietnam and all over the world are praying and hoping, for less than victory is inconceivable."

In the Philippines on his way home, the Cardinal said to other American veterans of Vietnam:

"I believe that, in these circumstances, you are not only serving your country but you are serving God, because you are defending the cause of righteousness, the cause of civilization and God's cause."

Naturally that made The New York Times editors hopping mad; but, then, it may not be fair to say "The New York Times editors" because The Times is not a monolithic body of thought, even at the top. Hanson W. Baldwin, the military editor, would not think the same "unthinkable thoughts" as John B. Oakes, the Editorial Page Editor, a title that has been introduced since Charles Merz was Editor. Mr. Oakes presumably writes most of the editorials on Vietnam. C. L. Sulzberger, Chief European Correspondent of The Times, differs with Mr. Oakes on Vietnam, Cambodia and nearly everything else in the political affairs of the world, so far as is apparent. In fact, C. L. Sulzberger, who is a nephew of Arthur Hays Sulzberger, chairman of the board of The Times, and a cousin of Arthur Ochs Sulzberger, president and publisher of the paper, stands out among the writers on foreign affairs as a man of great discernment, judgment, independence and courage—that is to say, he understands that even in a rapidly shrinking, unifying and integrating world the United States has a right to expect of its citizens certain loyalties, cohesions and support in the face of totalitarian nations with a hard inner desire to dominate others. James Reston, Associate Editor, who, like C. L. Sulzberger, writes a column for the editorial page, thinks somewhat independently of the rest of the paper but is not so far from the center as C. L. Sulzberger, who is sui generis.

There is, however, sufficiently similar thought in The Times to color the editorials and the news play as well as the news itself to permit speaking of "the editors" as hopping mad, for if they did not all join in the reaction they ended up by supporting it. In this case the collective annoyance at Cardinal Spellman resulted in the editorial, "The Words of a Cardinal," on December 29, 1966, which read in part as follows:

"Cardinal Spellman had every right as an American citizen to express his feeling that anything 'less than victory is inconceivable' in Vietnam. When President Johnson was in South Vietnam briefly after the Manila conference last October, he put somewhat the same tough sentiment into equally unfortunate if more homely language in his now famous incitement to the American soldiers to 'be sure to come home with that coonskin on the wall.'

"One might say: two Americans, two patriots, two men of heart and feeling under a very special emotional impact—so why should they not speak this way? Yet the reasons are obvious: one is a political leader of a great nation the primary object [according to the Times] of which in this war is less a military victory than an honorable peace; the other is a man of the cloth with an exalted rank in a great church whose Pontiff has pleaded not for victory but for a negotiated 'peace in the freedom and justice.'

". . . . what the Cardinal said has shocked a great many people. It would have been possible for him to have comforted, inspired and encouraged young Americans enduring a cruel and often agonizing experience so far from home without calling for what amounts to total [heaven forbid!] victory.

"Most students of the war, as well as military and political leaders, accept the fact [opinion] that in this kind of war an old-fashioned 'victory' is simply not possible."

The last paragraph is nonsense. "Most students of the war" covers a great deal of territory. One wonders how The Times knows the opinions of "most students" and that they accept "the fact" that victory is impossible. Very probably, most students of warfare would argue that victory is *never* impossible.

When President Johnson returned in November, 1966, from the Manila conference and his trips to Vietnam and Korea, The New York Times asserted in an editorial:

"It was inescapable that the journey should have brought about a glorification of Lyndon B. Johnson as the leader of the world's most powerful nation. Mr. Johnson would have had to be less than human to preserve an equanimity and sophistication while statesmen flattered, and millions observed, and young Americans who are risking so much and fighting so bravely listened in rapt attention to their Commander in Chief.

"The temptation could not be resisted to make pep talks, to exalt and glorify the soldier over the politician—as Mr. Johnson did in Korea—to depict Communism as pure black [how about very dark gray?] and Western democracy as pure white, and always to preach that the United States will never yield and never stop fighting until Communist aggression has been defeated.

"Leaving aside any evaluation of these sentiments, [why?] the question is whether the practical and expressed purpose of the Asian trip—to further the cause of peace—was fulfilled. The United States today is more deeply committed than before to fight to the finish in Vietnam and to what Mr. Johnson called yesterday in Anchorage (Alaska) a firm anti-Communist stand in Asia."

Here The Times makes it obvious that it does not accept the idea that Communism is an unrelieved enemy. It is not "pure black," nor is "Western democracy pure white." Was Nazism "pure black"? Communism does not live under a legal system such as is honored in Western democracies. As a result millions have died in Russia and in Communist China without due process of law. In 1966 and 1967 the Red Guards in China, a large band of hooligans, conducted kangaroo courts and perpetrated violence on a large scale. Did the victims of the Red Guards have a chance to speculate on whether their oppressors were "all black"? They had no more opportunity—or very little more—than American soldiers, sailors and airmen in the middle of a battle action to ponder the question whether the enemy was all black or only three-quarters nasty. Bullets, shells, flack and missiles are impersonal representatives, harder to duck than Communism's evils are in Times editorials. Communism as a system, or lack of it, is wholly inferior and must seek to dominate the more orderly and more productive and powerful Western democracy force. It is not an accident that the Soviet Communist party leaders seek to enlist and to unify the Communists of the world to counterpoise their weight against that of the Western democracies. It is not an accident that a prominent Soviet Government official, Premier Alexei Kosygin, on January 5, 1967, expressed the hope that the Communist Chinese would come to their senses, as he put it, and put their house in order. Nor was it accidental that Leonid I. Brezhnev, the Soviet Communist party chairman, on October 15, 1966, called it "a strange and persistent delusion" of President Johnson's to hope for closer Soviet-American relations while the war in Vietnam continued. The Soviet formula for ending the war is complete defeat for the United States.

Since it is hardly a Soviet delusion that the United States might accept such, it can only be concluded that the Russians want to keep the war in Vietnam going in order to bleed the United States and to tie down as much military muscle there as possible. There may also be internal Russian reasons, and there may be world party reasons. The idea that Ho Chi Minh or Le Duan of North Vietnam decides whether or not to continue the war is half-true at best, since the war goes on only with Chinese and Russian arms. On the other hand, the North Vietnamese Communists would leave themselves exposed to a merciless enemy if they turned their backs on the Chinese and Russian Communists. And the North Vietnamese alone do not have the war-making industry to sustain the conflict without supplies from those who want to see them fighting.

This war was as surely carried to the Americans as if the North Vietnamese and the Communist Chinese and Russian collaborators had attacked farther to the east of Vietnam. It is not a question whether Communism is all black or not (and so far as this writer is concerned it could not be blacker). Nor, indeed, was it a question whether Nazism was all black or not, coal black as it was. The United States did not attack the Nazis or join with the British until after Pearl Harbor and after the Nazis declared war on the United States. The United States is not fighting in Vietnam on a purely ideological basis; so the matter of the relative negativism or evil of Communism is really beside the point. A nation fights to protect itself or its interests, which in a rapidly shrinking world are the same thing, though Vietnam may seem a faraway country about which we know little (we know a great deal about it now).

What did The New York Times expect the President to do on his trip to the Far East in a time of war, with hundreds of thousands of American servicemen in Vietnam and many others in the region? Was President Johnson expected to say to the men on the battlefield: "Gentlemen, there is much to be said on both sides."?

Mr. Salisbury showed a majestic neutrality in writing about American bombing of the Hanoi area. He wrote in a dispatch printed in The New York Times December 29, 1966:

"President Ho Chi Minh has warned the country that it must be prepared to face the destruction of both Hanoi and its port, Haiphong, as will all other cities or towns of any size. [Prëemptive propaganda—"we can take it, so why bother bombing?" Salisbury should have seen through it.]

"The new capital will probably be built in any case, since the present city is small, shabby and incredibly run down after more than 20 years of almost continuous warfare involving the French, the Japanese and now the Americans."

Thus Mr. Salisbury put his own countrymen in the same boat with the French and the Japanese, although the reasons for their presence in Vietnam were entirely different from those of the Americans. Moreover, the present Japanese Government favors the action of the Americans in Vietnam. The French were colonialists who milked Indochina as much as they could, with no announced intention by the end of World War II of ever giving self-government and independence to the three countries involved— Vietnam, Laos and Cambodia. The French eventually were defeated and forced out of the region. Some persons who ought to know assert that the French have never forgiven the Americans for doing what they could not do. John Mecklin in his book *Mission In Torment* (Doubleday, Garden City, N.Y., 1965) wrote on page 10:

"Once he had consolidated his position Diem quickly eliminated what remained of French political influence in Saigon. France's last days in Vietnam were deeply humiliating. The French never forgot. Officially, of course, they supported U.S. efforts to save the South, but many Americans in Saigon had a visceral feeling that emotionally the French wanted us also to fail. There was surely a suspicion of this in President de Gaulle's 1963 proposal to 'neutralize' Southeast Asia, which probably would mean its eventual loss to the Communists."

The French do not understand what the Americans are attempting to do, which is something they ought to want to understand, since it concerns them as well as other believers in democracy (and not merely Western democracy). The United States wants to see a strong, self-governing South Vietnam, free of interference from North Vietnam or Communist China or the Soviet Government. The United States granted independence to Cuba and the Philippines, without compulsion. The United States took no territory in Europe, while the Russians still hold all but one (Austria) of the countries they overran. The Japanese were not known as kind colonialists; nor did they establish free nations, and then leave the territories of their own volition. But no matter what the facts, the basic attitude of The New York Times makes it keep hammering at the United States and not at the enemy, which is North Vietnam, Communist China and the Soviet Government.

One investigation after another has proved that the Asian countries want the United States to continue its action in Vietnam. The United States Government has made its own tests on this matter time and again, once by Henry Cabot Lodge, who was twice Ambassador to South Vietnam. Carl T. Rowan, a highly trained student of public opinion and a newspaper columnist, wrote in his column for the New York World Journal Tribune of January 6, 1967, that President Ferdinand Marcos of the Philippines had told him that "the American military presence not only restrains Red China by forcing it to defend its own borders, but it has enabled other Asian countries 'to contain the subversive elements within our own jurisdictions.' " Mr. Rowan said Mr. Marcos "had summed up three of my most conclusive observations on this Asian tour:

"1. Talks with the prime ministers of Korea and Malaysia and the Foreign Minister of Indonesia, as well as the Marcos interview, showed that the fear of Communist China is far greater in Asia than most Americans realize. It is a fear manifest not only in international actions, but in almost psychotic distrust of, and brutal discrimination against, the Chinese residents of Southeast Asia.

"2. These outspoken advocates of a U.S. military presence in Asia are convinced that the Japanese, Indians and even the utterly neutral Burmese share their fears—of China, and of the possibility that the U.S. will give up the fight in Viet Nam and withdraw.

"3. The horrors of the Viet Nam war that arouse American and European sentiment or intellectual revulsion mean nothing to these Asian leaders. They figure their countries' independence, and their personal necks, are at stake, and the hard, practical question of how to preserve them is all that matters."

A similar report by Ambassador Lodge after a tour of the whole Far East to ascertain the opinions of the governments was printed as a small obscure story at the bottom of an inside page of The New York Times. If that newspaper had been of a different mind about resistance to Communism the story would have made an ideal leading story on page one. The Times plays up anything it regards as a peace possibility, which is, in brief, irresponsible, for it gives rise to false hopes and depressing letdowns.

Within South Vietnam the most evident mistreatment and misrepresentation of the news concerns the activities of Thich Tri Quang, one of the leaders of the Unified Buddhist Church. (Thich is an honorific meaning "Venerable." Hereafter, therefore, he will be referred to most often simply as Tri Quang, especially since he seems the least likely person one would want to venerate.) His case, of immense importance in the affairs of South Vietnam, illustrates the wisdom of remembering this fact: He did precisely what avowed enemies of the Saigon regime would have liked to be able to do in order to discredit, wreck and ruin the South Vietnamese Government—any government there. He kept the heat on South Vietnam and away from North Vietnam as far as he was able, whether by design or not. The fact is that North Vietnam is not discussed, dissected, analyzed, criticized, attacked and condemned for being weak, disorganized, cruel to its "Buddhists," a military dictatorship or a civilian dictatorship (whichever kind of government happens to be in power in South Vietnam). The New York Times has not in its news columns or editorially made a serious study of the regime in North Vietnam, but the heat stays on the South Vietnamese Government—and the United States—all year around. In virtually everything one says about The Times, however, there is at least one eminent exception, as previously mentioned, and that concerns the work of C. L. Sulzberger, who goes wherever the news takes him and writes what and as he pleases, and usually he is deliberately tweaking the noses of the editors of the editorial page or raking some piece of "news" from stem to stern. You can know that Cyrus Sulzberger is right from the internal evidence presented in his stories—from the logic and news sense in them.

When Tri Quang's mobs stormed the streets of Saigon or blocked thoroughfares of Hue and Danang with altars in order to overthrow the existing governments, while the country was engaged in a most terrible war, only the simplest, most superficial facts were presented in the newspapers. Readers in America were informed that while their men were fighting a pitiless foe in South Vietnam, a completely undisciplined populace was raising hell at the behest of a group of Buddhist monks whose religion was being basely persecuted by the current government. Sophisticated Americans and others—from diplomats to military officers to information men and newspaper correspondents—were taken in by the monk Tri Quang and his militant followers in the Unified Buddhist Church, with a reported total membership of one million in a total South Vietnam population of 16,000,000. It was not always or even generally noted in the news stories that of the one million adherents of the Unified Buddhist Church only 100,000 followed Tri Quang and that a number of them were Vietcong (Communist) infiltrators using Buddhist militants to help defeat South Vietnam.

Regardless of how heavily the Unified Church was infiltrated by the Communists, the story of how the militant monks kept the government, if not the country, in a state of turmoil for years is one of the most astonishing in the annals of foreign affairs involving the United States. For the Americans were so far deceived by Tri Quang that he was given sanctuary in the United States Embassy at Saigon from September through November, 1963. He later avowed to the late Marguerite Higgins that he intended to get the Americans out of the country. Miss Higgins, a magnificent reporter, wrote a superb book, *Our Vietnam Nightmare* (Harper & Row, 1965), in which she described an interview with Tri Quang.

"Buddhism" in South Vietnam has been a large and well-nigh unbelievable area of confusion for the people of other countries and especially Western countries. When The New York Times carried a story from Saigon as late as December 19, 1966, saying that there were "roughly one million followers of Thich Tri Quang —a minority among the country's 13 million Buddhists," one had to wonder whether The Times was seriously seeking to convey the facts about this remarkable troublemaker and about the "Buddhists." That Vietnam dispatch, incidentally, under a 5-column headline with a picture of Tri Quang, managed to tell the story of "the swift collapse of the Buddhist movement" without mentioning the word "Vietcong" and without giving the vaguest hint of what "political action" Tri Quang and his followers sought to take. It said his "luminous brown eyes terrified a succession of Saigon regimes," which may by accident have summed up the aims of this inscrutable character in the terrible drama of Vietnam. The story had no reason for existence beyond a nostalgic New York Times desire to remember a man who had gained so much space in its columns over the years. It recalled an earlier piece by C. L. Sulzberger, published in The Times of April 24, 1966, which began thus:

"SAIGON, April 22—The Vietcong sees it has a good thing going in the Annamite north of this country and is now feeding troops into that region either to undermine it militarily or to encourage separatist tendencies. These tendencies have been fanned by Venerable Tri Quang, chief among the activist Buddhist bonzes of South Vietnam.

"Tri Quang is now in his stronghold, the cities of Hue and Danang, and announces that he will stay there until this summer's elections. He has formed a virtually autonomous administration under local 'Struggle Committees.' The Danang 'Struggle Committee' at least is known to have been infiltrated by Vietcong agents."

Why is it that the reader did not find this information in a regular news dispatch about Tri Quang and his "Buddhists"?

Compared to that absence, it certainly is odd that Cyrus Sulzberger never comes away from his long journeys empty-handed. Even in this dispatch, or column, he provided a bundle of information sufficient to keep a reader wondering until some other enterprising and open-minded reporter picked up some more useable data. The Sulzberger column added this bit of solid news (which belonged on the front page of The Times):

"Tri Quang claims that Buddhism is a rival to Communism but there is a parallelism at least in their short-term aims here. During the past two decades Communism has often sought to use for its purposes the Buddhist renaissance which arose almost simultaneously in Asia. Peking originally sought to employ Buddhism as a tool of subversion abroad but its efforts were crude and unsuccessful. Hanoi has done better.

"When Ho Chi Minh took over North Vietnam in 1954, its Mahayana Buddhism was sharply hit and there are now believed to be only about 100,000 practicants in a population of some 17 million. However, a special divinity school was established in Hanoi to instruct bonzes destined for evangelical work in South Vietnam.

"There is certainly no real evidence that the Buddhist apparatus of the south is subject to Communist control. But there is real evidence that some of its adjuncts have been penetrated—as in the recent instance of the Danang 'Struggle Committee.'

"Buddhist activities have played a major role in overthrowing three Saigon governments and they are now out to topple a fourth. The propaganda apparatus of the bonzes is skillful and produces a signal effect on the foreign press. This, of course, suits the Vietcong.

"As long ago as September, 1964, a directive was captured ordering Communist cadres in Saigon to join Buddhist organizations and, before joining, to sever party links. They were instructed to urge anti-Government and anti-American demonstrations. Similar instructions were given this month to Vietcong agents intruded into Danang among the bonzes.

"It is reckoned some of the momentum will run out of Tri Quang's autonomous movement in Annam and that moderate Buddhists will join with Catholics, other sects, military officers and some intellectuals to establish a nationalist regime capable of fighting the war to a successful end."

Tri Quang was forcibly taken to Saigon in the spring of 1966 after his power had been broken by firm action on the part of the Ky Government, which did indeed benefit from the good sense of the people of all shades of religious belief in the cities and the region. It is a peculiar fact that the Tri Quang faction's enormous contribution of confusion in the affairs of South Vietnam perfectly paralleled the plans of the North Vietnam Communist regime and aggressor. Therefore the possibility that Tri Quang himself was a Communist sent from North Vietnam to mess up things in the South was discussed in Miss Higgins' book, *Our Vietnam Nightmare*. Unfortunately, the information given by C. L. Sulzberger on Communist infiltration was not to be found baldly stated in the news columns of The Times. Indeed, Tri Quang found the choicest space always waiting for his antics, usually with smiling pictures. He seemed to be happy in his work, which included sending many monks and nuns to fiery deaths and he threatened to induce many more to die before he was summarily stopped by Premier Ky. Tri Quang himself never threatened to commit suicide by immolation.

Miss Higgins showed superior professional initiative and industry in seeking out the facts in regard to the man who led the successful efforts to topple three governments of South Vietnam, including that of the powerful and controversial Ngo Dinh Diem, and who appeared to be on the verge of bringing about the downfall of the Ky Administration when the unscrupulous monk was finally brought to heel. Miss Higgins, an American who was born in Hong Kong, visited Vietnam nine times. She had a knowledge of that country going back to her infancy, since her parents had been advised to take her there—to Dalat, a central mountain resort—when she had malaria.

On May 8, 1963, eight persons were killed during a demonstration in the Tri Quang stronghold of Hue by "Buddhists." Quotation marks are used advisedly in view of the following development of the facts—or at least the factual events. This development establishes a fallacy—a far-reaching and fatal fallacy—that was pursued by the United States State Department, by American (and other) newspapers, especially The New York Times, which ought to have known better; by some Vietnamese, and by a multiplicity of other persons.

Miss Higgins wrote on page 3 of *Our Vietnam Nightmare* and following pages:

"As a State Department spokesman put it at the time: 'We told Diem from the very first that if he were not conciliatory, if he did *not admit the army's guilt* and fire those responsible for the killing at once, he would be in for it. But he would not take our advice. And so now we have a full-fledged religious crisis. The United States is getting a black eye all over the world because of Diem's repressions of the Buddhists. Diem's stubbornness has enabled the Buddhists to turn the incident—and their grievances—into the cause célèbre. And if you have the Buddhists against you, you have a majority of the Vietnamese people against you, and therefore the Buddhist agitation is bound to hurt the war effort.'

"Even though I knew that both precolonial and colonial Vietnam were overwhelmingly Confucian (which to the simple villager meant ancestor worship), I had no reason at the time to question this official's statement that 'the majority of Vietnamese are Buddhists.' Perhaps in recent decades the Buddhists had made enormous strides in propagating their faith. Further, in the summer of 1963 almost all news dispatches out of Saigon stated that seventy, even eighty to ninety, per cent of Vietnamese were Buddhists. . . .

"General Victor H. Krulak, of the U.S. Marine Corps, who brought a keen, incisive mind to the problems of counterinsurgency, told me that the Buddhist situation in Vietnam was *not* religious, but political. The Buddhists were not a majority of either the population or the army. The agitation in the cities was *not* affecting the war in the countryside, which had started going some-what better in the spring and summer than at any time since the American operations began in earnest in February, 1962.

"General Krulak's views on the Buddhist situation—which I discovered to be shared by many at the Pentagon, Central Intelligence Agency, and the White House—were quite opposite to the prevailing State Department line. . . .

"Back home was the inherent drama of a situation in which President Kennedy was persuaded to do things that signaled the overthrow and murder of Diem (quite probably he did not realize that his actions led inescapably to these tragic ends) even though his own Vice President—Lyndon B. Johnson—strenuously opposed the toppling of Diem for fear of political chaos and disintegration of the war effort.

"And then, almost three weeks to the day after the murder of Diem, the world shuddered at the assassination of John F. Kennedy. And it was Lyndon Johnson who was left to pick up the already rapidly crumbling pieces resulting from a policy on Vietnam that he had bitterly and vainly opposed."

It has to be remembered—even though it is hard to believe—that beneath the vast political earthquake that was the fall of Diem in South Vietnam lay the evil hand of Thich Tri Quang. Yet it appears that Miss Higgins was the only American newspaper correspondent who at the time went to a great deal of effort to discover who he was. Soon after she arrived in Saigon in the summer of 1963, Miss Higgins had an interview with Tri Quang, which, in part, she describes on page 25 and following pages, thus:

"At the Xa Loi (Pagoda), which was reverberating as usual to the hum of its indefatigable mimeograph machines, I passed rows of politely bowing monks in saffron robes and was ushered into the innermost sanctum. It was a small, cozily furnished room in the business wing of the Xa Loi.

"There sat a monk in his forties, wearing gray robes. Deep, burning eyes stared out from a gigantic forehead. He had an air of massive intelligence, total self-possession, and brooding suspicion.

"Thich Tri Quang was obsequiously introduced by a younger monk acting as interpreter. . . .

" 'You are accredited to the White House,' repeated the interpreter. 'And since you are only here for a short time (six weeks), we have a message for you to take back to President Kennedy.' . . .

"It was an extraordinary exchange, long, lasting two and a half hours, always intense, sometimes acrimonious. It began with Thich Tri Quang conducting a virtual interrogation about President Kennedy's views on President Diem, Russia, Buddhism, etc.

"Warily I referred Thich Tri Quang to President Kennedy's press conferences, copies of which I said the embassy would surely be glad to furnish.

" 'But in his last press conference,' Thich Tri Quang said, 'President Kennedy spoke too favorably of President Diem. . . . We had reason to believe that President Kennedy was on our side. And so we were puzzled.'

"While I was digesting this remarkable claim, Thich Tri Quang's voice slid smoothly on. 'Besides, it would be most unwise for President Kennedy to appear to be associated with Diem's actions. There will be, for example, many more self-immolations. Not just one or two, but ten, twenty, maybe fifty. President Kennedy should think about these things. For these events will blacken President Kennedy's reputation as well as Diem's. . . .'"

" 'Are you,' I asked with some heat, 'asking me to blackmail the President of the United States by passing on this threat?'

" 'Not at all,' said Thich Tri Quang. 'I am merely telling you what is going to happen.' . . .

"Who, I wanted to know, was Buddhism's candidate for President of Vietnam if [Tri Quang's] campaign against Diem should be successful?

"Thich Tri Quang replied, 'There are many others who could run South Vietnam. . . . after all, it is a fact that men close to President Diem have tried to get rid of him before. . . . they must have had someone in mind to take his place. . . .' [That statement is of signal importance, as subsequent events were to prove, for Tri Quang sought to overthrow every government that followed that of Diem.]

"The next question was whether continued friction between the Buddhists and the government might not soften up the country for a Communist takeover.

" 'It might help the Communists to victory,' conceded Thich Tri Quang.

" 'But,' I interjected, 'do you realize what would happen to the Buddhist religion if the Communists took over?'

" 'If the Communists take over,' said Thich Tri Quang, 'it will be Diem's fault, not ours. And besides,' he added, 'we cannot get an arrangement with the North until we get rid of Diem and Nhu [Diem's brother-in-law, who was murdered with him].'

"If I had known more about Thich Tri Quang, I might have been less taken aback by his massive indifference to the fight against the Communists.

"Even today Thich Tri Quang's past remains very much of a mystery.

"Why did he emerge as the dominant monk at the Tu Dam Pagoda at Hue? Nobody knows for sure—or will say. . . .

"According to records of the French colonial office, Thich Tri Quang was twice arrested for his dealings with Ho Chi Minh (the Communist leader of North Vietnam). By his own admission he served after 1945 with Communist front groups, working with Ho's Viet Minh Army.

"In a recent report [1965] sent to Washington based on conversations with Thich Tri Quang, our embassy in Saigon noted: 'Tri Quang himself has said that he acceded to Viet Minh "invitations" to collaborate with them in the 1940's and that in response to their demands he served "passively" as chairman of the United Vietnamese Association, which was controlled by the Viet Minh and was located near his home village in Quang Binh province.' The U.S. Embassy further noted that Thich Tri Quang claimed he was able to leave the Viet Minh-controlled province 'by a ruse.' Thich Tri Quang also for a time led a Communist-front Buddhist organization collaborating with Ho Chi Minh. But this has to be measured against the fact that many non-Communist Vietnamese worked with the Viet Minh prior to 1954, out of a patriotic desire to rid the country of the French colonialists. In any case, Thich Tri Quang claimed to have fallen out with the Communists since then.

"Thich Tri Quang is a disciple of Thich Tri Do, who is now in Hanoi as a leader of the Buddhist puppet organization there. Buddhism in North Vietnam operates of course by favor of and for the purposes of the Communist regime."

North Vietnam would not for five seconds have tolerated the demonstrations and the induced "self-immolations" that would be regarded as homicides in the United States. There are no such disorders in the North. The suicides of the monks and nuns of the militant wing of the Unified Buddhist Church were deliberate actions of the Tri Quang group. They were announced and often threatened in advance, for they were used as human sacrifices in a political course that virtually always coincided with Communist purposes but were never of any evident utility in the affairs of the South Vietnamese. Alleged final statements by the alleged suicides were issued immediately after death by the militant monks. These called upon the current government to commit some act of hara-kiri in compliance with the arcane aims of Tri Quang, who did not hesitate to disclose that he was most interested in knowing how foreign governments, especially the United States, reacted to the latest series of human sacrifices. Nor did he shrink from revealing his great disappointment when President Johnson said that suicide as a method of influencing national and international affairs would not be recognized by the Washington Government. This was a bitter blow to Tri Quang.

So far as can be ascertained, The New York Times never advocated that Tri Quang discourage the practice; nor, indeed, did The Times editorially take a vigorous position against him. On the contrary, during the last months in the life of President Ngo Dinh

Diem, when Tri Quang was mounting an especially fierce campaign against the head of the country, The Times took the attitude that President Diem was persecuting "the Buddhists." True, at that time The Times was no more wrong than nearly everybody else, but The Times wants to be thought of as the greatest newspaper in the world. It is not the function of a newspaper to be in error in matters like this, but when the mistake becomes evident, surely it is the business of the paper to correct it.

On this head, The Times published a story on August 3, 1964, that is relevant. It said that Secretary of State Dean Rusk had asserted "that the purpose of United States foreign policy must be to win a 'worldwide victory for peace and freedom,' but 'without a great war if possible' and without a 'military orgy.' "

"He emphasized," the story said, "that the Administration of President Johnson had no illusions about Communist aims. 'No one has to convince us that the contest between freedom and Communist imperialism is for keeps,' he said."

The effort to "build bridges" to "Communist imperialism" does not seem to fit into that statement except on a broad basis of keeping the record straight, but at least the assertion that "no one has to convince us" was made. Mr. Rusk recognized that when the nation or a group of them is dealing with Communist imperialism at the front end of a missile or a mortar shell it is useless to argue whether it is all black. On the contrary, this period is more appropriate for the position taken by Alice Widener in the magazine U.S.A. on March 18, 1966, under the heading: "Needed: A Vietnam War Home Front." In that article Mrs. Widener quoted words from another statement by Secretary Rusk in which he said: "A certain kind of liberalism is jaded and cynical. Don't ask me to call a man a liberal who wants to turn over to a totalitarian regime more than 14 million South Vietnamese."

Mrs. Widener's remarks are so eminently sound, there would seem to be no controversy at all involved in them. Yet no one would expect to see them in The New York Times editorial pages. Mrs. Widener wrote:

"In every war the United States has fought abroad within living memory, there was a nationwide organized home front of volunteer civilians for moral support and material help to our fighting men and to our wounded.

"Today, in the Vietnam War, are we so sick with subversion that the only nationwide organized home front we can produce on the American scene is the beatnik, Vietnik, churchnik, peacenik front?

"I, for one, do not believe it. Probably, most Americans are unaware of our true situation, though why this should be so is a mystery, since almost everyone knows we have more than 235,000 [Some 540,000 by 1968] GI's in Vietnam and our service hospitals there and at home are crowded now with hurt, sick and lonesome soldiers, marines, sailors and airmen urgently needing warmhearted, solicitous civilian attention.

"During a visit this month to Walter Reed Army Medical Center, Washington, D.C., I had a personal talk with each of the 93 amputees then in Wards 34 and 35.

"Are we sicker than they?

"This is the question that haunts me.

"From a pillow on a bed in Ward 35, a 19-year-old GI just back from the Vietnam War without his right arm and legs looked up at me with eyes as blue as his pajamas. 'They call this a limited war,' he said drily, without any bitterness. 'What's limited about it?'

"An officer at Walter Reed Hospital asked the same question in a different way. 'Are we or aren't we in a war?' he said quietly. 'If we aren't, then why is this hospital choked up with our wounded? If we are, then why aren't our civilians backing up our fighting men with everything they've got?'

"Why aren't we?"

Mrs. Widener had an answer for this attitude in our times, as follows:

"The best explanation, I believe, lies in the intellectual influence which Marxists have been able to exert in our communications media. Recently, the present situation was clearly set forth by

Professor Eugene Genovese of Rutgers University, who retained his post there after he had publicly welcomed the idea of a Vietcong victory. At a forum held last month at the Riverside Plaza Hotel in New York City, under the auspices of the National Guardian, Genovese said that to achieve a Marxist revolution in the United States, the Leftwing intelligentsia must gain 'cultural hegemony.' He expressed optimism about their being well on the way, and said this is why there exists now in our country 'the necessity for open advocacy of socialism.'

"Hegemony is preponderant authority.

"In any society over which Marxists exert cultural hegemony, freedom of speech—so abused by Genovese and his ilk—does not exist, as was evidenced lately by the sentencing to hard labor in prison camps of two Soviet writers critical of the Moscow regime.

"This month, Secretary of State Dean Rusk exposed the true position of the so-called 'liberals' in our nation, when he told a Columbia University history professor that our American 'liberal intellectuals' have always made a distinction between Fascism on the one hand and Marxism on the other, with respect to the intensity of their feelings. 'They are more concerned with the Hitler type of problem,' said Secretary Rusk.

"Then he heaped scorn on the 'jaded and cynical' pseudo-liberals. They deserve it, for they are unwilling to denounce any political crimes except Nazi crimes. The Marxists' crimes—whose number of innocent victims far exceeds, within Red China alone, that of the Nazis—are excused by the jaded, cynical 'liberals,' or rationalized away or condoned as justifiable steps towards Marxist 'social progress.' Their unwillingness to point an accusing finger at any Marxist, no matter what he does, was extended even to Marxist Lee Harvey Oswald, assassin of President Kennedy."

The flaccid atmosphere in regard to the Vietnam War at home and the fumbling nature of many of the moves in Vietnam, some of which are as much the fault of South Vietnamese as Americans, have been terribly costly. By "costly," human lives are meant, not funds or materiel. True, every time the United States has stepped up ("escalated" is the invidious word) the pressure upon the aggressors in South and North Vietnam, the North Vietnamese and their Communist allies have matched the new moves. We have the word of Sir Robert Thompson, who was the British Adviser to South Vietnam from Malaysia and an authority on guerrilla warfare, that the North Vietnamese "had it made by the summer of 1965" but for the decision of the United States to send a large number of troops to save the situation for South Vietnam. Sir Robert spoke at the Overseas Press Club in New York in the autumn of 1966. It was a moving as well as immensely revealing address on Vietnam, where the former Malaysian Defense Minister had been serving for years before he became associated with the RAND Corporation. There was no mention of the address in The New York Times.

The confused and even befuddled nature of the free world's response to creeping Communist expansion in places far from the West was set forth by the brilliant Miss Higgins in a passage in her book. Here, with the wisdom of hindsight that is rare in some parts of the press, she admitted holding up her own great exclusive story for six weeks. Here are her words on page 32 and following pages:

"The Americans were not the only ones played for a fool by Thich Tri Quang.

"President Diem first began to make inquiries in depth about Thich Tri Quang in midsummer, 1963, when his insurrectionary activities had begun to alarm the government. Diem turned first to his brother, Ngo Dinh Can, who served as a kind of overlord of Central Vietnam, where Thich Tri Quang made his headquarters.

"Ngo Dinh Can's initial response to President Diem was to tell him not to worry. As President Diem recounted the episode to me, Ngo Dinh Can expressed complete confidence in his ability to 'handle' Thich Tri Quang.

" 'I have done him many favors,' Ngo Dinh Can was reported as saying. 'Therefore I feel he will be responsive to my counsel.'

"As it turned out, Ngo Dinh Can paid with his life for his inability 'to handle' Thich Tri Quang. After the *coup d'etat* it was Thich Tri Quang who led the pack in demanding Ngo Dinh Can's death by the firing squad.

"Gratitude is not one of Thich Tri Quang's strong suits. The Americans who had granted him asylum were disconcerted, for example, to find him in the forefront of the anti-American campaign. Soon after his departure from his U.S. asylum, his disciples in Central Vietnam even went so far as to accuse Americans of persecuting Buddhism.

"His contempt for Americans appears complete. A staff member of the Saigon *Post* reports a conversation in which Thich Tri Quang said: 'With the Americans, it is not so interesting any more. They are too easy to outwit. . . . some of them persist in thinking they can 'reform' me into agreeing with them. . . . It is useful to smile sometimes and let them think so. . . . We will use Americans to help us get rid of Americans. . . .'

"It seems strangely unreal, looking back on the summer of 1963, that anybody could have been still in doubt about short-term Buddhist aims.

" 'What do the Buddhists want?' I wrote at the end of my Vietnam tour. 'What they want is Diem's head, and not on a silver platter but wrapped in an American flag.'

"What I most certainly did not foresee that 'Diem's head, wrapped in an American flag,' was precisely what the Buddhists would get.

"As I emerged from the Xa Loi Pagoda, it was clear to me that Thich Tri Quang was hungry for power, exhilarated by the world's attention, and supremely confident of getting his way.

"I remember at one point saying, 'But if I repeat some of these things you are telling me, it could hurt you.'

" 'That is not possible,' said Thich Tri Quang, 'because nobody will believe you.'

"And he was quite right.

"In late August, 1963, I did print the key points of what he said, and few Americans believed me. Thich Tri Quang understood the automatic reflexes of Western opinion very well. The horrors of the self-immolation were such as to put world opinion automatically on the side of those from whose ranks the suicides came.

'Any suggestion that a few ambitious Vietnamese in Buddhist monks' clothing might deliberately incite their disciples to suicide for their own political ends and in defiance of the true state of affairs was simply beyond credulity in those days and in that atmosphere.

"But Thich Tri Quang was perfectly candid about what he was doing. When I asked him about the ethics of sending people off to fiery deaths for political purposes he merely shrugged his shoulders and said that 'in a revolution many things must be done.'

"Why did I wait six weeks to print the extraordinary story of this monk? It is a good question, because the delay was a mistake if conveying a realistic portrait of the extremist Buddhist to the American people was important. In July the United States had not yet made its decision to dump Diem. Perhaps even a minority report in a paper like the New York *Herald Tribune* would have stirred up a few doubts in those who automatically assumed that the Buddhist politico priests were totally in the right and Diem totally in the wrong.

"It was probably unfortunate that the confrontation with Thich Tri Quang took place on the third day of my midsummer visit in 1963. At that point I was still being mentally whipsawed by the confusing and conflicting versions in the U.S. government and the U.S. press about what was going on in Vietnam. And in all my U.S. briefings nobody had ever dropped a word about Thich Tri Quang. Indeed, as I left the Xa Loi Pagoda, I actually had doubts whether to take this monk seriously. Was he really, as his obsequious subordinate had said, the real power behind the Buddhist agitation? And what was to be made of his icily cool manner as he talked of 'ten, forty, fifty' horrifying suicides? Wasn't there a quality of madness here? There wasn't time that evening to test my impressions on embassy officials, for I was leaving at dawn for the fighting fronts. But the truth is that I, like many Americans, greatly underestimated Thich Tri Quang for a long, long time.

"In any case, by September the message I finally conveyed to President Kennedy about Thich Tri Quang was far different from what the monk intended. Instead of passing on his piece of blackmail concerning self-immolations and the Kennedy image, I tried at the White House to convey some of my own forebodings about these extremist Buddhists that had crystallized, finally, during my fact-finding tour of Vietnam. I think I made another mistake. If I had simply passed on the blackmail, it would have had more effect —if anything could by that time.

"It is clear that Thich Tri Quang understood the forces at play in the world at that time far better than I did. For even when I left Vietnam that summer I did not share Thich Tri Quang's conviction that the United States would take his side in the battle against Diem.

"But I was wrong."

I have taken the liberty of quoting Miss Higgins at such length because I regard her as the most perceptive journalistic observer that America has sent to Vietnam. This magnificent witness contracted an Asian disease from which she died at the age of 45 in January, 1966, leaving her husband, General William Hall, and two children. *Our Vietnam Nightmare* is suggested reading for all who wish to strengthen their background knowledge of Vietnam.

How many Americans (or others) know that those poor South Vietnamese monks and nuns who were induced to commit suicide were greatly assisted in their action? Others obligingly poured gasoline over them and sometimes applied the match. That made the action a form of homicide, not suicide. Two pills were supplied to each of the victims to reduce the excruciating pain of death by fire. The pills were found to be worthless. It is all but impossible to believe that the man who boasted and prated about these "suicides" was given sanctuary in the United States Embassy in Saigon for more than two months. Secretary of Defense Robert S. McNamara commented in the spring of 1965: "Thich Tri Quang has made serious trouble for us before and he will again. Perhaps the greatest mistake we made was when we gave Thich Tri Quang asylum at the U.S. Embassy."

After that the troublesome monk was feared more both by Americans and South Vietnamese leaders, most of whom regarded him as nearly untouchable, and so he was able to carry on his work of spreading confusion and mayhem on a broader and more sustained scale. Although United States military chiefs in Vietnam denied that his antics really seriously slowed the war effort, they certainly did not help it. His supreme indifference to the lack-logic of his position and the increasing vigor of his baffling efforts to unseat governments made the question of his reasoning powers a pertinent one. If he had a death wish he was not going to satisfy it by the method he supplied to some of his religious colleagues. He fasted, but not unto death.

There is a striking parallel between the suicides in South Vietnam and the calling in of foreign correspondents to North Vietnam to witness the alleged damage and to hear figures of alleged killings of civilians by American aerial bombs. The strange logic that assigns the guilt in a suicide to some one else is also present in the exhibition of ruined population centers. (They could have been hit by North Vietnamese antiaircraft shells.) Assuming that all the damage was done by American bombing, can one not reasonably ask why North Vietnam does not call a halt by agreeing to cease its aggression in the South and make peace? That, however, would be giving something for something. Apparently the North Vietnamese are finding it less easy to outwit Americans now than previously. Tri Quang complained that it was so easy that it was hardly amusing any longer. Thus, since there are always compensations, the North Vietnamese must find some attractions in the failure to enlist the United States in its own defeat. With Tri Quang, however, the *comedia e finita.* He wouldn't even see a New York Times correspondent in December, 1966, when one put a note under his door at his retreat from so many victories.

CHAPTER VII

More On The Times and the Vietnam War

• • •

NEWS DISPATCH TO THE NEW YORK TIMES: *"Saigon, April 20 (1966)—Some American officials hope to persuade Premier Nguyen Cao Ky to bring his rival, Lieut. Gen. Nguyen Chanh Thi, back into the South Vietnamese Government in a high post.*

"Informed sources said these officials hoped that through a reconciliation, Premier Ky and General Thi could prevent Buddhist elements led by the monk Thich Tri Quang from gaining control of South Vietnam.

"Other American officials privately regard the plan as almost totally unrealistic.

"Moreover, these officials said they believed that the United States must begin to accommodate itself to new political realities in South Vietnam, including the possibility of a government dominated by Thich Tri Quang."—From a special dispatch to The Times of April 21, 1966.

U.S. NEWS & WORLD REPORT: *"Military men suggest that the Communists have been trying out the so-called 'Pavlov principle' on the U.S. people, the reflex Pavlov (Russian scientist) developed on dogs, with the bait of something for which they hunger intensely—in this instance peace—and you can reduce their minds to pulp, readily manipulated and controlled.*

"So far it hasn't worked. Public pressure in U.S. is to get the war won."—February 20, 1967.

TIME *magazine: "Administration Democrats dismissed the proliferating anti-Johnson groups with bored shrugs. A White House staffer scoffed: 'All it takes is two people with a mimeograph machine and the cooperation of The New York Times. It looks like a movement, but the moment you touch it, it dissolves into thin mist.' Wyoming's Democratic Senator Gale McGee urged Johnson to put purely political considerations behind him and concentrate on winning the war. 'The issue is so critical that if I were in a position to talk to the President,' said McGee, 'it would be with the suggestion that he be prepared to lose, if necessary, on Eastern Asia, rather than tack with the political winds.' "—October 6, 1967.*

U.S. NEWS & WORLD REPORT: *"SAIGON—The toll of civilians in the Vietnam war is on the rise—chiefly from Viet Cong terrorist attacks.*

"In the week ended February 4, before the truce for the lunar new year, 34 South Vietnamese civilians were killed, 55 wounded and 131 abducted—a total of 220. The previous week's toll had been 122.

"Those killed by the Viet Cong included two members of the national police, four hamlet chiefs, a Buddhist leader, two hamlet officials and two relatives of hamlet chiefs.

"In one recent example of guerrilla terrorism in the South, five Viet Cong assassinated the school teacher of Quang Tin village.

"Viet Cong assassinations have averaged about 1,700 a year since 1962, far more than the few hundred North Vietnamese civilians killed accidentally in two years of U.S. bombing of the North."—February 20, 1967.

ARTHUR M. SCHLESINGER JR. in THE BITTER HER- ITAGE (*Houghton Mifflin, Boston, 1967*): *"The Vietnam War is just as frustrating as the Korean War and a good deal harder for most people to understand. The Korean War, after all, was a clear- cut case of invasion across frontiers; it entirely lacked the dimen- sion of internal revolt which gives the struggle in Vietnam its peculiar difficulties. Moreover, the United States fought in Korea as the representative of the United Nations with the unqualified blessing of most of the world, while today we fight in Vietnam substantially alone. Then we had a relatively stable local govern- ment as our partner in Seoul as against the parade of regimes in recent years in Saigon, many engaged in warfare against their own people. And then communism still seemed a united and mortal world threat, demanding the most urgent response—while today, as it degenerates into a scramble of warring tongs, it is losing its power and its momentum."*

GENERAL HAROLD K. JOHNSON, United States Army Chief of Staff: "The insurgencies in Malaya and Vietnam are very sophisticated wars. Every conceivable facet of human life and en- deavor and every function and agency of government have been taken under attack by every available means. Those wars are a blend of intense, political, economic, socio-psychological, and military activities—a blend conceived, practiced, and finally put into operation by experts. The result is total war, war more total in its effect on people than any ever fought before. . . .

"One of the key strategies of insurgency, or 'wars of national liberation,' is initially to create a disorder which can later be ex- ploited, penetrating every institution to the maximum degree pos- sible to promote confusion, disagreement, and uncertainty. The counterinsurgent's task is to maintain the established order while in fact waging war against the insurgents who are spread among the population. The counterinsurgent is thus constrained against the use of force which would normally be acceptable against a completely hostile population."—From General Johnson's Fore-

word (*February, 1966*) *to* THE LONG, LONG WAR, *by Brigadier Richard L. Clutterbuck (Frederick A. Praeger, New York, 1966).*

BRIGADIER RICHARD L.. CLUTTERBUCK: *"It needs only half a dozen dedicated clandestine Communists to provide the nucleus—the masses' executives—for a village organization. These half dozen will undoubtedly exist in almost every Malayan Chinese village, just as they do in other communities all over the world. For the time being, they are probably doing little more than keeping contact with each other, and doing some quiet work in front organizations; they will also be maintaining lists of potential supporters and targets for blackmail and subversion. They are well experienced in leadership, exploitation, and coercion, and they could quickly recruit a substantial masses organization if Chin Peng (head of the Malayan Communist party) were to need it.*

"Nevertheless, I believe that such an organization would be hard put to survive—anyway for some years to come—because the Chinese villagers remember the price that they and their families had to pay for guerrilla warfare (in Malaya) in the 1950's, and most of them will not want to see it start again."—From THE LONG, LONG WAR, *cited above.*

EDWARD HUNTER: *"Hanoi would be stupid to give up, for we have guaranteed as clearly as any government could that we do not intend to dislodge the communists from power in North Viet Nam. Indeed, we have pledged that it cannot lose, that at the worst we will pour American money into North Viet Nam to rebuild and strengthen it for the next try. Ho [Chi Minh] knows he faces either a stalemate or victory, whereas we have given ourselves the choice between a stalemate and defeat. Would any aggressor in his right mind cease fighting under such rosy conditions? This is the basic contradiction in our policy of negotiations without victory. It is the suicidal logic of the no-win policy."—From the magazine* Tactics *of March 20, 1967.*

THE INSIDER, in TACTICS magazine: "The supposedly 'modern' approach to newsgathering can be seen more vividly inside the State Department (of the United States) than anywhere else, for it is our most important policy-making agency. Its policy is anti-anti-communist, in opposition to anti-communism, which it opposes as 'right-wing-extremism.' Yet many in the State Department do not feel this way. Certainly the more experienced, older professionals are anti-communist, but the later, more recent wave of recruits are aggressively anti-anti-communist. These are the ones who consider news management as an inherent right of government. . . .

"The routine of news dissemination as seen from the inside is immensely more complex than the public realizes, more so than most newspapermen suspect. People take for granted, for instance, that the object of releasing a story is to have it published and read by the public at large. Actually, this may not be the intent at all. The originator of the news item may be utterly unconcerned over whether it is noticed by the public at all. The item might have been released for the benefit of only one reader. This is frequently the case where the N.Y. Times, Washington Post and the Baltimore Sun are concerned.

"The single reader for whom the news release is prepared is the President of the United States. This expedient is resorted to on numerous occasions when there is little likelihood of a fact or an idea reaching the Chief Executive 'through channels.' . .

"Often, an article may be leaked for its impact on members of Congress, when protocol prevents it from being brought directly to their attention. The originator of the item is concealed this way, too.

"Practically all political advertising in political campaigns, on the issues of the day as distinguished from advertising in political campaigns, appears in the N.Y. Times or the Washington Post, for the same reason. The President is sure to see it. . . . the intent is to snowball the President on an issue. The fake 'liberal' Eastern

Establishment resorts to this ruse quite often, as do the pro-reds generally. The avalanche of anti-Vietnam war advertising in these papers obviously was part of the worldwide, psychological warfare campaign of the enemy. The expectation was that the President would obtain a wholly exaggerated idea of the self-styled pacifist movement, that actually was part of the military action in communist-style guerilla warfare."—From the Tactics *issue of March 20, 1967.*

FRED SPARKS *in New York World Journal Tribune: "MOSCOW—First, it is important for American readers to understand that in the Communist world Sen. (Robert F.) Kennedy is the most popular and oft-quoted American public figure, and that the New York Times is the most respected and often-quoted journal.*

"A noted Soviet journalist, Eugene Poznyakov, said: 'When The Times opposes the war in Viet Nam, that means most intelligent Americans oppose it.'

"The recent reportorial adventure in Hanoi of Harrison Salisbury, a Times correspondent, was closely followed by the Soviet leadership. Salisbury reported that American bombs had demolished civilian areas and this was echoed on television and reprinted from Leningrad to Vladivostok with editorial delight.

" 'An American,' cried one commentator, 'has proven that Americans are barbarians.' "—From a Moscow dispatch printed March 1, 1967.

NEWS STORY *in The New York Times: "Harrison E. Salisbury of The New York Times, Ramparts magazine and Murray Kempton of The New York Post are among the winners of annual George Polk Memorial Awards in journalism announced yesterday by Long Island University. . .*

"The awards for excellence in journalism are a memorial to George Polk, a correspondent [a vigorous anti-Communist] for

the Columbia Broadcasting Company who was killed in Greece [by Communists] in 1948 . . .

"Mr. Salisbury, an assistant managing editor of The Times, was given the foreign-reporting award for a 'pioneering news mission' to North Vietnam in December and January that 'contributed a new dimension to coverage of the Vietnam War.'

"Ramparts magazine, a monthly published in San Francisco, was chosen for the magazine reporting award for its 'explosive revival of the great muckraking tradition.' The (March) issue of Ramparts, for example, described the Central Intelligence Agency's undercover relationship with the National Student Association."—March 1, 1967.

Mr. Salisbury was also awarded a prize of $500 *"for outstanding achievement in mass communications at the annual Sidney Hillman Foundation awards,"* according to the Bulletin of the Overseas Press Club of America for May 27, 1967. He narrowly missed receiving a Pulitzer Prize.

CARL T. ROWAN: Washington—A few days ago a brief, cryptic report out of Prague, Czechoslovakia, was passed among a handful of top officials in Washington.

"It said that an editor of Ramparts Magazine had come to Prague and held 'a long, secret session' with officers of the Communist-controlled International Union of Students.

"Ramparts is the magazine that exposed the fact that the Central Intelligence Agency has been financing the National Students Association, which in turn has worked for several years to prevent the IUS from dominating the youth of the world.

"The Prague report aroused deep suspicions here among officials who are privately shocked and dismayed at the damage to the CIA and to U.S. foreign policy interests caused by the endless series of busted intelligence 'covers' that has resulted from the Ramparts' expose. . . .

"I learned that the Prague visitor was supposed to be Robert

Scheer, Ramparts' managing editor. I telephoned him in San Francisco and asked if he had met with IUS officers in Prague a couple of weeks ago.

" 'Yes,' he said. 'How did you know?'

"I failed to reply, and he went on to volunteer that he had spent two days meeting with representatives of the National Liberation Front, political arm of the Communist Viet Cong in South Viet Nam, and with IUS leaders.

"Scheer hedged for a while when asked who controls the IUS, but finally said, 'It is essentially an organ of the foreign policy of the Soviet Union.'

" 'Look,' Scheer continued, 'I went to the IUS headquarters strictly for journalistic reasons. I was in Europe doing a piece for Ramparts on Bertrand Russell [the 94-year old British philosopher who fostered a Viet Nam "war crimes tribunal" of President Johnson] so I just went to Prague to check the international implications of our article on the NSA.'

"Until proof of something else is presented, I have to assume that Scheer went to Prague on a journalistic mission.

"But Scheer and Ramparts have intensified America's mood of suspicion. Before the suspicion fades, Ramparts may find it desirable to reveal who has provided the estimated million and a half dollars the magazine will have lost by the end of this year. And Scheer may have more to say about his mission to Prague.

"That might lay to rest the rumors that Ramparts is not only a muckraker, but a muckraker with a malevolent motive."—*From Mr. Rowan's column in the New York World Journal Tribune, Feb. 24, 1967.*

ALICE WIDENER: *"Fortunately for politically innocent Americans, the truth always comes out, but regrettably it sometimes comes very late. Thus the facts brought out by American intelligence concerning the ugly use of Communist statistics about alleged North Vietnamese civilian casualties of U.S. bombings at the city of Nam Dinh in an article by Harrison Salisbury of The New York Times—first U.S. newsman admitted in that enemy land in recent years—confirm what I myself heard about him on the evenings of April 13 and April 20, 1956, at American Socialist Forum meetings, 229 Seventh Avenue, New York City.*

"At the April 13 meeting—held to brief Leftist radicals on the significance of the 20th Congress of the Communist party Soviet Union—the main speaker, notorious radical Milton Zaslow, held up before the audience clippings of New York Times articles by Harrison Salisbury and praised them as having 'the correct line.' . . .

"At the American Socialist Forum meeting on April 20, 1956, the discussion wasn't about the Soviet internal situation, it was about the world situation and the 'capitalist United States.' Here is a verbatim quote of what I reported in my U.S.A. Magazine about Zaslow's briefing:

" 'Zaslow cleared his throat, held up a copy of the New York Times and said: "Before I forget, I want to call your attention to Harrison Salisbury's story today. It's right here on the front page. Don't miss it. I can assure you, it's entirely correct. A fine piece."

" 'It happened I had read the piece which Mr. Salisbury says is based on "information from Moscow" and "reports on the Soviet situation" now being assessed in Washington "by official experts as part of a general scrutiny of the new Soviet picture." He wrote that "the Soviet system of collective leadership (Khrushchev, Bulganin & Company) is working smoothly and well." '

"That was exactly what the Communist party Soviet Union wanted the outside world to believe. . . .

"To show the nature of Milton Zaslow's total adherence to the CP line and thus gauge what his recommendation of Harrison Salisbury's article as being 'the correct line' evidently signified, I then quoted in my magazine all of Zaslow's concluding remarks at the American Socialist Forum meeting. Zaslow said: 'As the 20th Congress (CPSU) pointed out, war is not inevitable. It is entirely possible to achieve a worldwide triumph of Socialism without war.

It all depends on the capitalists. Inevitably, of course, the Socialist World and the Capitalist World must clash. That is, unless the Capitalist World will surrender without a suicidal struggle.'

"Fellow Americans: Our nation is now engaged in a bitter, bloody struggle with the Socialist World in Vietnam. The enemy's objective is to achieve our American surrender and to mobilize public opinion throughout the world against our American military effort in behalf of freedom. The New York Times *article by Harrison Salisbury on North Vietnam casualties in Nam Dinh as alleged results of U.S. bombings has been proved by American intelligence to be based on enemy statistics furnished by the North Vietnamese Ambassador to Moscow on November 16, 1966—weeks before Harrison Salisbury used them in his article.*

"Evidently, Harrison Salisbury is still following what Leftist radicals applauded in 1956 as 'the correct line.' "—From Mrs. Widener's newspaper column distributed by U.S.A. Syndicate and published by U.S.A. magazine December 31, 1966.

"ARTHUR SYLVESTER as Pentagon spokesman in January, 1967, 'even went so far as to break the practically inviolable rule of the N.Y. Times never to use the word 'communist' or 'communism' in an unflattering way to the reds, except when absolutely unavoidable, or just 'for the record.' Obviously, Sylvester had had his fill, for the nonce, of such Machiavellianism.

"The specific case that turned Sylvester's stomach was slantedly 'objective' reporting from the enemy capital of Hanoi by Harrison Salisbury for the N.Y. Times, and through it for the important chain of newspapers served by its syndicate. Sylvester said he was shocked when the N.Y. Times 'published communist propaganda statistics concerning alleged civilian casualties on its front page, without attribution of any kind.' He also said 'the American public and the world was misinformed by Communist propagandists who cleverly took in The Times—lock, stock and barrel." —From the magazine TACTICS, February 20, 1967.

"THE BRITISH are pressing U.S. strongly to stay in South Vietnam, even if holding on means a bigger war there, on the ground that a U.S. defeat, or even a negotiated settlement, would upset the balance of power in much of Asia."—"Washington Whispers," in U.S. News & World Report, February 8, 1965.

THE INSIDER, in TACTICS magazine: "The American people must gear themselves for more humiliations, more defeats, and ever-mounting casualty lists of American troops, until our Administration is brought to recognize the reality of this integrated, centrally directed communist program for conquest, in which the red guerrilla forces constitute only one factor, with the disguised regular red forces the main element. Our policy must adapt itself to this actuality. A no-win policy, as presently followed, cannot fill the gap, for the enemy insists on our defeat. There is no alternative to victory."—From an article, "3-Phase War in Viet Nam," in TACTICS of February 20, 1967.

MARGUERITE HIGGINS in OUR VIETNAM NIGHTMARE (Harper & Row, 1965): "I extend thanks to the thousands of soldiers, sailors, airmen and marines—both American and Vietnamese—who have paused over the years to answer my questions. Finally, I am indebted to the specialist fourth class from Pleasantville, New York, who in a letter from Vietnam managed to sum up in a few lines much of what this book is about.

"'It is maddening,' the soldier wrote, 'to see clippings from the U.S. newspapers scorning our efforts. Vietnam is a long way from home, but suppose we were in, say Alaska, or Canada, or Mexico maybe. That's pretty close to home. It's easy to sit in front of that old TV and say, "Aw, to hell with Vietnam." I don't think anyone here feels that way. It's disheartening to know that many folks back home do. If we say "to hell with Vietnam," we might as well say to hell with Southeast Asia, then, maybe, to hell with Europe, South America, Africa, and then maybe, "to hell with freedom."' "

From the point of view of the reader's interests, not to mention the national interests, The New York Times coverage of the war in Vietnam has been consistently execrable, and it has been just as consistently inconsistent. There are two reasons for this. First, the overriding managements of the editorial page and the news sections have been against the purposes of the United States Government (all the Administrations involved) in making war in Vietnam. This has put the two arms of The Times—editorial and news—in the position of finding fault with whatever the United States and its allies were doing there, instead of finding the news and presenting it clearly or of supporting the United States and its allies editorially, rather than nit-picking and constantly demanding a coalition with the Communist enemies so as to be able to kick the whole thing under the rug. Of course, as has been shown in Korea and elsewhere, kicking things under the rug brings no solution.

The appearances of The Times policy in its news pages have been pictures showing children with or without their mothers in various stages of distress because of United States war actions in South Vietnam, and long articles by Harrison E. Salisbury, especially, describing the damage to civilian areas in North Vietnam. (What is published in The Times is, of course, official—for The Times. Since Mr. Salisbury is an assistant managing editor, his articles should make it a certainty that the way he presented his pieces was entirely official.) Investigation has turned up no Times pictures of Vietcong atrocities perpetrated in South Vietnam. These cruelties, exceeding anything inflicted by accident by the Allies, were deliberately done by the Communists with the aim of frightening the people into submission. Time magazine printed a picture of a South Vietnamese soldier whose head had been amputated by the Communists. It was not deemed fit to print in The Times.

Some time after 1954, North Vietnam under the pitiless leadership of Ho Chi Minh instituted a collectivization program among the peasants. They resisted it. Therefore, according to reports not prominently printed in The New York Times, if at all,

50,000 North Vietnamese farmers were executed by their Communist rulers, and about 100,000 other peasants were put into concentration camps (cf. *Our Vietnam Nightmare,* by Marguerite Higgins.)* David Halberstam, who was a New York Times correspondent in South Vietnam in 1963-64, wrote a book about his experiences, called *The Making of a Quagmire.* He found little to praise in the South Vietnamese regime, the people or the soldiers, and thus he reflected back to New York the unhappiness of the paper with Vietnamese events. (He did like the city of Saigon.) Mr. Halberstam wrote (on page 52) of "the dynamism, efficiency and motivation that Communism had brought to the North [Vietnam]." It is entirely possible that Mr. Halberstam knew nothing about the Communist atrocities in the North but his book shows he was well aware of them in the South. He wrote (page 64) that two types of village chiefs were killed by the Communist Vietcong —the good and the bad! He reported that hundreds of teachers were slain. He described the killings as "wholesale murders" (page 65), and he placed the figure of teachers and civil servants believed to have been murdered between 1959 and 1961 at 10,000. Obviously, when it comes to killings of civilians and civilian officials, nobody, but nobody, can outdo the Communists, on either side of any given curtain. Mr. Halberstam had not yet learned that when he wrote his book. He barely mentioned Tri Quang.

Given The New York Times' will-to-lose attitude, nothing could have been more natural than for it to have attached itself to the pointless but flagrant activities of the militant monks under the leadership of Tri Quang, whom Premier Ky has described as a Communist and whose following was infiltrated by Communists,

---

* United States Senator Robert F. Kennedy, Democrat of New York, stated in his book *To Seek A Newer World* (Doubleday & Co., 1967) on page 184: "The North Vietnamese regime is far more repressive, and more ruthlessly efficient, than any of the various Southern governments. Its 'land reform' program of 1954-55 was a forced collectivization on the Chinese model, so brutally carried out that the peasant rebellion that it caused could be suppressed by Ho's army only at a cost of over 100,000 lives. There is nothing we would recognize as freedom in North Vietnam today."

according to C. L. Sulzberger of The Times. Mr. Halberstam was one of the three correspondents accused by Pierre Salinger, press secretary to the late President Kennedy, of seeking the overthrow of the Government of President Ngo Dinh Diem. (The other correspondents named by Mr. Salinger are Malcolm W. Browne and Neil Sheehan. Both are now also members of the staff of The New York Times.) So far as is known, no correspondent was ever accused of working in South Vietnam to halt or expose the activities of Tri Quang. Marguerite Higgins wrote about him in her book *Our Vietnam Nightmare* with great courage and forthrightness, and she wrote some newspaper pieces about him, but they appear to have made little impression on the general public. No news articles in The New York Times undertook to expose the sinister monk as did C. L. Sulzberger on the editorial page of The Times.

Yet it came as a surprise and a profound shock when on April 22, 1966, The New York Times printed a dispatch from Saigon stating that some American officials felt that the "United States must begin to accommodate itself to 'new political realities' in South Vietnam, including the possibility of a government dominated by Thich Tri Quang." No greater tragedy could have been visited upon South Vietnam, other than outright conquest by the Communists, than the formation of a government dominated by Tri Quang. Nor had the newspapers of the United States ever sought to show that he had any of the requisite qualifications; nor had a single one ever suggested that this supposedly religious man, with a cynical disdain for human life, except his own, should become the power behind or in the South Vietnamese Government.

The inconsistency of The New York Times in its attitude toward the war is shown by a modest proposal made in an editorial published on April 11, 1965, called "Initiative for Peace." The editorial begins in a fashion that has now become familiar over the months and years:

"Negative Communist responses to President Johnson's peace plan for Vietnam were to be expected initially. It would be an error to assume that they are final and unalterable. Or even that these public statements accurately reflect the diverse views held privately in Hanoi, Peking and Moscow and within the Vietcong." (How does the Times know that "diverse views" are "held privately in Hanoi, Peking, Moscow and within the Vietcong?" One doubts that The Times has the faintest notion about these "diverse views," which in any case it has never printed.)

After discussing various avenues toward peace talks, the editorial makes this astonishing suggestion:

"Meanwhile, an ingenious plan prepared by a former high civilian official in the Pentagon seems to merit Administration study. It is a plan for 'air guerrilla action,' intended to cause maximum military and economic disruption in North Vietnam with minimum destruction of life. It would give 48-hour warning through leaflets that one in a group of towns and villages was slated for bombing, thus encouraging large-scale evacuation but limited actual bombardment."

However well-intentioned both The Times and the ex-civilian Pentagon official, it is hardly the slightest exaggeration to say that such studied, all-out war against civilians would rally opinion in the non-Communist as well as Communist countries against the United States. Nothing could be better calculated to inflame feelings everywhere and to bring about a speedy abandonment of such a project. Let it be said in charity that this was a mistake on the side of super-belligerency. It contrasts strangely with the mistake admitted by Mr. Salisbury that he failed to attribute to the Hanoi regime the figures he transmitted in the first four of his dispatches out of North Vietnam in December-January 1966-67. Those stories reported heavy casualties allegedly inflicted upon civilians by American bombing attacks. Mr. Salisbury stated that North Vietnamese were convinced that the Americans were deliberately bombing civilians. Publication in a Times editorial of the suggestion to do just that was reckless and irresponsible, as well as a mistake.

The Times advocacy of such an attack upon civilians is so

entirely out of character with the soft attitude of The Times toward North Vietnam and the constant urging by The Times to halt the American bombing indefinitely, that one wonders how that paragraph ever wandered into a Times editorial. It is quite possible that some member of the Times editorial family asked that it be used and that it was slipped into the article in order to placate that other force. At any rate, the idea never appeared again in The Times.

The Times has always asserted editorially that the more the United States bombs North Vietnam the more determined Hanoi and the people become never to give up or make peace until the attacks stop. But The Times has never once said that the more the Vietcong (with the full backing of North Vietnam) kill civilian officials, school teachers and just plain civilians in South Vietnam the more determined the South Vietnamese will be to fight on to victory against the invaders and aggressor. It comes down to the fact that The Times does not believe in freedom for all the people of the world. It has never given more than lipservice to world freedom but is greatly concerned over "world opinion." It has never really gone all-out against the North Vietnamese leaders for directing the assassinations, kidnappings, grotesque tortures and killings that are supposed to provide "examples" to fathers or brothers, sisters or mothers or friends in South Vietnam.

The New York Times news department's lack-logic in dealing with Vietnamese events has matched that of the editorial page. On April 20, 1966, in one of its farewells to the monk Tri Quang, the news pages gave a "Man in the News" biography to him. This started off by saying: "American officials, like the French before them, have watched with concern as Thich Tri Quang has again demonstrated that he is one of South Vietnam's most powerful leaders." This is an excellent example of what happens in the gathering and presentation of news when the wish is father to it. A few months later Tri Quang's "power" was stripped in a few bold and long-overdue strokes by Premier Nguyen Cao Ky. There was not a single demonstration in behalf of the sinister man as he was sent into retreat, which proved that his power, greatly aided in some areas of South Vietnam by the Communists, was overrated and overplayed, most especially in The New York Times in pursuance of its thesis that the Vietnam conflict is a civil war in the South.

That same Times story about Tri Quang said, astonishingly: "Having precipitated the virtual collapse of the military regime of Premier Nguyen Cao Ky, he made a tactical shift this week and called upon Buddhists to 'tolerate' the Government until elections were held."

The wrongness of all this is pitiful. Tri Quang was then precipitating his own collapse, not Premier Ky's. Moreover, his influence over the Buddhists of South Vietnam was minimal, not general, as implied in the story. He is regarded as "typical of the new Buddhist leadership," this fawning account related. It said American officials were uncertain about his political objectives but were impressed by his influence. Apparently no one stopped to recall that President Diem wanted to do exactly what Premier Ky did —that is, arrest the mad career of this man who progressed by human sacrifice—or to realize that Tri Quang's influence stemmed in part from what must have appeared to the Vietnamese to be great friendship for him on the part of the Americans. After all, they let him stay in the United States Embassy for 64 days to protect him from all enemies, no matter how powerful. Afterward, he overthrew or helped to overthrow three governments, in addition to that of Diem, which was ousted while Tri Quang enjoyed the sanctuary and repose of the embassy. This all was a fantastic boon to the Communists.

We have seen how the long arm of The New York Times reached out to help put Castro in power, and we seem now to see how The Times was suggesting that Tri Quang might come to power. For it was on the day after the appearance of this Times biography that the news article from Saigon was printed saying that unidentified American officials were turning over the idea that Tri Quang was one of "the new political realities" and he might have to be considered for the premiership. One of these days we may pay dearly for letting Castro come to power in Cuba. The idea of catapulting Tri Quang into a similar position of power in South Vietnam is repugnant and appalling. For, whether or not Tri Quang is a Communist or merely does things that help the Communists, there can be no shadow of a doubt that turning over the government in Saigon to him would mean the loss of the war. The Times biographical story said the American officials who were so impressed by his influence feared that "if the Buddhist leader achieves further power he will try to negotiate a quick end to the war and 'invite the Americans out.'" Presumably those same officials the next day thought he should be considered for premier.

In regard to that title, "the Buddhist leader," which The Times bestows upon him and which he does not deserve, some figures on the religious population of South Vietnam are relevant here. The loose use of "Buddhists" to describe the following of Tri Quang does no service to the American newspaper reader. To say, as The Times has often done, that there are 13 million Buddhists in South Vietnam's population of 16 millions, is to make a mistake and create misunderstanding. There is no accurate population count in South Vietnam, much less a census of religious groups. Here is the best breakdown that could be obtained from South Vietnamese and others:

Unified Buddhist Church ...... 1 million, of whom
    not more than 100,000 are followers of Tri Quang.
Catholics .... 1.8 millions
Protestants .... .5 million
(These include Mennonites, Baptists and others.)
Hoa Hao .... 1 million
Cao Dai .... 1.5 millions
Taoists .... .5 million
Hindus and Muslims .... .5 million
Animists (mainly Montagnards) .... 1 million
Buddhism overlaid with Confucianism ..... 4 millions
Other Buddhists .... 4.2 millions

If that breakdown is nearly accurate, 6.8 million South Vietnamese are not Buddhists at all but Catholics, Protestants, Cao Daists, Taoists, Hindus, Muslims, and Animists. Also, the Hoa Hao, formed in 1939, are an offhoot of Buddhism but they do not regard themselves as Buddhists, any more than a Lutheran looks upon himself as a Catholic simply because Lutheranism sprang from Catholicism. Thus not 13 millions but 9.2 millions would be nominal Buddhists in the population of 16 millions. The vast majority of the nominal Buddhists do not worship in a pagoda, much less do they subscribe either to the moderate or militant faction of the Unified Buddhist Church, of which Tri Quang is a member. It is fair to say that most Buddhists of nearly all shades would be horrified at the induced suicides among the followers of Tri Quang. Unfortunately, most of the people of South Vietnam do not get to read a newspaper every day or every month, and so they did not get to know about the suicides until weeks or months later, if at all. Tri Quang's idea was that the United States Government would mistake his actions for expressions of the South Vietnamese people as a whole. And that is largely how it seemed to the very end before Washington learned. The New York Times did not change its course. It never concealed its dislike of Premier Ky or its sympathy for Tri Quang, but Premier Ky was not going to be bulldozed by Tri Quang or The Times.

When a nation is at war and the actions of one group of its citizens seem calculated to prolong or to lose the war, criticism of such actions hardly falls into the category of "ungracious." My own disagreement with the actions of Tri Quang and The Times is entirely impersonal. The matter of graciousness does not arise. This writer's position is objective and altogether American in a world of hard-nosed nations and inscrutable individuals. One knows a person or a collectivity of persons by the movements, activities and friends of those persons. It is immaterial what label they wear. Tri Quang asserted that he did not like Communism because it is atheistic, but his actions betrayed not the slightest evidence that he would do anything to oppose it. He also said that he opposed the government—and this had meant every government or administration in South Vietnam since it attained its independence under Diem—because "it does not respond to the needs of the people." It really made no difference whether Tri Quang said he was or was not a Communist; his contributions to the work of the Vietcong could hardly have been greater had he been the Communist leader in South Vietnam. Thich Tri Quang has been called unscrupulous, sinister and evil. It would be of interest for the record to know whether he was anything else. The most important thing for the free world is that his enormous work of sabotage has been brought to a halt.

Tri Quang made another move to attain power or bring down one more government in the spring of 1966 soon after some American officials mentioned him as premiership timber. Following customary practice the kick-off began with the self-immolation of a number of persons, mostly monks and nuns, in the Danang area. Tri Quang had the temerity to denounce President Johnson for refusing to join him in this divisive and destructive effort. (Tri Quang never denounced Ho Chi Minh.) The political monk had even stronger words for Premier Ky because he used troops to occupy Danang and end a full-fledged mutiny. Tri Quang asserted that the fighting in Danang was a crime comparable in enormity to the use of the atomic bomb at Hiroshima—a charge that had two interesting aspects. One was the fact that that bombing was an American act. It is impossible that Tri Quang would have made the comparison without intentionally seeking to discredit the Americans, engaged in denying occupation of South Vietnam to the Communists. The second was the exaggerated character of the charge, indicating that the so-called Buddhist disorders in the Danang area were his final effort and that it was going badly.

Where would "militant Buddhism" be in Communist North Vietnam? The answer is that it does not exist there. There are no "Buddhist" disorders in North Vietnam, or plans for elections of any kind, nor guerrilla actions like those in the South, with their accompanying murders and atrocities. Outbreaks of any kind in

North Vietnam would be put down with a speedy ferocity. And what would "world opinion" have to say about that? In the city of Hue, where Tri Quang made a determined stand, the United States Information Center was attacked by a mob on May 26, 1966. The many books and documents were destroyed and the building was burned. The action paralleled Communist actions the world over.

Some day we may learn the whole story of what happened in South Vietnam under the fog of war. Now we can only guess. Meanwhile, we may remark, that Tri Quang did not find it so easy in the long run to use Americans to drive Americans out, although he did succeed in fooling many persons at home and abroad for all too many years, and no one will ever be able to measure the cost.

Tri Quang broke out of his isolation in the summer of 1967, and by October he was back at his old trick of seeking the over-throw of the current government. He was on a sitdown vigil in a park near the Presidential Independence Palace in Saigon. His ostensible aim was to cause Chief of State Lieut. Gen. Nguyen Van Thieu, then President-elect, to revoke a charter that gave recognition to the Buddhist section of the Unified Buddhist Church that has nine-tenths of the members. The New York Times story of October 3 spoke of that large group as "a rival Buddhist faction." It has always outnumbered the militant Tri Quang group by 9 to 1. General Thieu said he felt that the charter was an internal matter of the Unified Buddhist Church and that the members should decide it among themselves. But it would be quite unlike Tri Quang to do something with interior logic when he was undertaking the wholly extraneous action of overthrowing a government.

After the elections for President and Vice President and members of the South Vietnam Senate on September 3, Tri Quang quickly allied himself and his militant monks and nuns with the defeated candidates, especially Truong Dinh Dzu, the "peace" candidate. The New York Times story of Sept. 25 said: "Tri Quang is thought to have far fewer followers than he did last year. Some of his most able subordinates are in hiding, and some are in jail. Others have shown no stomach for a renewal of dissidence." While those lines did not get on page one, they were on page 3, with a subhead over them. That could have represented some kind of progress for The Times, but there were no editorials condemning Tri Quang for obstructionism in the middle of a war in which the nation of South Vietnam was fighting for its life.

It was not clear at this writing how Tri Quang made his way out of confinement, where he appears to have been placed by Premier Nguyen Cao Ky in 1966. (Not all of contemporary history is immediately clear, nor in fact of most history, although many facts do leak out over the years.) But the pattern of Tri Quang's activities was reemerging with much clarity. On October 2, 1967, a Buddhist nun committed suicide by burning herself to death in the city of Can Tho. the largest in the Mekong delta south of Saigon. She was said to have acted in protest against the Unified Buddhist Church charter. Tri Quang was reported by an Associated Press dispatch from Saigon to have expressed regret for the nun's suicide but "Tri Quang added that if the government did not rescind the charter there was a possibility of more self-immolations." Thus he was on both sides of that question. From his headquarters, the An Quang Pagoda, came threats of 100 more fiery suicides in the new militant Buddhist campaign. Both President Thieu and Premier Ky, then the Vice President-elect, appealed to the militants to end their gatherings and demonstrations.

One of the practices The New York Times has followed with fair consistency throughout this war has been to print prominently letters to the editor that denounced the war and sometimes the United States with it. Letters in support of the war policies of the Johnson Administration have been printed, to be sure, but they are not usually to be found at the top of the letter columns. How many letters backing the government on the war have not been printed at all is not known, but complaints have been made that letters were not used in The Times columns.*

---

* Whenever this writer goes to lunch, whether it be with a foreign diplomat or press officer, an American publisher or a New York physician,

"Two months ago (in August, 1966), following my return to the United States from Vietnam, Major General John Norton and the main body of his First Cavalry Division Air Mobile fought an important battle in the extreme west of the Central Highlands of South Vietnam," wrote Brig. Gen. S. L. A. Marshall in The New Leader of October 10, 1966. "The battle was remarkable for many reasons, including the fact that it did not make one lead headline in this country."

That is quite a commentary on the war reporting of American newspapers. In a later issue (Nov, 21, 1966) The New Leader gave pages of space to bitter articles in rebuttal by other war correspondents. General Marshall stood his ground in reply to them. Jim Lucas, a war correspondent for the Scripps-Howard papers, wrote in his book, *Dateline: Viet Nam* (Award House, 1966), page 11:

"No newspaperman can be very proud of the American press in this show. In the six months I lived in the Delta (in 1964) I was the only correspondent regularly assigned to—working and living with—combat troops. Now that I have come home there is no one. I can't explain why this is so.

"This is the only war of recent memory which has not been covered to saturation. We flew more than 300 correspondents (in 1958) to Lebanon, where no shot was fired in anger. In Viet Nam, 16,000 Americans are involved, with thousands more on the way, and well over 200 have been killed.

"Maybe I shouldn't complain. I had no competition. But after a while, I didn't particularly enjoy having the story to myself."

One gathers that Jim Lucas did not win a host of friends among the now much larger number of correspondents in Viet-

he is nearly invariably told a story about how The New York Times refused to publish a letter. The complainant generally asserts that The Times simply pigeonholed the letter and ignored pleas that it be published. One said that he had sent a certified check to The Times in an effort to get a letter published as an advertisement but that the letter and check were both returned, unused.

nam, for two reasons: he is older than most of them and he is very diligent in covering the news. The late Marguerite Higgins was also not the most popular correspondent for one excellent reason: she was so brilliant she outshone every writer around her, men and women; and, of course, she was industrious, clever and, of all things, patriotic. There appears to have been no concerted effort on the part of the American press up to the beginning of 1967 to seek, abroad or at home, to make the war appear worth while, much less popular in the sense of getting the people to give wholehearted backing to a necessary military operation in the life of the nation and of the free world.

The difference in the way the war news has been played at home was shown in its most exaggerated form on June 7, 1965, in the treatment of the same stories by The New York Times and the New York Herald Tribune. The Herald Tribune played the story in columns 7 and 8 on page 1 under the headlines:

U.S. MARINES'
GUNS SCORE A
VIET VICTORY

The Times played the story in column 1, page 1, under this headline:

8 U.S. MARINES DIE
AS 2 HELICOPTERS
CRASH IN VIETNAM

There was no mention of victory by the Marines.

Two other sets of headlines suggest the different attitudes of the two papers on one subject. The Herald Tribune gave a 6-column headline on page 1 to the subject, thus:

CRANK CALLS TO WIVES IN U.S. ANGER GIs IN VIET

The Times' headline, over a brief story on page 12 read:

PHONE CALLS TO KIN
ANGER VIETNAM G.I.'s

It seemed clear from the way the story was presented in The Times that it was much less concerned about the matter than the Herald Tribune.

The Times gives the reader to believe that the future belongs to the bearded beatniks, the psychedelic characters, the draft card burners, the student dissenters, and those who build ramparts for the defense of muckraking in the modern manner.

On October 17, 1966 (rather significantly late in the war) The New York Times published a story on page 6 with this headline: "Hanoi Seen as Confirming View That It Formed Liberation Front." The special dispatch of The Times from Saigon said that American specialists on Vietnamese Communism interpreted an editorial of that period in the North Vietnam Communist party organ as an admission that the National Liberation Front in South Vietnam was a creation of Hanoi's.

Previously, the story said, leaders of the Front and of the North Vietnam Communists had insisted that the Front was an indigenous autonomous organization of the South Vietnamese. The Front is the political body of which the Vietcong is the military section. Hanoi's admission was regarded as an effort by North Vietnam to meet the possibility of an "allied invasion from the South, and [a signal that] the Communists in the South must give top priority to preventing this," one American specialist said.

Yet the formation of a National Liberation Front for the invasion of Greece in 1947 and of Korea in 1950 by the Communists was well known. And students of the war in Vietnam had been asserting for years that the National Liberation Front followed the time-honored Communist pattern for infiltration and conquest. The war did not come about as a spontaneous uprising of the people after the Geneva conventions of 1954, which set up South Vietnam, North Vietnam, Cambodia and Laos as independent states. Undoubtedly the North Vietnamese Communists found some ready cooperation in the South because they were able to sell the idea that the aim was to drive out the French, who happened to be white as well as oppressive as colonial administrators.

To recall to the reader the circumstances of the French presence in South Vietnam after 1954, here is a capsule historical account from John Mecklin's *Mission in Torment,* page 10:

"At the Geneva Conference of 1954 the French gave up the northern half of Vietnam, accepting partition at the 17th Parallel and neutralization of Cambodia and Laos. Ho Chi Minh became President of the 'Democratic Republic of Vietnam.' But instead of accepting the evidence that they were finished in Vietnam, the French tried one last series of maneuvers in the South. They persuaded Ngo Dinh Diem, who was just about the last true nationalist of any weight who had not joined the Vietminh, to return from self-imposed exile to become Premier by promising real independence at long last. Then they tried to manage Diem, as they had his predecessors. When he refused to be managed the French tried to oust him by such trickery as their secret support for the Binh Xuyen gangster rebellion—and failed.

"Once he had consolidated his position Diem quickly eliminated what remained of French political influence in Saigon. France's last days in Vietnam were deeply humiliating."

The North Vienamese began their aggression in the South after 1954 by assassinating village leaders and others in an effort to stir up unrest and rebellions. Then they kidnapped large numbers of young men for impressment into the Vietcong, the guerrilla force. The assassinations continued and increased. By 1959 the North Vietnamese Communists had set up command posts in the jungles of the South and were ready for war. The "Hanoi Radio proclaimed that the objective was destruction of the Diem regime and achievement of 'national unity,' meaning reunification of Vietnam under Communist control." (*Mission in Torment,* page 13). President Kennedy in 1961 ordered additional United States military forces sent to Vietnam. Their number grew from about 600 in 1961 to 23,000 at the beginning of 1965, and to more than 400,000 by early 1967. The number was increased to above 500,000 in 1968.

In all this time The New York Times has done what it could

to discourage victory on the battlefield. What it could not accomplish in that area it later sought to achieve by setting forth conditions for peace talks that sounded very much like those we read about in the chapter on Korea. In commenting on the communique issued by the Allies after their conference at Manila in 1966, The Times said on October 26 of that year in its leading editorial, "Goals of Freedom":

"The pledge to withdraw the allied forces from South Vietnam in six months is a definite commitment in answer to the allegations of Hanoi, Peking and Moscow that the United States intends to stay in Vietnam. To this extent it is a modest advance from the previous position, but it is dependent on the long-established condition that the North Vietnamese first pull out of South Vietnam, halt their infiltration and stop the guerrilla violence.

"In other words, Hanoi must first give up, which is not a proposal calculated to tempt the North Vietnamese, nor is the very strong emphasis in the communique on North Vietnam's 'aggression.' While we certainly agree with the statement that the North Vietnamese have been guilty of aggression against the South, and every nation represented at Manila is also convinced of the North Vietnamese aggression, it is still not exactly conducive to a peace atmosphere to throw this idea repeatedly in Hanoi's face. In a document intended to persuade Hanoi to seek peace, the emphasis on its 'aggression' is simply going to make a peace move more rather than less difficult for Hanoi to take."

Such timidity even before the North Vietnamese have given the slightest sign of readiness to talk peace, truce or any other kind of tranquillity is foolishness. The Communists have proved over the years that blandishments and euphemisms about their actions will avail nothing. On the contrary, every single Communist move over the world proves that they believe in force as the final arbiter. There is nothing whatsoever to indicate that sitting down with them at a negotiating table will bring anything conclusive unless they are induced to withdraw from their aggressive positions before the talks start. To agree to a one-sided halt in the war would be almost certainly to lose it and therewith all the sacrifices made for freedom in Vietnam by the Allied forces. For the Communists would regard that as a fatal sign of weakness.

Then, just as unaccountably, The Times argued:

"The United States is not precluded from taking whatever further war or peace measures it sees fit: continuation of present tactics; escalation; or—the wisest course as we see it—a unilateral gesture toward peace from the American position of strength, in the form of a cessation of the bombing of North Vietnam."

This bankrupt method of fighting a war had by then been fully explored and demonstrated, and no one knows how many casualties on the Allied side resulted from the five pauses that had been tried by the spring of 1967.

The office of the Permanent Observer of the Republic of Vietnam (South Vietnam) at the United Nations in New York issues periodically the Vietnam Newsletter, the contents of which are almost never published in our newspapers. It nearly always contains items of interest and sometimes articles of great importance. It seems the proper place to go for a statement of the South Vietnamese position. The issue of June 22, 1966, printed excerpts from a speech made by Lieut. Gen. Pham Xuan Chien, chairman of the Vietnamese Veterans Legion, on March 19, 1966, in Saigon. The general said:

"Through the last 20 years, while the world has been enjoying peace elsewhere, our country, Viet-Nam, already underdeveloped from a century of colonial domination, must still endure destruction caused by the Communist-initiated war. The Communists have systematically destroyed our efforts to rebuilt the country; nothing is spared: roads, bridges, houses, markets, churches, pagodas, schools, hospitals. The Communists have sowed death in every sector of the population. Women, children, peasants, teachers, priests, journalists, writers, all those people without a single weapon in their hands to defend themselves have fallen under the strikes of the terrorists.

"Any observer, however absent-minded, can find that everywhere in the Republic of Viet-Nam, in any city, in any village, on any road, abundant proof that the Communists are determined to carry out the slogan which has been in their mind: 'Brute force is the midwife of proletarian revolution.' It is more evident in Viet-Nam than in other parts of the world. I am unhappy to admit that in our country, there are at present a number of our countrymen who can compare with the most bloodthirsty and bellicose people world history has ever known. It is precisely those bloodthirsty men who pretend to be the liberators. . . .

"We conceive that peace can be restored only when the Communists put an end to their aggression against South Viet-Nam, withdraw their troops and agents to the North, dissolve all subversive and terrorist organizations whatever their camouflage, and stop all violence."

It is well to have an expression of the South Vietnamese point of view, at least once a year. After all, a great deal depends upon it. A newspaper reader might get the idea that the Saigon regime was the enemy.

CHAPTER VIII

The Times' Balance of Power Falls on Its Face in the Mideast

● ● ●

JAMES RESTON: "GENEVA, MAY 30 (1967)—THE VICIOUS *Middle East controversy has startled our friends and allies in Western Europe. They have been saying the cold war was over in this part of the world (blaming Washington for not knowing it), but now they are not sure. [See editorial "Anglo-Soviet Detente," in New York Times of Feb. 15, 1967, cited in Chapter II, pages 33-34.]*

"The Arab-Israeli crisis is a little nearer Europe than Vietnam. It is in an area where Britain and France still have important interests. Moscow is backing the Arabs and Washington is sort of backing Israel, and this has produced some interesting reactions." From Executive Editor Reston's column in The New York Times of May 31, 1967.

EDITORIAL in The New York Times: "The issues in the Middle Eastern conflict are being confused by some commentators and critics with the very different issues involved in Vietnam. Just as spokesmen for the Johnson Administration have drawn false parallels between appeasement of Hitler and what was described as appeasement of Ho Chi Minh and Mao Tse-tung, so now the term 'hawk' and 'dove' are being loosely applied to the Middle East as if they had the same connotations as in Vietnam.

"It is neither accidental nor illogical that many of the same Americans who are calling for de-escalation and unconditional negotiations in Southeast Asia also call for firmness on the part of the United States in insisting on freedom of passage to the Gulf of Aqaba and on honoring American commitments to defend the sovereignty and independence of Israel."—May 31, 1967.

> Though the mills of God grind slowly,
>   yet they grind exceeding small;
> Though with patience He stands waiting,
>   with exactness grinds He all.—Lines from the poem
> "Retribution," by Baron Friedrich Logau, as translated
> by Henry Wadsworth Longfellow.

"L'AUDACE, l'audace, et plus l'audace."—Counsel of a French general for winning wars—and arguments.

EDITORIAL in The New York Times: "The responsibilities of power rest upon the United States in the Middle East crisis.

"Despite President Nasser's distorted accusations, Washington's responsibilities are not entirely of Washington's choosing. The United States has filled the vacuum left in the area by the decline of British power and the virtual withdrawal of the French. But whether one likes it or not, the facts are that the United States is the only power capable of the rapid projection of military force to the area of conflict.

"This is a sobering responsibility and not one to be met lightly. Korea and Vietnam prove that military intervention—even on a small, initial scale—can lead to open-end commitments and uncalculated costs in blood and treasure. As former President Eisenhower has said and Secretary Thant has recognized, the ideal mechanism for preserving peace in the Middle East is the United

Nations; no one—if it can be avoided—should take unilateral action."—May 29, 1967.

U.S. NEWS & WORLD REPORT: "The White House is no longer sure it acted wisely in using its influence to keep U Thant, of Burma, as Secretary General and operating head of the United Nations when he said he wanted to quit. Thant now is considered weak in critical situations and holding a strong anti-U.S. and pro-Communist bias.

" 'Doves' on the war in Vietnam are busy now striving to prove that they still are consistent when they suddenly become 'hawks,' demanding that U.S. go to any military length to save Israel from an Arab attack."—From the "Washington Whispers" page of June 12, 1967.

BARRON'S, in an editorial, "Legacy of Suez": "Overnight, it seems, those who used to blur issues are drawing sharp lines; after years of murky gray, black-and-white is suddenly in style. As anti-Nasserites of long standing—Barron's had the ruler of Egypt pegged as a tool of the Kremlin a decade ago, when most observers were hailing him as a symbol of Arab unity—we welcome the abrupt hardening of public opinion. However, at the risk of alienating our new-found friends, we venture to suggest that the onus for the latest crisis does not rest solely with Gamal Abdel Nasser. On the contrary, there is plenty of blame to go round.

"Part of it falls on so-called uncommitted countries like Yugoslavia and India, which rarely miss a chance to oppose the legitimate interest of the West and last week rallied behind the United Arab Republic. The United Nations, which packed up its peacekeeping mission in the Sinai Peninsula and Gaza Strip in unseemly haste, also shares the burden of responsibility. Guiltiest party of all is the United States, which for over 10 years, under Republican and Democratic Presidents alike, has abetted Egyptian subversion and aggression. Since Suez (in 1956), for example,

Washington has lavished more than $1 billion worth of foreign aid on Cairo. Food for Peace has underwritten Egypt's undeclared war on Yemen, while the U.S. almost alone in the non-Communist world, hastened to recognize Nasser's new puppet state. Even in a land of milk and honey, appeasement still bears bitter fruit.

"Since Suez the world has had more than one foretaste of things to come. In 1957, barely nine months after an unholy alliance between the U.S. and USSR had rescued Egypt from ignominious defeat, Syria (which subsequently became part of the United Arab Republic) fell to a Communist-inspired palace revolution. In the following year a Nasserite coup toppled the Iraqi monarchy, while U.S. Marines landed in Lebanon (and British paratroopers in Jordan) to save these unhappy fellahs from a similar fate. When fighting broke out in the fall of 1963 between socialist Algeria and the kingdom of Morocco, the latter's forces, to their surprise, wound up taking Egyptian prisoners. In Yemen, Cairo has deployed upwards of 60,000 troops in a revolt against the Royalist government, and, according to authentic reports, made savage use of poison gas. [Another Egyptian poison gas attack in Yemen was reported in July, 1967.] In recent months it has bombed unarmed towns in Saudi Arabia, which support the duly consituted Yemeni authorities. Emboldened by the lack of sanctions, it also is twisting the feeble British lion's tail in Aden.

"From the Straits of Gibraltar to the Red Sea, in short, Egypt repeatedly has violated international law. Yet somehow these outrages have failed to evoke a word of protest either from the peaceloving Parliament of Man or the pious diplomat who presides over its destinies."—May 29, 1967.

THREE EDITORIALS in The New York Times: "Most reprehensible of all, of course, is the adventurism of the Soviet Union. The power politics of the imperialist nations of the past is mirrored in Moscow's effort to exploit, if it did not instigate, the dangerous struggle now under way. The theory that the Soviet

Union no longer would risk involvement in a conventional war, lest it expand into a wider nuclear conflict, must now be revised along with all the illusions about the possibility of East-West detente, *unless Moscow begins to implement its peacekeeping responsibilities as one of the permanent members of the Security Council." June 6, 1967.*

"*No settlement, of course, can expunge a military humiliation that will make the losing side thirst for revenge. But every effort must be made in restoring peace to establish completely new conditions for the future that achieve stability rather than a basis for revived tension.*

"*Indications that Israel may be willing to cooperate in this direction can be seen in Foreign Minister Abba Eban's statement that 'more stable relationships' in the Middle East will be one of his country's peace aims and in Premier Eshkol's far-reaching promise to seek no territorial advantages from victory."—June 7, 1967.*

"*The disaster that has befallen Egypt and its Arab allies has created a situation of deep embarrassment for the Soviet Union that cannot be covered by its propaganda attacks on Israel or even a break in diplomatic relations.*

"*Moscow permitted itself to be dragged into a dangerous adventure in the Middle East over which it was unable to maintain close control. The Kremlin now is trying to cut its losses without too much damage to its posture as 'friend of the Arabs.' ...*

"*The Kremlin evidently believed that its huge arms shipments of the past decade to Egypt and the decline of British and French had changed the balance of power in the Middle East. Everything indicates that Moscow was taken by surprise both by Israel's decision to fight back and by the lightning destruction of the Egyptian and Jordanian forces. The loss of huge quantities of Soviet-provided military equipment was the penultimate humiliation, exceeded perhaps only by the fact that, having unleashed Nasser, Moscow is having trouble controlling his actions even in his hour of defeat.*

"All this does not add up to another Cuba, for the Soviet Union had avoided any direct military involvement. The Kremlin —wiser than Washington had been in Vietnam—has not chosen military escalation as the answer to its Middle Eastern difficulties. It has instead given private assurances to Washington that it is prepared to take parallel measures to restore peace to the area." —June 8, 1967.

WILLIAM F. BUCKLEY Jr.: "The crisis in the Mideast reminds us unpleasantly of the shapelessness of our foreign policy in the area, not only on the specific questions of how to treat the individual nations involved, but on the general question of what it is that we have to look out for. We have been so ardently convincing ourselves that the day is over when the Soviet Union will actually make trouble for us, that we seem to be caught completely off guard when we seem about to explode in the face of the world crisis generated almost exclusively by the Soviet Union."—From Mr. Buckley's column in the New York Post of May 27, 1967.

NEWS ITEM: "Washington (CDN)—Historian Arthur Schlesinger Jr., poet Robert Lowell, and former India Ambassador and chairman of ADA John Kenneth Galbraith, three illustrious 'doves' on Vietnam, refused to join an appeal to President Johnson to aid Israel in her war with the Arabs."—In New York Post June 10, 1967.

WILLIAM F. BUCKLEY Jr.: "Perhaps we should sign that mutual defense pact with Israel—if only for our own protection.

"Let's face it, that was a blood-stirring show she put on against the Egyptian swaggerer with all his Communist tanks and airplanes, and all his jingoistic rodomontade. One can hardly imag-

ine a better military machine to help us out of a jam than Israel's.

"*There is courage, tenacity, single-mindedness, skill—all of them put to essentially non-imperialist uses, if you grant the legitimacy of the Balfour Declaration which at this stage you might just as well do.*

"*Nasser declared that the Mideast was too small an area for the Arabs and Israelis, to which the Israelis' only response—always assuming they were not prepared neatly to dismantle their nation and march into the sea—was that under the circumstances, the Arabs would have to move over.*"*—From his column in the New York Post June 10, 1967.*

FOES OF ASIA WAR DIVIDE ON MIDEAST, Leftists Cool to Israel, but Moderates Support Her: Headlines for news story in New York Times of June 7, 1967, part of which follows—

"*A rift developed in the peace movement yesterday as Communists and other leftists sided with the Arabs in the Middle Eastern war while moderates deferred to Israel.*

"*Leftists who were asked to comment on the Mideast situation, among them Dr. Herbert Aptheker, the leading theoretician of the Communist Party U.S.A., sounded critical of Israel and her supporters here.*

"*Meanwhile, on the moderate wing of the peace movement, the National Committee for a Sane Nuclear Policy said it had postponed Washington demonstrations that were scheduled for this week because Jewish groups were planning a rally there Thursday. SANE also said it wanted to allow the Mideast situation to clear up.*

"*There were mixed reports about the impact of the Mideast war on Jewish opponents of the Vietnam War.*"

JAMES RESTON: "All the talk will not restore the balance of power that existed before the war [in the Middle East]." —From Mr. Reston's column in The New York Times on June 21, 1967.

The balance of power theory, along with the Arabs, took a tremendous beating in the Middle Eastern War in June of 1967. The New New York Times switched from a position of appeasing the Soviet Government on Vietnam (and just about everything else) to a hard stance of opposing the Soviet attitude in the Middle East. The writer of this volume found himself in some rare moments of agreement with Times editorials on matters involving the Soviet Government. But The Times made it clear that it was not abandoning its opposition to war and victory in Vietnam, while it advocated both in the Middle East. Nor did The Times see any contradiction in its advocacy of a balance of power in the Far East that posited a negative attitude toward resistance to the aggression of the Soviet-Red Chinese-aided North Vietnamese, while it shrilly opposed a balance of power in the Middle East, where Moscow supported Arab aggression. Or perhaps it should be said that The Times was for a balance of power in the Mideast but this time it should be tilted heavily against the Soviet Government through the military weight of the United States.

All this is not to say that The Times followed a consistent course in its positions on the paths of history in the Middle East. On May 29 The Times advocated that, "if it can be avoided," no one should take unilateral action, but the United Nations should be given the right of way in "preserving peace." Meanwhile, the Soviet Government, fishing in troubled waters with all the vigor of which it is capable, dispatched ten warships through the Bosporus from the Black Sea into the Mediterranean. Nasser was thus encouraged and emboldened to continue his shoddy game of inflaming Israel by blockading the Strait of Tiran and the Gulf of Aqaba. So on May 31 The Times demanded that the United States honor its "commitments to defend the sovereignty and independence of Israel." That editorial said: "It is neither accidental nor illogical that many of the same Americans who are calling for de-escalation and unconditional negotiations in Southeast Asia also call for firmness on the part of the United States in insisting on freedom of passage to the Gulf of Aqaba." There was no mention of the possibility that the United States might become involved in a war with Russia, as The Times so often mentions a danger of drawing Communist China and Russia into the Vietnam conflict through United States bombing of North Vietnam.

"The issues in the Middle Eastern conflict," said that Times editorial, "are being confused by some commentators and critics with the very different issues involved in Vietnam."

It was obvious that The Times was desperately anxious to maintain its position on Vietnam without impairing the new position in relation to the Soviet Government that The Times was taking or preparing to take on the Middle Eastern crisis. Indeed, the danger that the whole Times position on Soviet Russia would collapse in ruins was and is ever-present. The Times deemed it necessary to say some things that deeply undermined the appeasement structure so laboriously and so artificially erected. For instance, with the following words The Times destroyed one of the great bulwarks of its hopes and plans for the world order through American-Soviet amity:

"Most reprehensible of all, of course, is the adventurism of the Soviet Union. The power politics of the imperialist nations of the past is mirrored in Moscow's effort to exploit, if it did not instigate, the dangerous struggle now under way. The theory that the Soviet Union no longer would risk involvement in a conventional war, lest it expand into a wider nuclear conflict, must now be revised along with all the illusions about the possibility of East-West *detente,* unless Moscow begins to implement its peacekeeping responsibilities as one of the permanent members of the Security Council."

That The Times still clung to a wisp of hope for maintaining its old position, but not for facing the reality of the world situation, was shown in the concluding clause—"unless Moscow begins to implement its peacekeeping responsibilities" et cetera. The Times has spent so much time, energy and newspaper space on building bridges—or, rather, attempting to build bridges—that it cannot bring itself to burn any bridges, even though the plain facts pillory the Soviet Government. The "theory that the Soviet Union no longer would risk involvement in a conventional war, lest it expand into a wider nuclear conflict," is another weird invention, an artificiality that shields reality from The Times editors and those readers who accept their editorial views on Soviet actions and intentions. The Times asserts that this theory, "along with all the illusions about the possibility of East-West *detente*," must be "revised" unless—Will The Times become a revisionist in the matter of all the illusions it has fostered in regard to an East-West *detente?*

In the following forty-eight hours The Times had some second thoughts. So on June 8 came an editorial headed, "Russia's Unrealpolitik." Here the tone became almost apologetic for the behavior of the Soviet Government. Now readers were told that:

"Moscow permitted itself to be dragged into a dangerous adventure in the Middle East over which it was unable to maintain close control. The Kremlin now is trying to cut its losses without too much damage to its posture as 'friend of the Arabs.' . . . The miscalculations of recent weeks must be giving the Kremlin pause."

Now we were to see a general exculpation of the Soviet Government by The Times, in a move to get back to its old position of appeasement as soon as the Middle East crisis passed, thus:

"It is doubtful that Moscow expected the Egyptian show of military strength last month, which the Soviet Union supported, to lead rapidly to this succession of events: withdrawal of the U.N. Emergency Force, Egyptian occupation of the entrance to the Gulf of Aqaba and President Nasser's subsequent blockade which virtually assured war. Yet there is no sign that Russia's leaders seriously tried during this three-week period to terminate the crisis. Their initial errors were compounded by a naval demonstration that undoubtedly further encouraged Nasser's belligerence.

"The Kremlin evidently believed that its huge arms shipments of the past decade to Egypt and the decline of British and French influence had changed the balance of power in the Middle East.

Everything indicates that Moscow was taken by surprise both by Israel's decision to fight back and by the lightning destruction of the Egyptian and Jordanian forces."

Now we come to the crux of the matter:

"All this does not add up to another Cuba, for the Soviet Union has avoided any direct military involvement. The Kremlin —wiser than Washington has been in Vietnam—has not chosen military escalation as the answer to its Middle Eastern difficulties. It has instead given private assurances to Washington that it is prepared to take parallel measures to restore peace to the area."

So the returning sinner is embraced with open arms, while the upright one is condemned for an action in another area of the world where the sinner, unrepentant, continues with unremitting wickedness to sow disorder and death. The Times thus re-rolled the court and whitened the lines in preparation for a resumption of the games it plays with the Soviet Union. Linesmen ready? Play! The first move by The Times in this resumption of its own *detente* with the Soviet Union was to make a comparison between the Mideast and Vietnam—unfavorably to the United States.

Moscow made only one miscalculation in the Middle East. It miscalculated the strength and the determination of Israel to fight, with a stunningly new insight in warfare. The Soviet Government was not "dragged" into this affair. Although The Times shows some timidity about saying so, the Russians were the instigators of it. It was they who gave large quantities of arms and munitions of war to Egypt and Syria among others. It was they who sent warships steaming into the Mediterranean to spur the Arabs on. It is inconceivable that, had they spoken one discouraging word to Nasser, he would have kept on with his blockade of the Gulf of Aqaba. Where was the vaunted Soviet intelligence that it failed to discover the extent of Irsael's firepower and will power—and readiness to take on the whole Arab world in the sure knowledge that the Soviet Government would not intervene to insure a victory for the Arabs?

It is possible the Arabs were—and are—merely being used in Soviet world power plays, so that the disaster to the Arabs is only a setback for the Russians. James Reston suggested something like this in a column, written in Athens, that appeared in The Times on June 2, three days before the war started. He said that much guessing was going on in that part of the world on what the Soviet intentions were and that there seemed to be two popular theories, as follows:

"The first is that the Soviet Union is putting pressure on the United States in the Middle East in the hope of relieving U.S. military, and particularly bombing, pressure on North Vietnam. This has been China's charge to the U.S.S.R. for months—divert the Americans with new crises elsewhere.

"Nobody around here knows, of course, but the Soviets have recently gone out of their way to interfere with U.S. naval maneuvers in the Sea of Japan. The Chinese Communists have been stirring up trouble for the British in Hong Kong. There have been military incidents along the 38th Parallel in Korea. And we not only have the Russians backing the Arabs diplomatically, but the Soviet warships moving out of the Dardanelles into the Mediterranean to shadow the naval maneuvers of the U.S. Sixth Fleet in the Mediterranean. . . .

"So this is one theory: Moscow is saying to Washington—if you are going to increase the pressure on North Vietnam, which you obviously have the power to do, we will increase the pressure in the Middle East and elsewhere if necessary, in order to force a settlement in Vietnam.

"The second theory being discussed by the diplomats in Western Europe is even more ominous. It is that the United States is so involved in Vietnam—with more than half a million men committed in that war—that the U.S.S.R. feels that it can now risk or even achieve the ancient Russian dream of expanding to the south and breaking out of its frozen continental land-mass to the warm ports of the Persian Gulf and the Mediterranean.

"This is the historic issue the diplomats are talking about. As they see it and perhaps exaggerate it, the issue is not regional but global. It is not the balance of power in the Middle East but the balance of power in the world. It is not whether Nasser can cork the Gulf of Aqaba, but whether nations at the gates of the narrow seas of the Baltic and Black and Red Seas can control the commerce of their historic enemies."

Again it is to be noted that the expression "balance of power" means many things to many persons. It means different things to different editors of The New York Times, but it does not work for any of them. It is, however, a theory that can play havoc with the world's work. The meaning generally given to it in The Times editorial pages is a balance between the United States together with other nations of the free world and the Communist governments led by the Soviet regime—a balance, that is, between freedom and Communism, inside and outside of the countries involved. In this balance, which by its nature is a struggle, The Times seeks to maintain an equilibrium between freedom-democracy and Communism. But in the Middle East, "balance of power" means something very different to The Times. There it means that Soviet power machinations must be resisted—unlike Vietnam, Cuba, the Dominican Republic, and other areas, physical and mental, as described herein.

The Times did not resort to any nonsense about "incitement" of the Israeli soldiers to seek a victory. Out of the window went the alleged balance; the fresh air of reason and common sense began to blow in. Another Times development was the treatment of the war news. Three-line eight-column streamers on page 1 heralded the beginning of the military conflict in the Middle East on June 5, and for the next three days there were eight-column streamers on page 1, blazing forth the progress of the fighting. This was as it should have been. There have been no eight-column streamers, however, on the war in Vietnam. Much of the fighting news about the conflict has been relegated to inside pages. Nor did the Korean War, with its millions of casualties, rate eight-column headlines on page 1 of The New York Times. Some of the biggest news displays in the Vietnam War involved the activities of the monk Thich Tri Quang, which were essentially divisive, defeatist, disruptive, if not downright Communist and designedly inimical to the forces fighting the Soviet-Red Chinese-sponsored aggression.

The Israelis taught the whole world how to deal with a group of bullies, led by a great big one, the Soviet Government. Throwing aside all thoughts of no-win, limited war (with unlimited casualties), the Israelis went in with the power they had, to gain a quick and decisive victory. Jordan reported that her casualties in less than 48 hours of fighting were about 15,000 dead. Israel had no choice. She had to hit with all her might, since she had not a single ally to join her in the battle, and the consequences of defeat were too painful to contemplate. General LeMay remarked of the Korean War, after citing the 3,500,000 military casualties and one million civilians killed, that there must be some more humane way of fighting a war than that. A long-drawn-out conflict, with both sides forever bleeding, is obviously the Communists' aim in Vietnam, as it was their "achievement" in Korea. Israel would have none of this. She taught a lesson on how to deal with enemies that seek to destroy a nation piecemeal—she clobbered them.

In its rapid backpedaling pursuit of a return to its previous position—before the Middle Eastern War—The New York Times on June 11, 1967, made this editorial statement:

"Israel has now won a great victory with skill and bravery, but she is still 'bayed about with many enemies'—in fact, these enemies will hate her with all the more intensity after the humiliating defeats they have suffered. Military victory will be no solution in the Middle East any more than the military victory the United States is seeking in Vietnam would be in Southeast Asia."

The only certainty about that statement is that "Israel has now won a great victory with skill and bravery." There is bound to be a new respect and no doubt secret admiration for Israel in the Middle East—which nothing in the world except victory could have brought her. It is not to be expected that the Soviet Government is going to change a massive Russian policy that reaches back for centuries and gains support now in many countries of the world—a policy that has its own world philosophy, Marxism-Leninism-Sovietism, which in turn provides support for the divisive balance-of-power theory that has once again proved useless to the free world in a crisis.

Incidentally, if the first theory passed on by Mr. Reston from Athens in regard to the Middle East crisis is accurate, then the Communist Russians and the Communist Chinese are working together on Vietnam on a global basis, as they are cooperating amicably in Havana on Communist operations in the American hemisphere. Mr. Reston spoke of "China's charge to the U.S.S.R. for months—divert the Americans with new crises elsewhere." And the sudden flare-ups in Hong Kong and along the North-South Korean frontier, together with Soviet interference with United States naval maneuvers in the Sea of Japan and the Mediterranean, to coincide with the blockade of the Gulf of Aqaba, could hardly have been accidental. At any rate, it is idle to believe, in the light of our knowledge of Russia's behavior since the end of World War II (and during it) that any kind of solid *detente* is visible anywhere. It seems equally futile to expect that those who have pushed the appeasement line for so long will be able to give up their chimerical quest. A balance seeks no solution; it does not want one.

Unbelievably, The Times was already back at advocating another pause in Vietnam by June 14. Thus it completely ignored the fact that the Soviet Government had started the war in the Middle East, possibly as a backfire against the war in Vietnam, and it snuggled its head into the sands of know-nothingism in order to gain peace in Vietnam by not fighting. This would, indeed, be a payoff to the Russians for the upheaval in the Middle East. It would give them in Vietnam through inaction what they had been unable to gain in Araby through the catspaw of the Arab nations. The Times stated editorially on June 14, in an editorial headed, "Lest We Forget":

"Today, Americans have to think of the great price to be paid for a dubious victory that could not in present circumstances be a quick one. Until all efforts to introduce peace negotiations—such as trying a bombing pause in North Vietnam—are exhausted, there should be no thought of escalating the already greatly inflated war effort."

The lesson taught by Israel, that the most humane war is one that strikes with the greatest force to knock out the enemy, has been lost on The Times. Once again the hand of the United States would be stayed, and the only apparent reason is that the same powerful forces, including The Times, believe a balance of power can be maintained despite all the contradictory evidence and the demeaning character of the arguments in behalf of it.

Coincidentally, The Times reported on June 21, 1967, from the United Nations:

"Soviet sources said today that Moscow could not accept any controls on arms shipments to the Middle East until the military forces of the Arabs had been restored to a reasonable balance with the force of Israel."

Between detente-itis and balance of power fever, the world, then, will continue in a condition of violent unrest punctuated by localized wars. There is hardly a good reason to believe that the same conditions as those of the past will bring more peaceful events in the future. The fact is that Russia was willing to risk starting another Vietnam in the Middle East. Russia's sending of warships through the Bosporus was a signal to the Arabs that they had the fullest support of the Soviet Government. The only reason there was not more bloodshed and a continuing and most serious war in the Middle East was the quick and valorous action of Israel.

Chapter IX

The Times and 'The Final Conflict'

• • •

DAVID LAWRENCE: "The constitution of the United States defines treason as follows:

'Treason against the United States, shall consist only in levying war against them, or in adhering to their enemies, giving them aid and comfort.'

"The United States today is in the midst of a world-wide 'cold war' as well as a military war in Vietnam which is being fought by American troops against a regime aided and supported by Communist governments in Europe and Asia. Not only are these governments enemies of the United States, but they threaten the peace of the world. . . .

"There should be full disclosure of the methods by which subversive movements inside this country have been financed by foreign governments. If it becomes evident that embassies or legations or consulates are being used to foment treason in America, serious consideration should be given to the severance of diplomatic relations with such hostile governments. . . .

"We have too long floundered in trying to handle subversive and treasonable activities."—From an editorial, "Treason Unpunished," in U.S. News & World Report on Nov. 29, 1965.

HENRY J. TAYLOR: "A letter thrown over my [United States] embassy residence wall [in Switzerland] by a Polish Communist defector (handwritten in German) figured in the far-off arrest of foreign service officer Irving C. Scarbeck, accused of breaking security at the American Embassy in Warsaw.

"It was a brilliant achievement by the department's security experts. And if you do not think the espionage problem is always present everywhere, let me tell you that even neutral Switzerland shot 16 traitors during the second World War.

"America's internal security is vital, delicate (and often tragic) work against an enemy that never sleeps. Yet, the State Department security section, which Otto F. Otepka headed after serving under every Administration for 19 years, has been knocked into utter shambles by a left-wing element that moved into the State Department when the New Frontier took over.

"The result is the destruction of anti-Communist experts and tragic discouragement to courageous vigilantes. If such knowing men as Otepka are not getting out they are being knocked out—which is exactly what is happening to Otto Otepka.

"There are so-called 'liberal' personalities high among the New Frontiersmen who have been cracking at any internal security forces inside and outside the State Department, including Director J. Edgar Hoover and the FBI, for many years.

"They didn't like any of the security forces in the Alger Hiss case, the Robert Oppenheimer case. . . . They have their inside ways, their innuendoes and their devices of assassination which are relentless, far-reaching. . . .

"The knocking out of Otepka, and all it symbolizes, is a vicious desecration against his efficiency record, invariably re-garded as excellent, and the department's earlier proud bestowal on him of its meritorious award.

"Otepka now is accused of insubordination. But what kind of a country do we live in when a man like this can be railroaded the way Otepka's antagonists are now driven to confess?"—From Mr.

Taylor's column in the New York World-Telegram and Sun of November 18, 1963.

EUGENE LYONS: "Toward the end of September (1967), a group representing national, patriotic, religious, veteran, refugee and civic organizations met in New York City on the invitation of Citizens for Freedom, headed by the well-known American anti-Communist, Lady Malcolm Douglas-Hamilton. In order to counter the avalanche of pro-Soviet propaganda, then already pouring over our country, they decided to proclaim November 7th, the fiftieth anniversary of the Bolshevik seizure of power, a day of mourning for the victims of communism.

"The black-bordered proclamation outlined the appalling price paid by Russia and by the world for the Soviet half-century —in tens of millions of dead, terror, suffering, moral depravities and spiritual blackouts; in thought control and worldwide brainwashing; in wars, civil conflicts, guerrilla depredations and five decades of turmoil. . . .

"A press release on the action was issued early in October and another at the end of the month. By any journalistic test, it was 'news fit to print.' Normally, such joint action by leading organizations, backed by prestigious individuals with Cardinal Spellman heading the list, is a guarantee of press attention. Some newspapers and radio stations in many parts of the country did, in fact, carry the news.

"But the leading mouthpieces of the Liberal Establishment chose, deliberately and with malice aforethought, to ignore it. The N.Y. Times, which rarely overlooks even minor political activities of the far left, refused to report the proclamation emanating from the right-of-center."—From TACTICS, Nov. 20, 1967.

EDITORIAL in The New York Times: "The self-appointed next assignment of the tenacious House Un-American Activities Committee is an investigation of unrest in the nation's cities, a project remarkably ill-suited to bringing tranquillity to those cities.

"Before the hearings of the committee begin anew, this seems an approptiate time to question once again whether it should exist at all."—March 25, 1967.

NEWS ITEM in The New York Times: "*Newark, Oct. 9 (1964)—Richard M. Nixon said today that 'a State Department clique' was responsible for a 'debacle' of the Johnson Administration's foreign policy.*

"He said the 'clique' had also prevented President Kennedy from sending air support to Cuba during the Bay of Pigs invasion after he had made 'the right decision to send in troops.' . . .

" 'Yes,' Mr. Nixon said, 'Castro did come to power during the Eisenhower Administration.'

"But those responsible for the success of Premier Fidel Castro, he went on, were a 'State Department clique who thought Castro was a "liberal," a clique more interested in what world public opinion will be than in the security of our country, a clique that tried to sabotage (John) Foster Dulles.'

"The same group, he said, was responsible for 'one of the great series of foreign policy defeats in our history.

" 'Put a map of the world on the wall,' the former Vice President said, his right hand jabbing at the audience. 'Stand back 20 feet and throw darts and try to hit one part of the world where the United States hasn't been humiliated in the past four years.' "
—October 10, 1964.

EDITORIAL in The New York Times: "*The case involving the Harvard historian Prof. H. Stuart Hughes and his right to travel in Europe without snooping by American embassies has had one useful result. Secretary of State Rusk and Attorney General Katzenbach have been embarrassed into reviewing the procedures concerning security and freedom of travel for American citizens.*

"The involved affair is tied up with the controversial Frances Knight, director of the Passport Office; the now dismissed director

of the Bureau of Security and Consular Affairs, Abba Schwartz; the Senate Internal Security subcommittee and its aggressive chief counsel, J. G. Sourwine; the F.B.I., which asked for the 'shadowing' of Professor Hughes; the State and Justice Departments. . . .

"Miss Knight has devoted much of her official career to saying nasty things about her superiors—a habit that must occasion some wonderment about the State Department in foreign ministries. But she was, at least, quite right in saying that if someone with authority would give her instructions on what to do in cases like the F.B.I.'s request for a watch on Professor Hughes, she would follow them. In lieu of clear guidelines and a firm and open policy by the State Department, it has been possible for many years for Miss Knight either to apply her own criteria on traveling Americans or to pass along requests of the kind made by the F.B.I. 'as a matter of routine.'

"In the Hughes case, the embassies in Paris and Moscow were advised to keep an eye on him and report back on what he did. This is a procedure straight out of the McCarthy era."
—March 31, 1966.

MAX FRANKEL in a news story for The New York Times:
"Oleg V. Penkovsky's service to the capitalist world—considerable while he lived and still unfinished in death—reached a pecuniary culmination here [in New York City] yesterday.

"The mysterious forces of espionage and the obvious forces of commerce joined to promote a book that purports to be the secret journal of Colonel Penkovsky, the West's best-placed Moscow spy in memory. Thus they produced yet another extraordinary chapter in an extraordinary but slippery tale.

"With an expression of regret that the executed colonel was unfortunately 'not with us,' the publishers of the book, Doubleday & Co., presented the next best pitchman, Greville Wynne, just 19 months out of a Soviet jail for his contact work with Penkovsky in 1961 and 1962. . . .

"He was happy . . . to have flown the Atlantic to help drum

up business for the Penkovsky papers. . . . because, he said, he wished to call attention to a courageous man, to his warning that the West 'must show strength' to the Soviet Union and to the importance of their venture in espionage.

"Neither Mr. Wynne nor Mr. [Frank] Gibney [the editor of the papers] said enough to dispel the widespread doubts about the origin of the Penkovsky journal. It is said to have been smuggled out of Moscow just before the colonel's arrest Oct. 22, 1962. Mr. Wynne said that, in more than 50 meetings with Penkovsky, the colonel never mentioned the secret diary by which he allegedly wanted one day to reveal and justify his treason to the world."
—November 12, 1965.

"INTERNATIONALE:" Lines from the Marxist anthem—

'Tis the final conflict;
Let each stand in his place;
The international Soviet
Shall be the human race.

HERODOTUS, Book VII, 157:

Greece united will be strong and a match for the
    invader;
but if some of us betray and others stand aside
and the loyal are few,
then there is reason to fear that all Greece may fall.—

EDITORIAL in The New York Times: "More fundamentally, however, the United States is now torn by a confrontation between the two nations that inhabit it, the 11 per cent the census calls Negroes and the great majority, those whom many young Negroes call "Whitey.' "—July 16, 1967.

TRYGVE LIE, former Secretary General of the United Nations, in his book IN THE CAUSE OF PEACE *(Macmillan, New York, 1954), pages 438 and 444:*

"The ideological struggle between Communism and other forms of dictatorship on the one hand, and democracy on the other, will never cease. . . . the victory of democracy over world Communism in our time is possible if we win the trust of the 1,500,000,000 underprivileged persons now living in Asia, Africa, and several parts of South America. If, on the other hand, these millions—or a great part of them—are lost to democracy, our basic principles and our way of life, even our prospects for peace and freedom, will be exposed to the greatest pressures.

"Soviet Communism as a form of totalitarianism, like all other dictatorships, constitutes a source of pressure which, in my opinion, can be contained, in the first instance, only through the application of force. Experience has shown that, sooner or later, every dictatorship begins to suffer from claustrophobia and before long begins to exert pressure on its neighboring states."

LINES from 'Invictus'

In the fell clutch of circumstance
I have not winced nor cried aloud:
Under the bludgeonings of chance
My head is bloody, but unbowed.

It matters not how strait the gate,
How charged with punishments the scroll,
I am the master of my fate;
I am the captain of my soul.—

Wiliam Ernest Henley

It is a peculiar fact—and it is a fact—that fighters against Communists, whether domestic or foreign, do not ordinarily find favor with The New York Times. One of the most remarkable cases before the people of the United States today is that of Otto Otepka. Here is a respected man who was downgraded and virtually reduced to the hideous condition of a "non-person," to use diction introduced from the Soviet regime. Did he do anything against his country? On the contrary, he was serving it extremely well. He is a man whose appearance bespeaks the honest and devoted civil servant. Strangely, his picture has rarely appeared in the newspapers, despite the certainty that he is a *cause célèbre*. That ought to ring a bell.

Aside from his appearance and his stainless record, declared meritorious, the host of friends and objective students of government who have given him their support attests to his character and integrity. If The Times has written an editorial asking for his rehabilitation, to borrow another word from Russia, it has escaped a diligent search of the newspaper's files. Certainly there has been no campaign by The Times on behalf of Mr. Otepka.

Frank L. Kluckhohn, who for nearly 20 years was a highly respected foreign and Washington correspondent of The New York Times, wrote in his book *LYNDON'S LEGACY* (Devon-Adair, New York 1964), page 151:

"The last hurrah for the State Department's security setup came immediately after the advent of the Kennedy Administration, when the State [Department] Security Office ruled that now-Assistant Secretary of State Harlan Cleveland should not be given even a temporary security clearance, and this ruling was upheld by the State Department's Acting Administrator of Security. [Mr. Cleveland is no longer in the position.]

"However, Secretary of State Dean Rusk overrode the evidence against Cleveland and personally waived security requirements for Cleveland. . . .

"Indeed, a Senate Internal Security Subcommittee report issued in the autumn of 1963 revealed that up to mid-1962—more than a year before—Dean Rusk had personally waived security checks for 152 new key State Department employes, most of them over the violent objections of State's security office. In fact, many others had been personally 'cleared' by Rusk and were working in the State Department without the security office's even knowing them.

"After the State security office had refused clearance to Cleveland, the security division was 'reorganized,' reportedly along the lines planned by William Wieland, the 'Ex-President of the Fidel Castro Fan Club.'

"The first 'reorganization' move of the Kennedy Administration was to abolish the jobs of 23 of State's professional agents. They were given 30 days to 'show cause' why their jobs should not be abolished. Other security men were given minor and meaningless jobs calculated to make them resign. Many key security professionals, who had memorized dozens of security files and who could be 'troublesome' if they were accorded too much of 'the treatment,' were sent abroad to meaningless jobs. Some of these were given foreign assignments on 'security,' which were so laughable, they could be compared with giving J. Edgar Hoover a job as a traffic cop.

"One top security official who received a 'show cause' notice was Otto Otepka, chief of all personnel security, whose 'security risk' findings at State skyrocketed into headlines across the nation in the summer and autumn of 1963, when Otepka revealed to the Senate Internal Security Subcommittee that Assistant Secretary of State Harland Cleveland was trying to worm Alger Hiss and a number of other known security and loyalty risks back into the State Department. Otepka told the Senate subcommittee a lot more about the hanky-panky at State, too.

"Otepka was no mere cog in the wheel in the State Department's security setup. He was the top man, the ranking Deputy Director of the Security Office, and was in charge of the entire personnel security organization of the U.S. State Department, both in Washington and in American embassies and consulates throughout the world. . . .

"As chief of personnel security, it was Otepka's duty to investigate State Department 'mistakes' about hailing Castro as a Robin Hood and letting Fidel establish a Communist bastion and staging area for communizing all of Latin America, 90 miles from American shores. Of course this involved investigating William

Wieland, who had been chief of the State Department's Office of Middle-American affairs during the Eisenhower Administration and who is a carryover into the Kennedy and Johnson Administrations. Otepka did a thorough investigation of Wieland and wrote a sizzling report on him, which has never been published; but it is known that Otepka said Wieland definitely should be dismissed.

"Wieland has not been fired by the Administration; in fact, President Kennedy made it clear that he was pleased with Mr. Wieland. . . .

"Indeed, far from being dismissed, Wieland was, in fact, the senior officer (with two others, one of whom was J. Clayton Miller) who reportedly planned the Kennedy Administration's 'reorganization' of the State Department's security setup. Naturally, the State Department has denied that Wieland even had a hand in helping to smash State's security organization. Even putting aside Wieland's hideous pro-Communist record, it was a case of a man under investigation as a loyalty and security risk firing his chief investigator, Otto Otepka!

"As soon as the State security office had been effectively smashed, the Foreign Service officer in charge, William Boswell, was one of those transferred overseas. [William Wieland was later sent overseas, too.]

"What security against loyalty and security risks now remains in the State Department? Even those few experts still in State's security office are so subjected to pressures from the top that there is no longer any effective security in the State Department. Actually, the New Frontiersmen and the Foreign Service are still policed, except that they now police themselves—politically, but certainly not for security and loyalty, most observers declare."

There is more to the Otepka case than can be dealt with in this book.* Mr. Kluckhohn has described much of it in his book. (For some sharp details there is the document, State Department

---

* I am advised that it will be treated comprehensively by William J. Gill in *The Ordeal of Otto Otepka* to be published by Arlington House in the summer of 1969.

Security—1963-65, The Otepka Case—XIII, Hearings before the Internal Security Subcommittee, Part 15, U.S. Government Printing Office, Washington, D.C.) Edward Hunter has done much to keep the case alive in the pages of the magazine TACTICS. The financial weekly Barron's has also shown a lively and continuing interest in it, and on June 12, 1967, printed the following paragraph bringing the matter up to date:

"Otto F. Otepka, a high State Department official who lost his job when he objected to lax security procedures decreed by Dean Rusk some six years ago, finally got a hearing last week. A State Department hearing examiner presided, and a Justice Department lawyer acted as prosecutor. Over objections of the defense, laying the basis for subsequent appeal to the courts, the examiner ruled that the hearing record would be 'classified.' Justice dropped 10 of the original 13 charges, leaving only those accusing Otepka of having breached the wall dividing the executive and legislative branches of the U.S. government by handing over State Department documents to a Congressional investigation. One hostile witness called by the defense may not answer the summons. (He has good reason to hide behind the Fifth Amendment, a plea which might cost him his job.) Meanwhile, the number of 'doves' among those for whom Mr. Rusk waived security checks gives the watchful citizen food for thought."

Mr. Otepka continues at this writing to be in a limbo, still out of a job. He was happy to have the hearing, which The New York Times reported in a very brief story on the inside of the paper at the bottom of a page. There was no picture. Mr. Otepka was bewildered by the fate that had befallen him. The Johnson Administration had not undertaken summarily to correct the injustice done to him; much less had it restored the security system in the State Department. How can this be justified with such favorable words as have been written in this volume about Mr. Rusk? The answer can only be another question: How could the installation of Castro in Cuba have begun while so well-known and undoubted an anti-Communist as John Foster Dulles was Secretary of State? It is a mystery, lost in the labryinthine maze of the State Department. Mr. Nixon's statement quoted in the paragraphs preceding the beginning of this chapter explains the happening in part, but if a clique can do such important things, then the systems and methods in the department preclude the guarantees necessary to the security of the United States. The American press—and not merely The New York Times—has been largely indifferent to this case.

In contrast to The Times' attitude in the Otepka case, the New York newspaper has shown an eagerness to rehabilitate Alger Hiss and restore him to acceptance by American society without apology or admission by Hiss of his betrayal of the United States by handing over to Whittaker Chambers secret documents, taken from archives of the State Department, for transmission to the Soviet Government. There are volumes of evidence to prove Hiss's guilt, if any proof were needed at this point. Let us merely recall what President Harry Truman thought at the time, in 1949, as cited in the book *SIX CRISES* by Richard M. Nixon, the former Vice President, who as a Representative in Congress was most responsible for bringing Hiss to justice. The following quotation is from page 64 (the book was published by Doubleday & Co.):

"I have no doubt that President Truman personally had just as much contempt for Alger Hiss as I when the full import of his activities became known to him. An indication of his attitude was a report Bert Andrews [able and trusted reporter of the New York Herald Tribune] gave me shortly after Hiss's indictment. He said Truman was shown copies of the stolen documents by a representative of the Justice Department. As he thumbed through page after page of incriminating evidence, he muttered, over and over, 'Why, the son of a bitch—he betrayed his country!' " Yet when asked in his next press conference if he still thought the [House Un-American Activities] Committee's investigation of the Hiss case was a 'red herring,' he replied in the affirmative! When a friend asked him how he could possibly make such a statement in light of the new evidence, his reply was: 'Of course Hiss is guilty.

But that damn Committee isn't interested in that. All it cares about is politics, and as long as they try to make politics out of this Communist issue, I am going to label their activities for what they are—a "red herring." ' "

Is it any wonder that one Representative in disgust said, "Communism is poison!" [meaning dangerous to tackle]? Is it any wonder that a book was published in 1966 that sought to prove that Hiss was framed by Whittaker Chambers? A more fantastic undertaking, which would involve the collusion or deception of hundreds of men from the President of the United States down, could hardly be imagined. Is it not amazing that so clearcut a case as that of Alger Hiss is still hazy in the minds of a considerable section of the public? And is it not surprising indeed that an effort was made only a few years ago in the United States State Department to put Hiss back into the department? Is it not one of the unthinkable thoughts that Benedict Arnold would have been restored to his commission in the United States Army after his perfidy? Let those who still have doubts about Hiss read *SIX CRISES*, and also *SEEDS OF TREASON* and *LAMENT FOR A GENERATION*, the latter books written by Ralph de Toledano (*SEEDS OF TREASON* in collaboration with Victor Lasky); and of course, *WITNESS*.

Now on September 16, 1967, The New York Times published on its so-called second front page, also known as the split page, a story under a B head, the largest one-column head used by The Times for an inside-page story. The head read: "HISS NOW WRITING BOOK ON NEW DEAL. Takes First Cautious Steps Back into the Public View Since '50 Perjury Case. HE ALSO WILL LECTURE. Maintains His Innocence of Passing State Department Documents to Russia." That story said that Hiss would deliver four lectures on the New Deal at the New School for Social Research. It added simply that he had been convicted of perjury in 1950. The next chummy paragraph put Whittaker Chambers in the darker light—which has been the strategy of the pro-Hiss faction from the first. It reads:

"He [Hiss] said in an interview over lunch Thursday that he believed the public climate had changed sufficiently so that he could now teach without the publicity that has surrounded virtually all of his public words and actions since Whittaker Chambers, a confessed Soviet spy courier, said that Mr. Hiss had passed him State Department documents."

That is precisely what Hiss was convicted of doing. That is to say, he was convicted of lying in asserting that he did not pass such documents to Mr. Chambers. That is a quite different matter from mere perjury. Moreover, while Mr. Chambers was "a confessed Soviet spy courier," he was not a Soviet spy courier at the time of the trial of Hiss, as the story seems to suggest. Mr. Chambers had purged himself of guilt by admitting to the United States Government what he had done in the 1930's in collaboration with Alger Hiss and others in the Communist party in Washington. Since then Mr. Chambers had become a highly respected editor of Time magazine. Hiss has never admitted his guilt, as affirmed by a Federal jury; nor ever revealed what he did as a Communist who, as Mr. Truman said, "betrayed his country."

The Times story carried a benign picture of Hiss and was so long that it jumped from the second front page, page 35, to page 52 with a four-column line over the jump section. The story treated Hiss as a man who had been put upon and was now attempting to return to the good graces of his fellow-citizens with an honored place among them as a professor giving new insights into the New Deal. This is upside-down business indeed.

Another public figure for whom The New York Times has reserved special treatment is Owen Lattimore, now a professor at the University of Leeds, England. The treatment in his case involves non-coverage of his activities when they would expose him as a vigorous foe of the policies of the United States and a leading defender of the actions of Communists and Communist governments. The journal that used to pride itself on being "the newspaper of record" sent no reporter to cover the proceedings of the Third Annual Conference of Socialist Scholars at the New York

Hilton Hotel, Rockefeller Center, only a few blocks from Times Square, on September 9 and 10, 1967. Mrs. Alice Widener, publisher of the magazine U.S.A., who lives quite a few blocks away, managed to attend the sessions, at which Dr. Lattimore was a guest of honor. He spoke to the well-heeled radicals, including two guests from the Soviet Union, Timor Timofeev and Yuri Zamoshkin of the Institute of World Labor in Moscow. (There are no strikes in Soviet Russia and no real labor unions.) Mrs. Widener reported in U.S.A., issue of Sept. 8-Sept. 22, 1967, that the Leeds professor, in the hotel's Sutton Ballroom, addressed "a capacity crowd of fashionably dressed Socialist Scholars and friends" who "dined by candlelight at $12.50 a head and then sat back, full of food and in a relaxed spirit of *camaraderie* to listen to Dr. Owen Lattimore." Her article continued:

"Nothing would be more easily understandable than the intellectual spell that Owen Lattimore seems to have cast over the major foreign policy makers in our country during the crucial years between 1941 and the fall of China to the Communists.

"The mild-mannered, smiling way in which he says the worst and ugliest things about our country must be very disarming to all those intellectuals who believe it isn't what is said that counts, but the way it is said."

Mrs. Widener said Dr. Lattimore was "civilized, cultivated, cultured and urbane. He looks like a bank president, not a professor. Above all, he is clever, very, very clever." She added:

"Listening to Owen Lattimore in the Sutton Ballroom of the New York Hilton on the evening of September 9, 1967, one could grasp the full significance of what the U.S. Senate Internal Security Subcommittee had in mind when it reported to the American people, fifteen years ago, that he was one of the persons active in and around the Institute of Pacific Relations who 'knowingly and deliberately used the language of books and articles which they wrote or edited in an attempt to influence the American public by means of pro-Communist or pro-Soviet content of such writings.'

"Listening to Lattimore, anyone thoroughly familiar with the

Senate Subcommittee's 'Report on the Institute of Pacific Relations' and loving his or her native land, the United States of America, could well wonder whether some day a congressional investigating committee might describe the Socialist Scholars Conference in precisely the same manner as the Senate Subcommittee described in the IPR: 'The net effect of IPR activities on United States public opinion has been such as to serve international Communist interests and to affect adversely the interests of the United States.'

"Dr. Lattimore's main thesis, at the Socialist Scholars dinner, was that it is the United States, not the Soviet Union or Red China, which is 'expansionist.' The present borders of the Soviet Union and of Red China are merely their historic ones, he alleges, dating back to the great eras of the czars and Chinese imperial dynasties. Dr. Lattimore never once mentioned Czechoslovakia or East Germany or Tibet as being subject to Red expansionism, but he identified as subjects of present day United States' expansionism 'Guam and Japan and the Philippines.'

"This was the 'scholar' that the Socialist Scholars paid homage to as their guest of honor! He said that in international affairs, 'the active principle at work today is the expansionism of the United States.' He accused our country of seeking to make Asia 'the privileged reserve of white men.' He derided the intellectual ability of American scholars and foreign policy molders and their 'amateur geopolitical thinking since the beginning of the Cold War,' and he lauded, 'the great Lenin's mature, sophisticated understanding of world politics.' Lattimore described the Chinese Communist party as 'nationalistically patriotic,' but he criticized every attitude of the U.S. Government that loyal Americans could regard as nationalistically patriotic.

"Dr. Lattimore belittled the idea that the present chaos in Red China and dissension among Communist leaders signify a breakdown there. He said that what is taking place is 'turbulent debate—not the precursor of general massacre.' He described the Red Guard terror as an 'egghead exercise.' . . .

"All notions that there will be a Sino-Soviet conflict over border regions between the Soviet Union and People's Republic of China are sheer nonsense, according to Dr. Lattimore. He said the present frontiers of both Communist nations 'are of an enviable stability.' He said neither nation seeks expansion. 'Expansionism,' he said, 'is in areas where American forces are.'

"After his speech, the audience of Socialist Scholars was invited to ask questions. Someone inquired when the Chinese are going to take Hong Kong from the British imperialists.

"Dr. Lattimore beamed with delight at the question. Here was an opportunity for him to be himself at his scholarly best. A most apt historical analogy, he said, could be found in a true anecdote about Lawrence of Arabia. When he was defending the Arabs against the Turks, he would bomb the Turkish railroad across the desert in intermittent attacks, a strike here, a strike there.

"A subordinate asked, 'Why don't you blow the whole bloody thing all at once and get it over with?'

" 'Ah,' replied Lawrence, 'I want them to suffer a permanent hemorrhage.'

"Dr. Lattimore paused and looked all around the Sutton Ballroom, beaming at the Socialist Scholars and their dinner guests.

" 'A permanent hemorrhage,' he repeated with utmost satisfaction, smiling benignly as if he were a minister pronouncing the benediction.

"Those were just about his last public words to the Socialist Scholars at their Third Annual Conference. They found them inspiring. Their appluase was rapturous. Dr. Corliss Lamont of Columbia University, seated next to Yuri Zamoshkin of the Soviet Union, looked pleased as Punch."

Mrs. Widener also reported this:

"Just across from the Hilton, along the Avenue of the Americas, are the skyscraper offices of the Columbia Broadcasting System and American Broadcasting Company. Within a few blocks are the Time-Life Building and National Broadcasting Company.

Nearby the Hilton are the offices of the Associated Press; within walking distance is The New York Times.

"Not a single reporter from any of these great communications enterprises covered the first, second or third annual conferences of the Socialist Scholars, though the gatherings took place in such easily accessible places as the McMillin Theatre, Columbia University, the Hotel Commodore and New York Hilton.

"Why?"

A good question. The answer no doubt has something to do with bridge-building. This is straight out suppression and concealment of news. It is one more instance of a deception of the people. This is in remarkable contrast to the voluminous coverage given to Lattimore when he was in trouble with the United States Government and faced trial for contempt of the Senate. Edward Hunter in *TACTICS,* October 20, 1967, remarked upon this as follows:

"The movements of Owen Lattimore have been consistently covered by the press. He has been a cause celébrè for the entire 'liberal' establishment. Its organs usually ignore his involvement with the Communists, or else declare, as have the N.Y. Times and Newsweek, that he was absolved by a U.S. court. Of course, this is untrue. Lattimore was saved from trial by one of those legal technicalities that have nothing to do with guilt or innocence, but which have become time after time the device allowing the obviously guilty to go scot free. The Senate Internal Security Subcommittee unanimously concluded that he was 'a conscious, articulate instrument of the Soviet conspiracy.' "

Americans in general would prefer not to believe in plots and conspiracies, spies and agents, infiltrators and the grim and horrible possibilities of the kind of thing that has happened in Europe, especially Germany and Russia in our time. Let us pray that we need not worry about grossly treasonable occurrences. Yet we cannot forget so recent a case to the contrary as that of Alger Hiss, which some persons are still trying to portray as a "non-event." Here are a few more paragraphs from the column of Henry J.

Taylor, written for the New York World-Telegram and Sun of November 18, 1963:

"The prize—and priceless—information needed by any enemy nation is: What are America's intentions and capabilities?

"This requires continuously tapping into our top-secret circles of decision, if possible—penetration at the highest possible level.

"Soviet agents deal in two commodities, information and people. And they deal in these here on the largest scale of anywhere in the world.

"Because the United States is the only country Russia fears, it is impossible to overstate the skill, cunning and patience, the resources and ruthlessness of this attack upon us.

"Yet, where are the bulwarks against this in the State Department today?

"If the raising of this question sounds sinister, it is nevertheless unavoidable. For I have lived an important part of my life too close to the Red hand not to know the power of its fingers."

There are some persons—perhaps, many—who feel it is superficial to deal with newspaper columnists for guidance in such important matters. Where else shall we turn? It is Henry J. Taylor, Alice Widener, Joseph Alsop, C. L. Sulzberger, Jeffrey St. John, Edward Hunter, Ruby Hart Phillips, Paul Scott, Hanson W. Baldwin, William S. White, Victor Riesel, Edith Kermit Roosevelt, Robert Considine, Leon Dennen, William F. Buckley Jr., Jim Bishop and many other fine, able, honest and patriotic writers that we must turn to for the sense of things left out of The Times and other papers. Indeed, the professional historians are usually poorly equipped and altogether unsuited for the task of telling the people about contemporary events. In any case, the people have no choice—they must rely upon their daily newspapers, the radio, and the television. The television is an excellent source of news, but heaven forbid that we should be forced to rely upon this no-permanent-record medium for our news in entirety. One day it may become the main source of news, but only when it has absorbed the medium of the newspapers, not bypassed it.

The grasping, power-seeking hand of The New York Times in the State Department was well seen in the case of Mrs. Frances G. Knight, head of the Passport Office. This came to pass in the matter of Professor H. Stuart Hughes, Harvard historian, in March, 1966. Messages, requested by the Federal Bureau of Investigation, were sent to the U.S. embassies in Paris and Moscow saying that Professor Hughes "reportedly in the past has had strong convictions toward Communism" and asking that "pertinent information" received about his activities be sent to the F.B.I. This news was given in a Washington dispatch to The New York Times of March 26, 1966. Obviously this information was never expected to be found in the public press. The publication brought about a hassle between Mrs. Knight and Philip B. Heymann, acting director of the Bureau of Security and Consular Affairs, of which, The Times dispatch said, the Passport Office is a part. There followed an exchange of memorandums between Mrs. Knight and Mr. Heymann. In one of them Mrs. Knight wrote:

"As far as I am concerned, it is an established fact that The New York Times had deliberately been made privy to classified information of the 'official use only' and 'confidential' category in an effort to discredit me and cause embarrassment."

Later, in an interview with The Washington Star, Mrs. Knight said:

"This leak to The Times was not a leak; it was a handout. . .

"They are so concerned about Professor Hughes that no one has mentioned the leak of classified information to The New York Times. This is not the first time. There is a New York Times coterie in here which is virtually part of the State Department."

Five days later The Times printed the vitriolic editorial saying, "Miss Knight has devoted much of her official career to saying nasty things about her superiors—a habit that must occasion some wonderment about the State Department in foreign ministries." Such an angry and obviously ridiculous attack could only have been designed to bring about the dismissal of Mrs. Knight. She had asserted—and The Times agreed in the same editorial—that she had no other course to follow in such matters. It was, indeed, a matter of "routine" to follow such a request. It was a rule of the department, and Mrs. Knight had said, with a pardonable bitterness, that she would issue a passport to a "baboon" if such a rule were given to her. This kind of aggression against civil servants can only result in chaos, and one must ask in all seriousness, is that the aim?

The New York Times has the right to print or not to print, to slant and curve the news as it pleases, to take any editorial position it wishes. That is the basis of a free press. It is also the right of the free citizen to criticize and complain, to analyze and pillory the actions of the press. In any case, this book has only scraped the surface, and I know some of my friends will be disappointed that I failed to cover some area in which they had a special interest. One of them feels that I ought to say that The Times makes a special pitch to school pupils, high school and college students, teachers and professional men, and other opinion-makers and leaders, not excluding the President of the United States, a regular reader of The Times during all the administrations. Let it be said.

This book is not designed to damage The New York Times but to point it back on the course that was followed so successfully by Adolph S. Ochs and Arthur Hays Sulzberger. For The Times is the leader among American and world newspapers. If it fails its readers in the long run, it could hurt us all. It cannot but do that if it continues on its present path. I am not a lone voice in my criticism of The Times. "The world is out of joint, O cursed spite, that I was ever born to set it right." That has been the cry of all the ages of man. Yet some one must undertake the task. Always he finds he has many associates and co-workers.

The Russians have exploded a 100-megaton hydrogen bomb. The Chinese Communists reported in June, 1967, that they had detonated a 3-megaton thermonuclear bomb. (One megaton has the value of 1 million tons of TNT.) The largest bomb the United States has exploded was in the range of one megaton, although the United States no doubt could set off as large a bomb as either

Russia or Communist China. This is not to suggest the relative strength of the three powers. Red China does not have the capability of hurling the bomb by intercontinental ballistic missiles now, and that country is torn by deep and widespread internal rifts. But there is in the world this unimaginable might of destruction. It is this power that I believe to be at the bottom of The New York Times attitude. It feels that the United States can somehow sneak up on the Russians and gain their assent to some general *detente*.

The course of self-destruction that could follow from this attitude cannot be gauged. It means, in my opinion, that we should go from one kind of decay to another. One nation after another would be sacrificed, until in the end we would have no friends—and then, no nation. This book has attempted to describe some of the ways in which this has already been accomplished.

Bibliography

The Story of The New York Times by Meyer Berger, Simon & Schuster, N.Y. 1951

Raymond of The Times by Francis Brown, W. W. Norton & Co. 1951

The House of Adolph Ochs by Roger Kahn, The Saturday Evening Post, September, 1965

The Kingdoms, The Powers, And The Glories of The New York Times by Gay Talese, Esquire magazine, November, 1966

"All the News That's Fit to Print," an article by Prof. George Lichtheim in Commentary magazine, September, 1965

Student Disorders and Responsibility: Analysis of N.Y. Times by Edward Hunter in magazine *Tactics,* November 20, 1965

The Forgotten People by Seymour Freidin, Charles Scribner's Sons, N.Y. 1962

Eastern Europe in the Sixties, Edited by Stephen Fisher-Galati, Frederick A. Praeger, 1963

A City in the Darkness by Andras Pogany, Literary Guild, 1966

Rumbles Left and Right by William F. Buckley Jr., G. P. Putnam's Sons, New York, 1963

A History of Russia by George Vernadsky, Yale University Press, 1961

Workers' Paradise Lost by Eugene Lyons, Funk & Wagnalls, N.Y., 1967

USSR: A Concise History by Basil Dmytryshyn, Scribner's, New York, 1965

The Soviet Economy Since Stalin by Harry Schwartz, Lippincott, 1965

Soviet Foreign Aid by Marshall I. Goldman, Frederick A. Praeger, N.Y., 1967

Juggernaut: A History of the Soviet Armed Forces by Malcolm Mackintosh, Macmillan, 1967

How Russia is Ruled by Merle Fainsod, Harvard Press, 1953

The Volga: A Political Journey by Marvin Kalb, Macmillan, 1967

Red Pawn: The Story of Noel Field by Flora Lewis, Doubleday & Co., 1965

The Kremlin's Human Dilemma by Maurice Hindus, Doubleday & Co., 1967

In the Cause of Peace by Trygve Lie, Macmillan Co., 1954

Attack by Mail by Edward Hunter, Bookmailer, 1966

Red Spies in U.N. by Pierre Huss and George Carpozi Jr., Coward-McCann, 1965

Behind the U.N. Front by Alice Widener, Bookmailer, 1955

Betrayal at the U.N., the Story of Paul Bang-Jensen, by DeWitt Copp and Marshall Peck, Devon-Adair, 1961

Soldiering for Peace by Maj. Gen. Carl von Horn, David McKay, Inc., New York 1967

Writers and Politics by Conor Cruise O'Brien, Pantheon Books, 1965

Lament for a Generation by Ralph de Toledano, Farrar, Straus and Cudahy, 1960

Waging Peace by General Dwight D. Eisenhower, Doubleday & Co., 1965

Six Crises by Richard M. Nixon, Doubleday & Co., 1962

Design for Survival by General Thomas S. Power, Coward-McCann, 1965

Floodtide in Europe by Don Cook, G. P. Putnam's Sons, New York, 1965

Hostile Allies, FDR and De Gaulle by Milton Viorst, Macmillan, 1965

Oppenheimer: The Story of a Friendship, by Haakon Chevalier, George Braziller, 1965

China and the Bomb by Morton H. Halperin, Praeger, 1965

The Thought Revolution by Tung Chi-ping and Humphrey Evans, Coward-McCann, 1966

China: Empire of the 700 Million by Harry Hamm, Doubleday, 1966

The Ageless Chinese: A History, by Dun J. Li, Scribner's, 1965

Mao Tse-Tung: Emperor of the Blue Ants, by George Paloczi-Horvath, Doubleday & Co., 1963

Mao and the Chinese Revolution by Jerome Ch'en, Oxford, 1965

Red Star Over Cuba by Nathaniel Weyl, Hillman-Macfadden, 1961

The Cuban Dilemma by R. Hart Phillips, Obolensky, 1962

Cuba and Castro by Teresa Casuso, Random House, N.Y., 1961

I Was Castro's Prisoner by John Martino, in collaboration with Nathaniel Weyl, Devin-Adair, N.Y., 1965

With Kennedy by Pierre Salinger, Doubleday & Co., Garden City, N.Y., 1966

Reminiscences by General of the Army Douglas MacArthur, McGraw-Hill, N.Y., 1964

MacArthur: 1941-1951 by Maj. Gcn. Charles A. Willoughby, McGraw-Hill, N.Y., 1954

Our Vietnam Nightmare by Marguerite Higgins, Harper & Row, 1965

Mission in Torment by John Mecklin, Doubleday, 1965

The Long, Long War by Brigadier Richard L. Clutterbuck, Praeger

The Green Berets by Robin Moore, Crown, 1965

To Seek a Newer World by Robert F. Kennedy, Doubleday & Co., 1967

Viet-Nam Witness by Bernard B. Fall

Why Vietnam? by Frank N. Trager, Praeger, N.Y., 1966

The Making of a Quagmire by David Halberstam, Random House, N.Y., 1964

I'm the Lucky One by S/Sgt. Barry Sadler, Macmillan, 1966

Dateline: Viet Nam by Jim Lucas, Award House, 1966

The Lost Revolution by Robert Shaplen, Harper & Row, 1965

Report of the Warren Commission, New York Times Edition, McGraw-Hill, 1964

The Unanswered Questions About President Kennedy's Assassination by Sylvan Fox, Award Books, 1965

Lyndon's Legacy by Frank L. Kluckhohn, Devin-Adair, 1964

Communist Threat to the United States Through the Caribbean,
    Part 16, March 7, 1967, U. S. Government Printing Office,
    Washington, D.C.

Communist Threat to the United States Through the Caribbean,
    Part 17, March 7 and 8, 1967, U.S. Government Printing
    Office, Washington, D.C.

Communist Party, U.S.A.—Soviet Pawn (1967) U.S. Govern-
    ment Printing Office, Washington, D.C.

Inside South America by John Gunther, Harper & Row, 1966

The Whole Truth by Robert Daley, The New American Library,
    1967

Index